CORPORATE MANAGEMENT IN DEVELOPING COUNTRIES

The Challenge of International Competitiveness

Alvin G. Wint

QUORUM BOOKS
Westport, Connecticut • London

OBN 1336790

Library of Congress Cataloging-in-Publication Data

Wint, Alvin G.
    Corporate management in developing countries : the challenge of
international competitiveness / Alvin G. Wint.
        p.   cm.
    Includes bibliographical references (p.   ) and index.
    ISBN: 0–89930–929–1 (alk. paper)
    1. Industrial management—Developing countries.   2. Competition,
International.   3. International economic relations.   I. Title.
HD70.D44W56   1995
658'.049—dc20   95–7519

British Library Cataloguing in Publication Data is available.

Library of Congress Catalog Card Number: 95–7519
ISBN: 0–89930–929–1

First published in 1995

Quorum Books, 88 Post Road West, Westport, CT 06881
An imprint of Greenwood Publishing Group, Inc.

Printed in the United States of America

∞™

The paper used in this book complies with the
Permanent Paper Standard issued by the National
Information Standards Organization (Z39.48 1984).

10 9 8 7 6 5 4 3 2 1

To Masie

Contents

Tables

Preface

At a time when developing countries are increasingly concerned with issues of international competitiveness, this book takes as its organizing theme the question of how the effective management of international business activities in developing countries can improve the competitiveness and development prospects of these countries. In this regard, the book differs significantly from the typical book on the subject of international business that is written from the perspective of the manager in a developed country and does not see a need to examine the linkages between the competitiveness of firms and of developing nations. This is not to suggest that there is not a significant overlap between the theory and practice of international business in developing and developed countries. There clearly is such an overlap, but it is even more clear that there are important areas of difference between the pressing issues in these distinct sets of countries. This book will seek to identify and discuss both the similarities and the differences, while taking its starting point from the problems of developing countries.

This book, therefore, is not an effort to replicate existing material. Rather, it is an effort to provide information and an analytical perspective that will more readily resonate with those individuals who are interested in the issues of international business and competitiveness in the context of developing countries. These individuals include managers operating in developing countries or considering engaging in such operations, academics with an interest in developing country issues, and graduate students in international business whether in developed or developing countries.

Many colleagues have assisted me both in the development of my own ideas on the subject of international business and national competitiveness and in the production of this particular book. Louis T. Wells, Jr., of Harvard Business School has been a constant source of inspiration. My colleagues at Northeastern University, in particular, Ravi Ramamurti and Heidi Vernon Wortzel, have been extremely helpful and supportive. Eugene Salorio of Georgetown University provided particularly detailed comments on the manuscript that I found to be very helpful. In addition, my colleagues at the University of the West Indies, in particular, Gordon Shirley, have also imparted useful insights. I thank all of these individuals for their assistance.

Chapter 1

International Business and Economic Development

Managers in developing countries, whether operating in the private or public sectors, are constantly aware of the problems of underdevelopment. Managers in tourism enterprises are aware of the potential problems of tourist harassment that result from the fact that few of the residents of tourist locations have viable economic opportunities. Managers in information service companies suffer because of the limitations of the telecommunications infrastructure. Managers in many manufacturing enterprises face a limited pool of innovative and creative technical talent. Managers in export agriculture face deficiencies in transport and port facilities and a paucity of intelligence about international marketing networks.

Managers in the public sector are similarly cognizant of the problems typical of stagnating economies that are growing only slowly, if at all. It is clear, for example, that such economies breed high rates of unemployment and underemployment. In addition, however, they are also often breeding grounds for spiraling inflation as governments unwilling to accept the reality of slow growth and unable, or unaware of how, to overcome the fundamental obstacles to growth seek to create the illusion of growth through expansion of the country's money supply. Inevitably, this inflationary process leads to currency depreciation, which, in turn, leads to greater inflation. As conditions of macroeconomic instability reign supreme, the result is likely to be even less production than obtained prior to the onset of an inflationary spiral.

The effects of an unstable macroeconomy lend merit to the proposition that the development process requires that public-sector managers stabilize their economies as a precursor to a movement toward economic growth. A principal theme of this book, however, is that beyond economic stabilization, it is the successful pursuit of international business activities that leads to increased national competitiveness and, ultimately, economic growth and development.

These international business activities could involve international trade as in the export of goods and services to an array of countries. They could be investment activities in which firms use international investments as listening posts from which they gain market intelligence or learn how to meet the demands of a more sophisticated market; or they could be intermediate forms of international business that are more than the arm's-length, short-term relationships that are represented in international trade transactions but less than the commitment of risk capital to an international venture that occurs in the context of international investment. The programs of licensing of technology used to great advantage by Japan and Korea in the development of internationally competitive firms represent an interesting case of the use of intermediate forms of international business in the development of internationally competitive industries. It seems obvious that it is such industries that are the basis for economic development, even though this link is rarely explicit either in the work of international business analysts or in the writings of development economists.

ECONOMIC DEVELOPMENT

The economic development literature has focused on the results of the economic development process and the generic strategies countries might pursue in order to achieve the goal of economic development. This process is said to involve a systematic rise in a country's real national income and the living standards of its residents through increases in the productivity of its resources typically associated with a shift of factors of production and national production away from agriculture and toward industry or services. An improvement in living standards as a component of development incorporates the presumption that development includes not only increases in per capita income but also declines in the level of absolute poverty, declines in unemployment, and a national income that is not only growing but is also becoming more equally distributed over time.

Other economic trends are viewed as accompanying economic development. There is a trend, for example, toward urbanization. Social and demographic trends tend to complete the description of the economic development process. The population becomes more literate, its health improves, and birth rates decline. Obviously, economic development is never regarded as a tidy, straightforward concept. The foregoing are seen as representing tendencies and trends, not scientific formulas. It is not clear, for example, in which direction causality runs when discussing these trends. Indeed, the tendencies tend to become circular and self-reinforcing, creating virtuous cycles that lead to development and vicious cycles that forestall development.

It is important to note that despite the frequency with which the world is divided between developed and developing countries, there are no official efforts to divide the world in this way. The World Bank (WB), for example, uses the designation of low-income economies with 1992 per capita incomes that vary from US$60 to US$670; lower middle-income economies with 1992 per capita incomes that vary from US$670 to US$2,700; upper middle-income economies with 1992 per capita incomes that vary from US$2,700 to US$7,500; and high-income economies with 1992 per capita incomes that vary from US$7,500 to US$36,080. See Table 1.1 for per capita income and other data for most of the countries upon which the WB provides information. Table 1.1 also provides information on the proportion of a country's national productive capacity devoted to agriculture, adult literacy rates, life expectancy for residents, and proportion of citizens living in urban areas.

Also provided in Table 1.1 is a Human Development Index (HDI) developed by the United Nations Development Program (UNDP). This index was designed to complement the gross national product (GNP) per capita index developed by the WB. The HDI index combines indicators of life expectancy, educational attainment, and income into a composite index. A country's HDI is based on its position in relation to a target expressed between 0 and 1. Minimum and maximum values are fixed for each component that affects the HDI value. Life expectancy is measured between a minimum of twenty-five years and a maximum of eighty-five years; adult literacy between 0 percent and 100 percent; mean years of schooling between zero and fifteen years; and income, in purchasing power parity terms, between US$200 and US$40,000.

The UNDP uses this index to divide the world into areas of high human development, with 1992 HDIs that vary from 0.801 to 0.932; medium human development, with 1992 HDIs that vary 0.511 to 0.798; and low human development, with 1992 HDIs that vary from 0.191 to 0.489.

Despite the fact that official statistics tend not to divide countries into two broad camps of developing and developed, there has been a strong tendency to divide the world in this manner. According to this division, developing countries would be largely those with per capita 1992 incomes in the range of US$80 to US$12,000, 5 to 64 percent of their productive resources devoted to agriculture, adult literacy rates of 35 to 90 percent, life expectancy for residents from forty to seventy-three years, 10 to 75 percent of their populations living in urban areas, and HDIs of 0.191 to 0.875. Developed countries, on the other hand, are primarily those with per capita 1992 incomes in the range of US$12,000 to US$36,000, 2 to 5 percent of their national productive capacity devoted to agriculture, adult literacy rates of about 99 percent, life expectancy for residents at about seventy-six years, about 75 percent of their citizens living in urban areas, and an HDI of more than 0.875.

The countries that meet all the characteristics associated with the description "developed countries" are primarily countries of Western Europe, North America, Australasia, and Japan. Some countries that do not meet these cri-

Table 1.1
Development Indicators, 1992

Country	Per-Capita Income (US$)	HDI	Percentage in Agriculture	Percentage Literate	Life Expectancy	Percentage Urban
Mozambique	60	0.252	64	33	44	30
Ethiopia	110	0.249	48	NA	49	13
Tanzania	110	0.306	61	NA	51	22
Sierra Leone	160	0.209	38	21	43	34
Nepal	170	0.289	52	26	54	12
Uganda	170	0.272	57	48	43	12
Bhutan	180	0.247	42	38	48	6
Burundi	210	0.276	54	50	48	6
Malawi	210	0.260	28	NA	44	12
Bangladesh	220	0.309	34	35	55	18
Chad	220	0.212	44	30	47	34
Guinea-Bissau	220	0.224	44	36	39	21
Madagascar	230	0.396	33	80	51	25
Lao PDR	250	0.385	NA	NA	51	20
Rwanda	250	0.274	41	50	46	6
Niger	280	0.209	37	28	46	21
Burkina Faso	300	0.203	44	18	48	17
India	310	0.382	32	48	61	26
Kenya	310	0.434	27	69	59	25
Mali	310	0.214	42	32	48	25
Nigeria	320	0.348	37	51	52	37
Guyana	330	0.580	NA	96	65	NA
Nicaragua	340	0.583	30	NA	67	61
Haiti,(1991 data)	370	0.354	NA	53	55	29
Togo	390	0.311	36	43	55	29
Benin	410	0.261	37	23	51	40
Central African Republic	410	0.249	44	38	47	48
Pakistan	420	0.393	27	35	59	33
Ghan	450	0.382	49	60	56	35
China	470	0.644	27	73	69	27
Tajikstan	490	0.629	NA	NA	69	NA
Guinea	510	0.191	33	24	44	27
Mauritania	530	0.254	29	34	48	50
Sri Lanka	540	0.665	26	88	72	22
Zimbabwe	570	0.474	22	67	60	30
Honduras	580	0.524	22	73	66	45
Lesotho	590	0.476	11	NA	60	21
Egypt, Arab Republic	640	0.551	18	48	62	44
Indonesia	670	0.586	19	67	60	32
Sudan	NA	0.276	34	27	51	23

Table 1.1 *(continued)*

Country	Per-Capita Income (US$)	HDI	Percentage in Agriculture	Percentage Literate	Life Expectancy	Percentage Urban
Zambia	NA	0.352	16	63	48	42
Cote d'Ivoire	670	0.370	37	54	56	42
Bolivia	680	0.530	NA	67	60	52
Azerbaijan	740	0.730	NA	31	71	NA
Philippines	770	0.621	22	90	65	44
Armenia	780	0.801	NA	NA	70	NA
Senegal	780	0.322	19	38	49	41
Cameroon	820	0.447	22	54	56	42
Georgia	850	0.747	27	NA	72	NA
Uzbekistan	850	0.664	NA	NA	69	NA
Papua New Guinea	950	0.408	25	52	56	NA
Peru	950	0.642	NA	85	65	71
Guatemala	980	0.564	25	55	65	40
Congo	1030	0.461	13	57	51	42
Morocco	1030	0.549	15	49	63	47
Dominican Republic	1050	0.638	18	83	68	62
Ecuador	1070	0.718	13	86	67	58
Jordan	1120	0.628	7	80	70	69
Romania	1130	0.729	19	NA	70	55
El Salvador	1170	0.543	09	73	66	45
Syrian Arab Republic	1160	0.727	30	64	67	51
Turkmenistan	1230	0.697	NA	NA	66	NA
Moldova	1300	0.714	NA	NA	68	NA
Lithuania	1310	0.868	NA	NA	71	NA
Bulgaria	1330	0.815	NA	NA	71	69
Colombia	1330	0.813	16	87	69	71
Jamaica	1340	0.749	5	98	74	54
Paraguay	1380	0.679	24	90	67	49
Namibia	1610	0.425	12	NA	58	28
Kazakhstan	1680	0.774	28	NA	68	NA
Tunisia	1720	0.690	18	65	68	57
Ukraine	1820	0.823	NA	NA	70	NA
Algeria	1840	0.553	15	57	67	54
Thailand	1840	0.798	12	93	69	23
Poland	1910	0.815	7	NA	70	63
Latvia	1930	0.865	24	NA	69	NA
Costa Rica	1960	0.848	18	93	76	48
Turkey	1980	0.739	15	81	67	64
St. Vincent	1990	0.732	NA	NA	71	NA
Iran, Islamic Republic	2200	0.672	23	54	65	58

5

Table 1.1 *(continued)*

Country	Per-Capita Income (US$)	HDI	Percentage in Agriculture	Percentage Literate	Life Expectancy	Percentage Urban
Belize	2220	0.666	NA	NA	69	NA
Grenada	2310	0.707	NA	NA	71	NA
Panama	2420	0.816	11	88	73	54
Russian Federation	2510	0.858	13	NA	69	NA
Dominica	2520	0.749	NA	NA	72	NA
South Africa	2670	0.650	4	NA	63	50
Mauritius	2700	0.778	11	NA	70	41
Chile	2730	0.848	NA	93	72	85
Estonia	2760	0.867	17	NA	70	NA
Brazil	2770	0.756	11	81	66	77
Botswana	2790	0.670	5	74	68	27
Malaysia	2790	0.794	NA	78	71	45
Venezuela	2910	0.820	5	92	70	91
St. Lucia	2920	0.709	NA	NA	70	NA
Belarus	2930	0.847	NA	NA	71	NA
Hungary	2970	0.863	7	NA	69	66
Uruguay	3340	0.859	11	96	72	89
Mexico	3470	0.804	8	87	70	74
Trinidad & Tobago	3940	0.855	3	NA	71	66
St. Kitts & Nevis	3990	0.730	NA	NA	68	NA
Suriname	4280	0.677	NA	95	69	NA
Gabon	4450	0.525	9	61	54	47
Antigua & Barbuda	5980	0.796	NA	NA	74	NA
Argentina	6050	0.853	15	95	71	87
Oman	6480	0.654	4	NA	70	12
Barbados	6540	0.894	NA	NA	75	NA
Puerto Rico	6590	NA	1	NA	74	75
Korea, Republic	6790	0.859	8	NA	71	74
Greece	7290	0.874	NA	93	77	64
Portugal	7450	0.838	NA	85	74	35
Saudi Arabia	7510	0.742	7	62	69	78
Cyprus	9820	0.873	NA	NA	77	NA
Bahamas	12070	0.854	NA	NA	72	NA
Ireland	12210	0.892	10	NA	75	58
New Zealand	12300	0.907	NA	NA	76	84
Israel	13220	0.900	NA	NA	76	92
Spain	13970	0.888	NA	95	77	79
Hong Kong	15360	0.875	0	NA	78	94
Singapore	15730	0.836	0	NA	75	100
Australia	17260	0.926	3	NA	77	85
United Kingdom	17790	0.919	NA	NA	76	89
Italy	20460	0.891	03	NA	77	70

Table 1.1 *(continued)*

Country	Per-Capita Income (US$)	HDI	Percentage in Agriculture	Percentage Literate	Life Expectancy	Percentage Urban
Netherlands	20480	0.923	4	NA	77	89
Canada	20710	0.932	NA	NA	78	78
Belgium	20880	0.916	2	NA	76	96
Finland	21970	0.911	5	NA	75	60
United Arab Emirates	22020	0.771	NA	NA	72	NA
France	22260	0.927	3	NA	77	73
Austria	22380	0.917	3	NA	77	59
Germany	23030	0.918	2	NA	77	86
United States	23240	0.925	NA	NA	77	76
Norway	25820	0.928	3	NA	77	76
Denmark	26000	0.912	4	NA	75	85
Sweden	27010	0.928	2	NA	78	84
Japan	28190	0.929	2	NA	79	77
Luxembourg	35160	0.908	NA	NA	76	NA
Switzerland	36080	0.931	NA	NA	78	63

Sources: World Bank, *World Development Report, 1994* (New York: Oxford University Press, 1994); United Nations Development Program, *Human Development Report, 1994* (New York: Oxford University Press, 1994).

NA: Information not available.

teria are often viewed as developed because of historical reasons (e.g., the Western European countries of Portugal, Ireland, and Greece). Others, based upon these criteria, have entered the group of developed countries, even if they are not so designated by analysts (e.g., Singapore, Hong Kong, and Israel). Indeed, Singapore has, for almost a decade, had the long-term objective of being designated a developed country by the beginning of the twenty-first century. The world's other 4 billion people live in countries that are depicted as developing and are seeking to emulate the characteristics of the developed countries. Note that the range of characteristics of the developing countries is much broader than the range associated with the developed countries.

One additional factor that tends to differentiate the developing countries from the developed countries is the greater income inequality that exists in developing countries. This greater degree of income inequality seems evident to many individuals who compare living standards across these sets of countries. Increasingly, there are those who insist that developing countries are becoming the home of the "dirt poor and the filthy rich." The gap in income equality between developed and developing countries is supported by data on income distributions collected by the WB in thirty-six developing countries and twenty developed countries during the 1980s and 1990s (see Table 1.2). Beyond the data presented in Table 1.2 on the distribution of income by quintiles, whereas the top ten in developing countries earned, on average, 35 percent of their countries' national income, the equivalent decile in developed countries earned 24.8 percent of their countries' income.

It is worthwhile to point out that while there is a development plateau that countries can reach with regard to the indicators described previously, this does not represent some economic nirvana. Developed countries contain groups or regions that do not share in their countries' prosperity, keeping economic development on the policy agenda. Furthermore, it is quite easy for an entire country to slip and fall from the development plateau. Thus, many developed countries today sing the mantra of improving economic competitiveness to ensure that they maintain their positions atop the economic world. Although economic development is relevant to all countries, this book takes as its point of reference the economic problems of the developing countries of the world. In these countries, economic development problems take on particular urgency.

While there is some consensus on the characteristics of development, there is much debate about the strategies countries must pursue to achieve the goal of development. Development strategists have tended to be divided into four camps with respect to their analysis of the process by which countries develop.

One camp, reflected in the work of Rostow, Harrod, and Domar, sees development taking place in linear stages. Critical to this perspective is the identification of the takeoff point for development. Once there is "takeoff," then there is a certain automaticity to the development process. The development

Table 1.2
Percentage of National Income Earned by Each Quintile

Type of Country	Quintiles				
	1*	2	3	4	5
Developing Countries	50.6	20.6	13.8	9.5	5.6
Developed Countries	40.5	23.9	17.3	12	6.2

Source: World Bank, *World Development Report, 1993* (New York: Oxford University Press, 1993).

* Quintile 1 represents the 20 percent of the population earning the most income.

dilemma, according to this approach, is to identify the preconditions necessary for takeoff and ensure that these are in place. The contribution of the Harrod–Domar model to this perspective was to identify an injection of capital as the principal precondition necessary to allow developing countries to take off on a developmental path. The empirical justification behind the conceptual writings of this genre, which were published in the 1950s and 1960s, was the success with which the war-torn economies of Europe were rebuilt with the aid of the injection of U.S. capital in the form of the Marshall Plan.

Although this camp focused primarily on capital—either through domestic or foreign savings—as a precondition for economic growth, it is a church that is open enough to admit a variety of related parishioners. Thus, preconditions in the form of an educated citizenry or developed legal or commercial systems could also be captured in this approach to development.

A somewhat related school of thought sees the development dilemma encapsulated in the need to engage in a structural shift of the economy. This model of structural change, incorporated in the largely conceptual work of Lewis and the primarily empirical work of Chenery, views development as an identifiable process of growth and change with similarities across countries. The predominant structural shift identified in the work of these authors as necessary for, or synonymous with, development is that in which the economy shifts from an agriculturally driven economy to one powered by industry.

It is important to note that writers in this camp and economists, in general, do not argue that the shift away from agriculture and toward industry be accomplished by neglecting or taxing the agricultural sector. Rather, the empirical evidence suggests that countries with the better development records have focused on improving the productivity of the agricultural sector through increases in technology, improvements in the skill base of agricultural workers, and programs of land reform and worker relocation designed to create agricultural plots of a scale that allows for efficiency with ownership structures that provide incentives for efficient operations.

The shift, it is argued, is necessary because countries that are spending most of their productive resources on agriculture are likely to be affected by the commodity nature of most types of food. This characteristic ensures that demand for food does not increase proportionally with income—in the jargon of the economist, food has an income elasticity of less than 1—a phenomenon also known as Engel's law. Thus, if national income increases, the increased internal demand is likely to be for products other than food (e.g., industrial goods or services).

In a situation where a country exported the bulk of its agricultural products, one might anticipate a different result. Such a country could ostensibly pay for those industrial products or services its population demanded with the foreign exchange earned from its exports. Countries such as Denmark, Australia, and New Zealand are viewed as countries that have been able to develop based primarily on the export of agricultural products. Interestingly, however, even these countries have a relatively small proportion of their productive resources in the agricultural sector. As Table 1.1 indicates, for example, the proportion of gross domestic product (GDP) accounted for by agriculture in Denmark and Australia in 1992 was 4 percent and 3 percent, respectively.

Indeed, one possibility is that even those countries that export significant quantities of agricultural products will suffer from Engel's law applied internationally; that is, as worldwide incomes increase, there will not be a proportional increase in the demand for the agricultural products, so that over time it will take more of that country's agricultural exports to purchase the industrial goods and services that its population demands. This is likely to be the case particularly where the agricultural products are commodity-like. Clearly, not all agricultural products are commodities. Countries that can differentiate their agricultural products might be better able to avoid the problems associated with producing products with negative income elasticities.

A third school of development thought can be termed the dependency school. Analysts in this camp, which, in its heyday, was broad enough to admit Marxist and non-Marxist analyses, see underdevelopment primarily as an externally induced phenomenon rather than one that can be attributed to various forms of internal constraints. Dependency theories, popularized by Latin American economists and the development economists of the Plantation School of Economics in the Caribbean, view the situation in which developing countries find themselves to be an inevitable consequence of their relationship with developed countries. In particular, it is a relationship between colonial powers that created a structure of production and trade for themselves and their colonies designed to enrich the mother country at the expense, and ultimate impoverishment, of the colony.

Dependency theorists view multinational corporations and multilateral organizations such as the WB and the International Monetary Fund (IMF) as institutions that, after the demise of formal colonial relationships, continued to perpetuate a colonial-type economic structure that operates to the detriment of developing countries. Dependency theory, developed almost exclusively by economists from developing countries, was the primary intellectual force behind the calls from the developing world for a new international economic order to be discussed in greater detail in subsequent chapters.

The final development camp may be termed a neoclassical camp. This school of thought sees underdevelopment resulting from poor resource allocation in developing countries because of incorrect pricing policies. Those who support this view of the development problem argue that if governments in developing countries would only "get the prices right" and reduce the state's direct involvement in economic activity, then developing countries would experience economic growth and development. Getting prices right involves ensuring that the price of foreign exchange is realistic and determined by market forces and that prices for factors of production such as labor, land, and capital reflect their scarcity value. In general, this camp espouses the primacy of the market over state intervention.

One of the fundamental contrasts among these various models of the development process surrounds the trade and investment strategies countries should pursue. In particular, the various models have different prescriptions about the extent to which developing countries should open their economies to the developed world. It is these trade and investment strategies that provide the greatest insights into the role that international business plays in economic development.

TRADE AND INVESTMENT STRATEGIES

Debate on which trade strategies are more conducive to economic development has focused on three different strategic approaches. The first approach suggests that developing countries should follow the dictates of neoclassical comparative advantage or countries specializing in producing goods they have historically been very good at producing because of their natural endowments. This trade strategy has emphasized a specialization in the production and export of primary products, such as agricultural crops—sugar, bananas, coffee, cocoa, and so on—and raw materials—tin, rubber, bauxite, petroleum, and so on. This strategy, in its earlier years, relied on colonial powers and later on multinational firms. Over time, many governments in developing countries have taken over the operations of multinationals, although many multinationals still play an important role, often in joint operations with businesses in developing countries that are actually owned by the state.

The foregoing trade strategy corresponds most closely with the neoclassical development camp. It requires little in the way of government intervention, either in terms of direct involvement in the economy or with respect to the determination of various prices within an economy. This strategy that prevailed in many developing countries during colonial years was largely abandoned during the 1960s and 1970s but has become popular once again in the 1980s and 1990s.

A strategy of trying to use primary exports as an engine for development was abandoned by many developing countries during the 1960s, largely in response to the influence of the dependency and structuralist schools of development. Both of these schools of thought saw industrialization as synonymous with development. The implication was that developing countries should shift their economic structures toward industry and away from agriculture (structuralists) or from the production of commodities based on a neocolonialist orientation (dependency theorists). Such a shift toward industry required protection of new industries from external competition. Thus was created the trade strategy of import-substitution industrialization. This trade strategy eventually came to be popularly hailed by economic planners and academics in developing countries and by the development advisers and specialists from multilateral organizations such as the WB, and academic institutions in developed countries.

The import-substitution trade strategy involved protection, often applied in very liberal doses, for firms in developing countries that were willing to produce goods locally that could substitute for imports. Protection was often initially applied to firms that produced consumer goods from imported materials—the "easy" stage of import substitution. The expectation was that firms over time would move backward to different points along the vertical chain of production.

In the 1980s, a counterrevolution occurred in trade strategies. Arising out of a disenchantment with the effectiveness of the import-substitution programs of the 1950s to the 1970s and the success of several developing countries in East Asia that had apparently followed an export-led growth strategy, many developing countries—with the prompting and advice of developed-country economists and the international financial institutions—engaged in a strategic backlash that involved the move to a "new" strategy of export promotion.

According to this strategy, developing countries should remove protection of their economies and seek to promote industries in which they have a current or potential competitive advantage. The term *competitive advantage* is often deliberately used instead of *comparative advantage* to differentiate this strategy from the blind following of the dictates of comparative advantage, especially with regard to what is felt to be one of the critical disadvantages of comparative advantage—its static nature, or inability to recognize that countries can significantly improve their international competitiveness in a particular sector or industry over time. This trade strategy is most allied with the neoclassical development camp, but its adherents would identify themselves as modern neoclassicals, if you will, since they claim to accept the fact that government intervention may be necessary at times in order for a country to pursue its competitive rather than comparative advantages.

It is clear that some types of international business activities are required regardless of which of these strategies a country adopts. Both export-oriented strategies, whether the export of primary products or that of less traditional products, require the existence of domestic or foreign firms that can produce goods and export to world markets.

The strategy of import substitution would seem to involve far less in the way of international business activities. While this may well be true, one must recognize that developing countries pursuing such a strategy have often allowed multinational firms to invest in the country to produce goods that would substitute for imports, although the countries that have been most intent on pursuing an import-substitution strategy have tended to be relatively hostile to the operations of foreign investors. Even where governments have pursued this strategy primarily through the productive activities of indigenous firms, however, these firms have often relied on international business activities.

Such activities include importing the capital and raw materials they need for their production processes and licensing the technology of foreign firms as the means by which they acquire the technology they need to produce internally goods that were, until this time, imported.

The most notable difference between the strategy of import substitution and the export-oriented strategies is that the former strategy does not require that the firms, whether domestic or foreign, operate at internationally competitive levels in the short term. Theoretically, they should achieve internationally competitive levels of operation in the long term, but theory and reality often diverge in this, as in other instances. The experience of countries pursuing import-substitution strategies was that most such firms never achieved internationally competitive standards, as evidenced by their ability to compete against imports without government subsidies or protection, or as evidenced even more strongly by their ability to enter export markets and export goods to a wide array of countries.

THE ROLE OF INTERNATIONAL BUSINESS IN ECONOMIC DEVELOPMENT

It is clear, then, that for most countries, international business has a fundamentally important role to play in economic development. The only group of countries that would conceive of economic development other than through international business are those that would opt for autarky, or the cessation of trade with the rest of the world. These countries would seek to substitute, through indigenous firms, domestic production for imported goods. This would be an extreme response to the arguments of the dependency school. Since underdevelopment is a function of structural relations with the rest of the world, then the solution to underdevelopment would be to rupture those relations in the direction described previously.

If the previous approach, with its obvious deficiencies, is not to be the development strategy, then international business transactions will play the most critical role in spearheading the thrust to develop. International business, whether in the form of trade, licensing, or investment, is the medium that allows a country to stay in touch with the rest of the world. In the absence of such contacts, countries—in their efforts to develop—will be unable to tap into technology, capital, products, and management skills developed in other parts of the world. Developing countries, by definition, are seeking to close the gap between developed countries and their own economies. It is easier to close this gap if they can take advantage of what the developed countries already know. If they cannot, they are forced to reinvent technology, products, and management practices.

This is true, albeit to somewhat different degrees, regardless of the trade or development strategy pursued by a country beyond the extreme position outlined earlier. The objective of the import-substitution strategy was not to close off a country from the world but, rather, to close off the country from imports in order that a domestic industry could be established. In practice, for many developing countries, this distinction was not made; and these countries were effectively shut off from the rest of the world with negative consequences for their ability to narrow the gap between the competitiveness of their firms and that of firms in other parts of the world. In the more successful pursuit of closed-market strategies, there were continuous attempts to import current best-international practices and technology into the country. This was often done through the international business practice of licensing technology.

Interaction with the global economy, however, is a two-way street. The country that seeks to interact with the global economy must have something to offer. It must host some internationally competitive businesses whose international earnings allow the country to acquire products, skills, and technology developed outside its borders. No country will find that all of its sectors are internationally competitive, nor is it likely that a country will find that it has no internationally competitive sectors. The issue as it relates to economic development is the proportion of the economy that is competitive versus that uncompetitive segment of the economy that is subsidized by the competitive segments of the economy. Clearly, economic development of a country results as the internationally competitive operations of firms within the country increasingly outweigh the uncompetitive operations of other firms.

This is especially true when one recognizes that economic development has relative as well as absolute dimensions. The peoples of the developing world are, in many cases, much better off than they were several decades ago. This has proven to be little consolation, however, since they continue to be much worse off than the developed countries of the world. Improvements in economic performance relative to other countries, however, are most easily achieved if one understands and, more important, has access to the elements that helped improve the performance of these other countries.

Interaction with the economy outside the borders of the country becomes more important the smaller is the country in question. Further, the smaller the country, the more likely it is that an important part of the process of interaction will come through trade. Small countries, for example, will find it more difficult than larger countries to persuade companies that have been denied the opportunity of trade or investment to license their technologies as their last option for taking advantage of the country's market.

The greater relative importance of interaction and trade for smaller countries is no more than the theory behind all economic specialization. The smaller the unit in question, the less likely it is that such a unit can do many things very well. Whereas a town might be able to be self-sufficient in many functions and still perform them well, this is less likely to be possible in a community within that town and very unlikely within one family in the town. Similarly, where a large country—albeit not usually a developing one—might be able to host many industries that are competitive by world standards, a small country would be unlikely to have such a range of resources to make such an achievement possible. As a consequence, international business becomes particularly important for the economic development of smaller countries.

The information in Table 1.3 makes this point with respect to international trade. The largest countries in the world, irrespective of levels of development or developmental strategies, are less engaged in trade with the rest of the world than are the smallest developing countries. In Table 1.3, large coun-

Table 1.3
Importance of Trade to Large and Small Countries, 1991

Country	GDP (US$ Millions)	Imports and Exports (US$ Millions)	Imports and Exports/GDP (Percentage)
Large Countries			
Bangladesh	23,394	5,188	22.17
India	221,925	38,082	17.16
China	369,651	136,666	36.97
Pakistan	40,244	14,967	37.19
Indonesia	116,476	54,866	47.10
Brazil	414,061	54,569	13.18
United States	5,610,800	903,947	16.11
Japan	3,362,282	548,498	16.31
Average			_25.77_
Small Countries			
Guinea-Bissau	211	106	50.2
Mauritania	1,030	908	88.15
Congo	2,909	1,979	68.03
Jamaica	3,497	2,924	83.61
Panama	5,544	2,014	68.03
Mauritius	2,253	2,768	122.85
Trinidad & Tobago	4,920	3,652	74.23
Gabon	4,863	3,989	82.02
Singapore	39,984	124,853	312.26
Average			_101.96_
Average (exluding Singapore)			_75.68_

Source: World Bank, *World Development Report, 1993* (New York: Oxford University Press, 1993).

tries are defined as those with a population of 100 million or more in 1991; small countries are those with populations of 3 million or less in 1991, for which data were readily available. Note that in the world's champion of free trade (i.e., the United States), trading activity represents a relatively small proportion of the country's GDP. The United States could loosen its trading ties with the rest of the world at far less dislocation to the nation than would be true if a much smaller country such as Mauritius or Jamaica sought to loosen its trading ties to the rest of the world.

The remainder of the book continues along the path taken by this chapter by examining the interaction between international business, international competitiveness, and economic development. It does so by examining the theories, concepts, and systems of international business from the perspective of developing countries; continuing and deepening the discussion of international trade, international investment, and intermediate forms of international business; and also discussing the financial systems that provide the lubrication that allows the cross-border movement of goods and capital. The book also continues the focus on economic development and international competitiveness—particularly in Chapters 10 to 15—by examining how firms operating in developing countries, whether indigenous firms or the subsidiaries of multinationals, can manage their international operations so that they become or remain internationally competitive.

FURTHER READING

Beckford, George L. *Persistent Poverty: Underdevelopment in Plantation Economies of the Third World.* Oxford: Oxford University Press, 1972.

Chenery, Hollis B., and Lance J. Taylor. "Development Patterns: Among Countries and over Time," *Review of Economics and Statistics* (November 1968): 391-416.

Lewis, W. Arthur. *The Evolution of the International Economic Order.* Princeton: Princeton University Press, 1977.

Todaro, Michael P. *Economic Development in the Third World.* New York: Longman, 1989.

United Nations Development Program. *Human Development Report, 1994.* New York: Oxford University Press, 1994.

World Bank. *World Development Report, 1993.* New York: Oxford University Press, 1993.

World Bank. *World Development Report, 1994.* New York: Oxford University Press, 1994.

Chapter 2

International Trade Theory, Practice, and Policy

The choice of free trade versus protection policy that has dominated issues of trade policy over the last few decades has been debated with even greater intensity in developing countries than in developed countries. In order to assess the policies of developing countries toward trade, it is useful to return to "first principles" and examine trade theories, with the objective of understanding the implications of theory for trade policy. Since in both developing and developed countries there are typically various perspectives on the extent to which the country should engage in trade, it is appropriate to begin any discussion of trade with the fundamental question, "Why do countries trade with each other?" The answer to this question lies in the analyses of the eighteenth- and nineteenth-century classical economists, the "neoclassical" theories developed more recently by twentieth-century economists, and newer classes of trade theories introduced by economists and business scholars only during the last few decades.

ABSOLUTE ADVANTAGE

It is well known that the first important classical trade theorist was Adam Smith. In his 1776 treatise, *The Wealth of Nations,* Smith suggested that countries would gain from trade, both exporting and importing, as long as each country had an absolute advantage in the production of a particular good. Such an advantage would be recognized in that country's ability to produce the good more cheaply than every other country. This conclusion was interesting at the time because it disagreed with the prevailing notion of mercantilism in which each country emphasized the advantages of exporting over importing. Since countries received gold as payment for their exports during the period of mercantilist philosophy (circa 1500–1800), this trade strategy allowed countries to expand their holdings of wealth in the form of gold. Smith's theory of absolute advantage, on the other hand, disagreed with the mercantilist philosophy of national wealth. Instead, he suggested that a country's wealth was reflected in the living standards of its residents. Consequently, importing was not only necessary but also beneficial to a country if it imported goods that other countries could produce more efficiently.

Using an illustration that corresponds to the reality and imagery of the era in which Smith developed his theory, let us assume, as indicated in Table 2.1, that England and France had equal quantities of productive resources and that England could produce with all its productive resources either 100 units of machinery or 40 units of wine, and France using all of its productive resources could produce either 30 units of machinery or 120 units of wine. Under these conditions, with England having an absolute advantage in the production of machinery and France an absolute advantage in the production of wine, England should specialize in machinery, France in wine, and both countries should export their surplus production and import the wine or machinery that their residents demand.

Table 2.1
Absolute Advantage

	Units of Output by Sector of Economy		
National and Global Production	**Machinery**		**Wine**
England	100	or	40
France	30	or	120
	——		——
Pre-Trade Global Production*	65	and	80
Post-Trade Global Production	100	and	120

* Assuming both countries split their available resources equally between the production of machinery and the production of wine.

In this example, note that the potential welfare of both countries clearly improves after trade. If there were no trade between these countries and they each decided to split their productive resources equally between machinery and wine, their combined production would be 65 units of machinery and 80 units of wine. If, on the other hand, both countries specialize in the area of their absolute advantage, recognizing that they can export their surplus production and import the good that they desire but do not produce, their combined production increases to 100 units of machinery and 120 units of wine. Joint production has increased by 35 units of machinery and 40 units of wine, and both countries can increase their consumption of machinery and wine. Thus, the case for specialization and trade is clear in the context of the theory of absolute advantage.

COMPARATIVE ADVANTAGE

Implicit in Adam Smith's theory of absolute advantage is the suggestion that a country that can produce all goods more efficiently than any other country should never import. Of course, were this to be the case in a world of two countries, no trade would ever take place. This seems like a very reasonable conclusion: Why should a country import a good that it can produce more efficiently than can the country from which it would be imported? In 1817, the political economist, David Ricardo, provided an answer to this question in his book, *The Principles of Political Economy and Taxation,* and indicated that the apparently reasonable conclusion was wrong. In so doing, Ricardo developed the theory of comparative advantage.

In his theory of comparative advantage, Ricardo argued that trade between any two countries was beneficial as long as these countries produced goods with different relative efficiency. In the Ricardian framework, differences in relative efficiency were based on differences in the productivity of labor across countries. The concept of producing goods with different relative efficiencies is best explained by an example.

Suppose that the world comprised two countries—Bolivia and the United States—and that both countries could produce two products: computer software and shoes. Suppose further that the United States used four units of resources to produce a unit of software, and ten units of resources to produce a unit of shoes, while Bolivia used twelve and fifteen units of resources, respectively, as shown in Table 2.2. According to absolute advantage, since the United States produces both goods more efficiently (with fewer resources) than does Bolivia, the United States should import neither product from Bolivia. According to comparative advantage, however, this example meets the test of a situation where two countries can benefit from trade. The United States and Bolivia produce two goods with different relative efficiency. The United States has a comparative advantage over Bolivia in the production of computer software relative to shoes because it produces computer software

Table 2.2
Comparative Advantage

Country	Units of Resources Required to Produce One Unit	
	Computer Software	Shoes
United States	4	10
Bolivia	12	15
Relative cost & efficiency	*United States is one-third as costly and three times as efficient as Bolivia*	*United States is two-thirds as costly and 1.5 times as efficient as Bolivia*

three times as efficiently (with one-third—4 units/12 units—of the resources) as Bolivia, while it produces shoes only 1.5 times as efficiently (with two-thirds—10 units/15 units—of the resources) as Bolivia. It is important to note that—based upon these figures—although Bolivia has an absolute disadvantage in the production of both products, it has a comparative advantage over the United States in the production of shoes relative to computer software.

To see the implication of these relative differences in efficiency, think of what happens if the United States gives up shoe production (its area of relative inefficiency) in favor of computer software production (its area of relative efficiency). If the United States produces one fewer unit of shoes, it releases ten units of productive resources that can be used to produce 2.5 units of computer programs. Since Bolivia would use thirty units of productive resources to produce those 2.5 units of computer programs, the same as it would use to produce two units of shoes, it would be willing to give up two units of shoes in exchange for the computer programs. Consequently, the result of the United States releasing shoe resources in favor of producing computer software is to increase the supply of shoes that both countries produce by one unit while holding constant the supply of computer software. Theoretically, this process of shifting resources should continue until the world's output can no longer be increased by an internal shift of resources in either the United States or Bolivia.

Since "world" production has increased, both countries have the potential to benefit from this specialization and trade. Both countries might not benefit. The United States might be able to negotiate with Bolivia so that it receives all of the extra unit of shoes. The important point to note, however, is that, in the context of the assumptions of comparative advantage theory, the world cannot lose from trade and that both countries have the potential to gain from trade.

Note also that the possibility of gains from trade does not require one to assume that the countries have equivalent quantities of productive resources. The basis for trade lies in differences in the ratios of productive efficiency not in the quantity of resources a country has available. If, for example, Bolivia had 300 units of productive resources available, while the United States had 3 million, this would reduce neither the desirability of trade nor the direction of trade. It would only reduce the amount of trade. Although Bolivia would continue to specialize in shoe production, the United States may be unable to completely specialize in computer software production because Bolivia, with its limited resources, might be unable to supply all of the U.S. shoe requirements or consume all of the U.S. excess computer software production. Thus, in this two-country world, the United States might continue to produce shoes but only after it has imported all of Bolivia's excess shoe production, which, in this two-product world, is equivalent to the exporting of all of its excess computer software production.

Not only is trade not dependent upon countries having similar quantities of productive resources; it is also not dependent upon them offering similar payments to the factors of production, including wages to workers. In fact, differences in real payments to the factors of production, land, labor, capital, and enterprise can be expected when there are differences in the productivity of the countries' factors of production or in the relative availability of, and demand for, those resources. In the previous example, the greater productivity of factors of production in the United States relative to Bolivia would suggest that these factors of production would generate higher incomes in the United States compared with Bolivia. These differences in payments to factors of production, including wages paid to workers, do not reduce the potential gains from trade.

One of the important neoclassical advances to comparative advantage theory was developed by two Swedish economists, Eli Heckscher and Bertil Ohlin, writing in the twentieth century. Together, they developed the factor endowments base for international trade. Using simplifying assumptions, they developed what has come to be known as the Heckscher–Ohlin theory, which suggests that a country has a comparative advantage in the good that uses intensively the factor of production of which it has an abundant supply. The theory is based upon the proposition that different products require productive factors in different proportions and that countries have different endowments of these productive factors. Thus, the theory suggests that a country with a large pool of capital will find that capital is cheap relative to other factors of production and, therefore, such a country should have a comparative advantage in capital-intensive products. Similarly, a country with abundant supplies of labor will find that labor is relatively cheaper, providing that country with a comparative advantage in labor-intensive products.

Classical trade theories and, to a lesser extent, neoclassical theories rely upon assumptions that diverge from reality. At issue is whether this divergence affects the generalizability of the theories.

ASSUMPTIONS OF COMPARATIVE ADVANTAGE THEORY THAT DIVERGE FROM REALITY

There are certain assumptions of the simple Ricardian model of comparative advantage theory that do not correspond to reality. Some of these assumptions are easily incorporated into neoclassical versions of the theory and may be viewed as weakly realistic; others are unrealistic and are not easily incorporated into classical or neoclassical trade theory.

Multiple Countries, Multiple Products

The assumptions most easily dispensed with are those of a two-country world in which there are only two tradeable goods. The Ricardian model easily expands to take into account multiple countries producing multiple goods without any loss of generality.

Mobility of Factors of Production

The Ricardian model also assumes that factors of production are completely mobile within a country and completely immobile across countries. Of course, neither assumption is correct; and both inaccuracies reduce the power of the model. Since resources are not freely mobile within countries, it is more difficult for countries to specialize by switching from the production of one good to the production of another. In the foregoing thought experiment using the United States and Bolivia, some of the laborers used in the production of computer software in Bolivia might find it difficult to switch to shoe production. Alternately, factors of production move more easily across countries than the theory suggests. Thus, some of the highly productive computer software experts in the United States might be willing to take their professional skills, their capital, and their entrepreneurial abilities and relocate to Bolivia.

Although both assumptions about factor mobility are inaccurate, however, they are also closer to reality than their extreme opposite assumptions. Thus, factors of production within a country are more mobile than immobile, especially over the long term. Further, factors of production, especially land and labor, find it relatively difficult to move among countries. Thus, these assumptions reduce the doctrinaire prescriptions of the theory without reducing its underlying explanatory and prescriptive power. In some cases, these reality checks can be incorporated formally. Thus, the reduced mobility of factors of production within a country is incorporated into neoclassical trade models by assuming that each productive resource that is transferred from one use to another will be transferred at increasing cost. (In the jargon of the economist, the production possibility curve becomes concave from the origin in contrast to the use of a straight-line production-possibility curve.)

Transport Costs

The simple Ricardian model ignores transport costs, but these are also easily incorporated into the theory. The result, however, is that for certain types of goods with high transport costs, the benefits of specialization are negated by the costs of transporting goods across countries. Other unrealistic assumptions of comparative advantage theory present much greater threats to the explanatory power of the theory.

Demand Factors and Consumer Tastes

Classical and neoclassical comparative advantage theory is concerned principally with production and supply issues. There are two important assumptions with respect to demand. The first is that there is assumed to be sufficient demand for goods that are produced. Second, it is assumed that consumers in different countries have similar tastes in goods. Of course, neither of these assumptions reflect reality. Consumer demand constrains the extent of specialization, although it does not affect the direction. The United States may have a comparative advantage in the production of commercial aircraft. The resources it places into commercial aircraft production, however, are likely to be constrained by the demand for this product, even worldwide demand.

The other significant demand-related assumption is that of monolithic consumer tastes. Clearly, consumers around the world do not have the same tastes in goods despite apparent trends to create global products and markets. These differences in taste may provide an opportunity for production and sale of a good to be based on an ability to identify the particular tastes of consumers rather than be based only on least-cost production, as is true of export production according to classical and neoclassical trade theories.

Constant Returns to Scale

If firms produced according to constant returns to scale and did not benefit from a learning curve, then the early identification of a market segment interested in a different type of product would not represent a competitive advantage. Once this market was identified, other firms could seek to serve it, thus forcing competition to return to least-cost considerations. Because these assumptions do not hold, there are advantages to being the first company to move into new markets. Firms do not produce according to constant returns to scale; that is, as the firm increases production, the cost per unit of output does not remain the same. On the contrary, in most industries, firms benefit from increasing returns to scale or economies of scale; that is, as output increases, there is a decline in the unit cost of producing that output.

Experience–Learning Curve

A concept that is related to increasing returns to scale is the learning curve, or its first cousin, the experience curve. Both curves convey the notion that as a firm learns more about a production process because of its experience producing the product, it will be able to reduce the costs of producing the product. In contrast to the message of these curves, comparative advantage theory assumes that there are no cost-reduction benefits associated with experience and learning in the same way that there are none associated with volume.

Each of these three unrealistic assumptions significantly reduces the explanatory and prescriptive power of comparative advantage theory. The prescriptions that have built upon the intellectual underpinning of comparative advantage theory include the notion that rational governments should specialize in the goods they produce most competitively based on their natural endowment of factors of production. Further, it is said that they should maintain open borders that allow the export of their surplus production and the importing of the other goods their residents demand. Implicit in comparative advantage theory with its traditional factor-endowment focus is a pattern of trade in which most of the trade flowing across national borders would be in dissimilar products and between dissimilar countries, that is, countries with different factor endowments.

TRADE PRACTICE AND NEW TRADE THEORIES

In fact, the practice of trade is quite different from the prescriptions implicit in comparative advantage theory. Most countries restrict trade using a plethora of techniques. In using these techniques, countries seek to "create" comparative advantage instead of relying on nature's endowments.

Where trade does take place, a significant proportion takes place among countries with similar factor endowments (e.g., some 80 percent of world trade takes place among industrialized countries). Further, instead of the interindustry trade that is implied by comparative advantage theory, much of worldwide trade is of the intraindustry variety. For some products, the degree of intraindustry trade is particularly high. In the mid-1980s, for example, Yoffie reports that some 70 percent of worldwide exports of antifriction bearings, a critical component in most manufactured products, went to countries that also exported antifriction bearings.

New Theories of Trade

While classical and neoclassical comparative advantage theories do not explain these worldwide trading patterns, they are explained by new theories of trade that have attempted to build trade models that incorporate more realistic assumptions than those of comparative advantage theory. These models, developed by economists and business scholars such as Paul Krugman, Ray Vernon, and Michael Porter, suggest that increasing returns to scale and product differentiation furnish a basis for trade independent of comparative advantage. Increasing returns to scale and the learning curve phenomenon suggest, unlike comparative advantage, that a country's pattern of trade may be determined by acquired expertise rather than naturally endowed factors of production.

The Product Cycle theory, for example, places special consideration on the impact of demand factors in determining trade patterns. It argues that products tend to be developed to meet the needs of a market close to the home of the producer. The idea is that firms do not have perfect information on all markets around the world and that they are most likely to respond to the opportunities close to home. Further, not all countries are likely to spawn innovating firms. Rather, they are likely to emerge in countries with plentiful supplies of skilled labor that can be employed to produce the product and high-income consumers that are likely to purchase the innovative good. It is usually the developed countries that meet these criteria.

Thus, innovations will be spawned in a developed country; and during the new product stage of the product cycle, these products will principally be sold in that home market with exports beginning to other developed countries. As the product matures, exports will increase and will include exports to developing countries. Over time, the product becomes standardized and competition becomes driven by cost. In many such cases, the product may be produced in developing countries to take advantage of lower costs and be exported back to the original innovating country. This view of trade patterns suggests that comparative advantage is driven by demand as well as supply and that it is not static. A country's relative ability to produce a product can change over time and is as dependent upon acquired skills as it is on natural endowments. This theory—with its recognition of the probability of product differentiation—also explains the reality of intraindustry trade.

Generally, product differentiation furnishes a basis for trade independent of comparative advantage, and this trade may well be intraindustry trade. Station wagons, for example, are more popular in the United States than they are in most other countries. Demand factors within the United States are particularly conducive to this type of automobile. Americans have access to a very well-developed interstate highway system, the country is large, and Americans travel extensively by automobile. While there are individuals in other countries that purchase station wagons, the largest concentration of consumers of these automobiles resides in the United States. Consequently, the Japanese automobile company, Honda, builds station wagons in the United States, close to its most demanding customers, and exports these to Japan. At the same time, Honda builds sedans in Japan and exports them to the United States.

Increasing returns to scale and learning also furnish a basis for trade independent of comparative advantage. A country could become competitive in a particular product because of a historical accident or because the product appealed to its consumers. Once the firms in this country begin producing the product, the country's "first-mover" advantages become quite significant because of increasing returns to scale and the ability of these firms to climb a learning curve. These firms will be able to lower their unit production costs because of their ever-expanding operations and their continuous learning about how best to produce the product. These cost advantages will allow firms in this country to out compete their rivals elsewhere. One should note that in trade theories that rely on increasing returns to scale the direction of trade is indeterminate; that is, it is not possible to predict based on any characteristics of any two countries which country will eventually export or which will import. That is entirely dependent upon which country happens to be the "first mover."

A final set of new theories surrounds the role of multinational corporations. These corporations dominate several industries in which there is a significant level of international trade. In fact, trade among affiliates of multinational corporations amounts to some 40 percent of worldwide trade flows. In such cases, contrary to the assumptions of comparative advantage theory, trade cannot be assumed to be a series of discrete arm's-length transactions. Rather, international trade, in these cases, results more from the competitive strategies of these companies and the strategic actions of governments in these countries than it does from the inherent characteristics of a nation, whether these are supply characteristics or demand characteristics. This leads Yoffie to suggest that "when industries become globally concentrated, visible hands rather than anonymous market forces emerge to guide trade."

For example, Wells points out that bauxite is mined in Ghana and that Ghana is the site of a world-class aluminum smelter built and operated by Kaiser. Ghana imports alumina from Jamaica to feed its aluminum smelter, and it exports bauxite to North America and Europe for conversion and smelting in facilities that are owned by the same companies that own mines in Ghana—this, despite the fact that each step in the conversion process cuts the weight to be shipped by one-half. These trade effects that would not be predicted by traditional trade theory are explained by the actions of companies operating in oligopolistic industry settings. Much of the world's bauxite is mined and processed by a few vertically integrated firms. These firms, argues Wells, opted to separate their mining and smelting facilities as a hedge against nationalization. It is this set of corporate strategies that explains some components of trade patterns in this industry.

These are the new theories of trade. Note that these theories do not displace comparative advantage. Rather, they complement comparative advantage; that is, countries specialize and trade with other countries because of differences in factor endowments, but they also trade with other countries because they were or were not able to capture the economies of scale and learning in a particular industry, because their consumers have tastes that differ from those of consumers in other countries, and because of the corporate and governmental strategies pursued by firms in highly concentrated industries.

These new versions of trade theory are captured in the recent work of business scholars. Porter adds to factor endowments the effect of demand patterns, of the competitive structure of industries, and of linkages among industries in explaining patterns of trade competitiveness. Yoffie argues that country-based factors, such as factor endowments and demand patterns, are appropriate for explaining trade patterns in competitive and fragmented industries in which government intervention is low.

In oligopolistic industries where scale and learning effects are critical, however, and in industries in which there is a significant amount of government intervention, it is the dynamics of the global oligopoly, the strategies of these global firms, and the strategies of national governments that will determine the nature of trade flows. The role of national governments is a particularly controversial one with respect to the impact on trade patterns. There are certain industries, such as commercial aircraft, where the late-mover disadvantages were so great because of the significant economies of scale and steep learning curve that it was inconceivable that a firm could challenge the dominance of the U.S. aerospace industry without government support. It was this argument that, of course, led the European governments to establish the Airbus Consortium in an effort to compete with U.S. firms, Boeing and McDonnell Douglas. It is the subject of the government's role in trade policy to which the remainder of the chapter is devoted.

IMPLICATIONS OF TRADE THEORY FOR TRADE POLICY IN DEVELOPING COUNTRIES

Independent governments in developing countries had never felt particularly comfortable with classical and neoclassical theories of trade. They looked around at developed countries and noted that, without exception, all of these countries were also industrial countries; yet it seemed that comparative advantage trade theory would consign them to forever following their "comparative advantage" in minerals; agricultural products; and light, labor-intensive manufactured goods.

In the 1950s, under the intellectual tutelage of Raul Prebisch, Hans Singer, and other economists that spawned the dependency school of development, many developing countries decided to ignore the dictates of comparative advantage and instead to restrict trade in an effort to develop their industrial base. The theoretical contribution of Prebisch and Singer was the development of the concept of the declining terms of trade.

A country's terms of trade represents the relationship between the price of a typical unit of exports and the price of a typical unit of imports. Trends in the terms of trade over time are identified by comparing export and import price indices calculated using the same base period. Prebisch argued that developing countries exported primarily mineral and agricultural commodities with low income elasticities (i.e., products for which demand, and therefore price, increased less than proportionately to increases in income). Developed countries, on the other hand, manufactured and exported goods with higher income elasticities, which saw greater price increases over time. Consequently, developing countries faced declines in their terms of trade. Prebisch's policy advice was that developing countries should seek to avoid this situation by moving into the production of manufactured goods.

Prebisch's analysis found a ready audience throughout the developing world. Jamaica's former prime minister Michael Manley writes in his book, *The Poverty of Nations,* for example, that when Jamaica became independent in 1962, a tractor could be financed with the proceeds of 18 tons of sugar; by 1980, it took 60 tons of sugar to finance the same tractor. Even though evidence is sketchy and this issue is hotly debated along North–South lines especially, it does appear that there has been a long-term decline in the terms of trade for nonfuel commodities.

During the period of Prebisch's original analysis (1870–1936), Prebisch calculated that England experienced a 36-percent increase in its net barter terms of trade, implying that the countries with which England traded—primarily colonies producing agricultural commodities—experienced a decline in their terms of trade. Between the mid-1950s and 1980, there was little change in the terms of trade for nonpetroleum-exporting developing countries. Between 1980 and 1990, however, there has been a relatively significant deterioration in the terms of trade for nonpetroleum-exporting developing countries.

Some analysts would explain away any apparent declines in the terms of trade by suggesting that manufactured products have changed over time. Thus, they would argue that it is inappropriate to compare, as Manley did, a ton of sugar—which is essentially the same in 1980 as it was in 1962—with a tractor that may have changed significantly over the same period. One suspects that Prebisch and his supporters would have said that whatever the cause of the declining terms of trade, the fact that declines are taking place lends support to the idea that developing countries should move away from commodities and move toward goods that are more likely to increase in price over time. This could be accomplished either by further refining, and thereby adding more value, to resource-based products or by shifting from resource-based products to manufactured goods.

Many developing countries did follow the prescriptive advice of Prebisch and the dependency school and engaged in attempts to develop their economies by shifting from an open trading strategy in which they imported manufactured goods and exported raw materials and commodities to an import-substitution development strategy. In a program of import substitution, countries placed high tariffs on imported goods in an effort to stimulate the production of domestic goods that would substitute for imports. This trade strategy was exactly the opposite of the open trade strategy prescribed by comparative advantage principles.

This strategy tended to occur in phases. The first, known as the easy stage of import substitution, involved the substitution of domestic production for the import of consumer goods. The development strategy of import substitution was accomplished through the trade strategy of protection. Governments throughout the developing world placed tariffs on imported goods. In the heyday of the import-substitution strategy, these nominal tariffs were often as high as 100 percent on consumer goods. These nominal tariffs, however, actually understated the extent of protection. This is because governments often allowed firms to import the raw materials that would be used for the assembly of the final products at low or, in extreme cases, zero rates of duty. Such a combination had the effect of making the degree of effective protection much higher than the rate of nominal protection.

Effective protection measures the protection afforded to the value that is added in the production or assembly process locally, compared with the value added to this process overseas. Essentially, it identifies to what extent the sum of local labor, materials, and other local costs can exceed the value that would have to prevail if the firm faced open competition from world markets.

Thus, for example, if a product faces a nominal protection rate of 100 percent, if the imported raw materials that are used to produce this product face no import duties, and if the value that is added in the country granting the tariffs is 50 percent, then a nominal duty of 100 percent translates into an effective rate of protection of 200 percent. That is, if e is the effective tariff rate, n is the nominal tariff rate, and v is the amount of value added internationally, then

$$e = n \, (1/1 - v).$$

To take this example further, if a local company was producing a car for $10,000, in which 50 percent of the production cost represented local costs, then a 100-percent duty on car imports, coupled with duty-free entry of imported raw materials would allow this company to increase its local costs from $5,000 to $15,000 and still remain competitive with imported cars.

During the period when import substitution was a popular development strategy, rates of effective protection in developing countries were, in fact, quite high. Average effective rates of protection were at about 200 percent for India and Pakistan during the 1960s. In the early 1980s, the average effective rate of protection in Indonesia was 124 percent for all sectors; but for the manufacturing sector, effective protection was an astounding 305 percent.

Not surprising, in retrospect, the development strategy of import-substitution industrialization had many unintended consequences. Firms producing in domestic markets with the high effective rates of protection that prevailed in most of the developing countries that undertook this strategy had little incentive to operate efficiently. Indeed, as Chapter 8 points out in greater detail, many of the firms that benefited from this protection and operated inefficiently behind high tariff walls were foreign firms invited into developing countries by governments following the path of import substitution by invitation.

Further, these firms invariably stayed at the easy stage of import substitution, rarely developing backward linkages to other sectors because of the attractiveness of the consumer goods sector. Consequently, imports of raw materials continued to burden the balance of payments of developing countries. Last, in concert with the import-substitution strategy, many developing-country governments maintained overvalued exchange rates that made it less costly to import raw materials; but that hurt those entities seeking to export to world markets. This was not an automatic consequence of an import-substitution industrialization strategy, but most countries that pursued such a strategy maintained overvalued exchange rates.

By the 1980s, most developing-country governments were admitting that import-substitution strategies had not been particularly successful. That is not to say that there were not pockets of success. Particularly in large countries, import-substitution strategies created a rather broad industrial infrastructure. India, for example, has probably the broadest and deepest industrial infrastructure in the developing world, producing a range of products from pins to satellites. In part, this is because of the intensity with which India pursued an import-substitution strategy, maintaining extremely high nominal and effective rates of protection for decades. Although India achieved a measure of self-sufficiency through this development strategy, the Indian experience also points to the inadequacies of this strategy. Some forty years after the initiation of an import-substitution strategy, Indian industry continued, in large part, to operate quite inefficiently by world standards. For example, in the late 1980s, most automobiles driven in India were produced within that country, a feat matched by only one other developing country—Korea. In contrast to Korea, however, Indian cars were produced based on 1950s automotive technology.

Table 2.3 provides data that help dramatize the fact that restrictive trade regimes seemed to have a detrimental impact on a cross-section of projects within the countries that operated such regimes. Other data reported by the World Bank indicate a strong positive correlation between productivity growth and open trade strategies in a sample of developing countries in the periods of 1960 to 1984 and 1977 to 1988.

The mounting evidence pointing to the problems associated with a highly protectionist trade strategy in pursuit of development through import substitution has led many countries to reconsider this strategy and to move, instead, to a strategy of development via export promotion. The principle behind this strategy is to promote exports from the developing country by putting in place certain elements. One important element associated with an export-promo-

Table 2.3
The Impact of Trade Policy on Project Returns in Developing Countries

Trade Restrictions	All Projects	All Public Projects	Public Agricultural Projects	Public Projects in Nontradeable Sectors	All Private Projects
High	13.2	13.6	12.1	14.6	9.5
Moderate	15.0	15.4	15.4	16.0	10.7
Low	19.0	19.3	14.3	24.3	17.1

Source: World Bank, *World Development Report, 1991* (New York: Oxford University Press, 1991).

Note: These returns represent average economic rates of return for 530 projects financed by the World Bank and its private-sector subsidiary, the International Finance Corporation, between 1977 and 1988 in thirty-two developing countries for which comparable data were available on tariffs and nontariff barriers.

tion strategy has been the establishment of a realistic exchange rate, that is, an exchange rate that is not overvalued. In fact, some countries have gone further and deliberately maintained undervalued exchange rates to assist the export sectors of their economies.

Other policies include a nationwide commitment to exporting, access to foreign exchange for exporters, programs of government export subsidies and assistance, and access to raw materials and capital at world market prices for exporters. In order to allow exporters access to raw materials at world prices and to increase competition as an incentive for domestic firms to improve their competitiveness, there has been an almost universal trend among developing countries to liberalize trade regimes by reducing protection. The universality of this move among developing countries is evident by the fact that even India, possibly the last bastion of import-substitution industrialization among developing countries and the country that arguably experienced the most success through this strategy, moved to a program of liberalization of trade in 1991 in order to improve the competitiveness of the Indian manufacturing industry.

Complete import liberalization has not been the path many countries pursuing an export-promotion strategy have chosen. Part of an export-promotion strategy may involve short-term protection for particular industries operating under the principle that producers of certain manufactured goods may need a breathing period to gain an appropriate production scale and climb to an appropriate point on the industry learning curve before they are able to penetrate export markets. Indeed, this is no more than the classic infant-industry argument for protection. The countries of East Asia that are held out as models of export promotion—particularly Japan and South Korea—did, in fact, use protectionist trade strategies in an effort to create new industries. These countries employed a pragmatic rather than an ideological approach to the issue of trade and development strategies, practicing principles that they believed would lead to competitiveness and that were expedient at particular times.

Given the use of protection, some elements of an export-promotion strategy might resemble a strategy of import substitution. The major difference with respect to protection is in its scope and timing. In a strategy of import substitution, a significant portion of the economy is protected. In a strategy of export promotion, specific targeted sectors are protected for specified periods of time. The key to the protection was that it would be temporary and that governments, as far as possible, would use protection to complement the market rather than ignore market mechanisms completely.

The strategy of export promotion follows the principles of trade theory but not classical and neoclassical comparative advantage. Rather, this strategy takes its intellectual justification from the newer trade models, often encapsulated in the term *strategic trade policy,* that add to comparative advantage theory. These models postulate that, in addition to trade taking place because of static comparative advantage, trade can also take place as a result of increasing returns to scale, product differentiation, and learning.

These theories suggest that comparative advantage can be created, that this process of creation can be assisted by the protection of imports coupled with government support for exports, and that it is particularly important for a country to create comparative advantage in certain strategic industries. Countries that appear to have used this strategy quite successfully include Japan and South Korea. In practice, however, there are many who debate whether governments in developing countries can pick the appropriate industries to protect or subsidize and whether they can ensure that these industries become internationally competitive and not forever addicted to and dependent upon government support. Indeed, there continues to be debate about whether countries such as Korea and Japan have developed because of or in spite of governmental policies that seek to protect or support particular sectors of the economy.

Even as many developing countries have tried to move to a strategy of export promotion, there are concerns by many analysts that such a strategy is not feasible for most developing countries and that the East Asian countries which are often held up as models—the four tigers of South Korea, Singapore, Taiwan, and Hong Kong—and increasingly the Southeast Asian countries of Malaysia, Thailand, and Indonesia are exceptions. As more countries seek to export to the same markets, the argument goes, developing countries will find that they are in a zero-sum game in which markets gained by one country will be at the loss of another. A significant concern also is that developed countries are restricting their markets at the same time as developing countries are seeking to increase their exports. This is an important development, and it is this issue of the impact of barriers to trade and the multilateral trading system on the prospects for exports from developing countries that is taken up in the next chapter.

FURTHER READING

Krugman, Paul. *Rethinking International Trade.* Cambridge: MIT Press, 1990.

Manley, Michael. *The Poverty of Nations.* New York: Andre Deutsh, 1990.

Porter, Michael. *The Competitive Advantage of Nations.* New York: Free Press, 1990.

Prebisch, Raul. *The Economic Development of Latin America and Its Principal Problems.* New York: United Nations, 1950.

Singer, Hans W. "The Distribution of the Gains from Trade between Investing and Borrowing Countries." *American Economic Review* 40 (May 1950): 473–485.

Vernon, Raymond. "International Investment and International Trade in the Product Cycle." *Quarterly Journal of Economics* (May 1966): 190–207.

Vernon, Raymond. "The Product Cycle Hypothesis in a New International Environment." *Oxford Bulletin of Economics and Statistics* (1980): 255–268.

Wint, Alvin G., and Louis T. Wells. *Indonesia: Choice of an Industrialization Strategy.* Boston: Harvard Business School, 1987.

World Bank. *World Development Report, 1991.* New York: Oxford University Press, 1991.

Yoffie, David B., ed. *Beyond Free Trade: Firms, Governments and Global Competition.* Boston: Harvard Business School Press, 1993.

Yoffie, David B. *Power and Protectionism: Strategies of the Newly Industrializing Countries.* New York: Columbia University Press, 1983.

Chapter 3

The Framework
for International Trade

The institutional and administrative framework for the international trading system reflects the contradictions in trade theory and policy discussed in Chapter 2. On the one hand, virtually every country in the world restricts trade in goods and services in some form or another. On the other hand, at the heart of the current trading system is the World Trade Organization (WTO)—formerly the General Agreement on Tariffs and Trade (GATT). This institution takes as its operating principle the notion that countries should move consistently toward a free market in goods and services and that this movement would be most rapid if negotiations toward this end were held on a multilateral rather than a bilateral basis.

Both developed and developing countries have experienced and contributed toward the conflicts in trade policy symptomatic of the post–World War II era. Developed countries, while championing free trade, have systematically restricted trade in industries such as agriculture, automobiles, textiles, footwear, and commercial aircraft. Likewise, developing countries, though eager to export their products to the markets of developed countries, have not been sanguine about their prospects for development if they allow the products of developed countries unfettered access to their own markets. Indeed, they have contributed to the collection of institutions and policies that represents the framework for international trade by trying to create, within the United Nations System, an organization to assist them in their quest for an international trading system that would be equitable according to their perspective.

The manager operating in a developing country needs to understand the nature of the trade regime in the country within which he or she operates; the regime that applies in the developed country markets that he or she seeks to penetrate; and the trends, whether toward protection or liberalization, in both sets of countries. Developments in both trade environments are likely to have an important impact on the competitiveness of the firm. It is with these issues in mind that this chapter is organized around the components of the international trading system listed in Table 3.1.

Table 3.1 summarizes the components of the current international trading system: national regulations on trade that primarily take the place of trade barriers; a multilateral trading organization in the form of the WTO that strives for a circumscribed form of free trade; several nonreciprocal trading regimes that, within the general ambit of WTO legislation, allow for one-way free trade (albeit often with severe restrictions) from developing countries to industrialized countries; and institutions such as the United Nations Center on Trade and Development (UNCTAD) that seek to represent the cause of the developing countries in negotiations on trading rights and obligations.

NATIONAL REGULATIONS ON TRADE

Nations typically regulate trade by erecting barriers to imports. Countries, at times, also establish controls on exports. This has been particularly true of industrialized countries in areas such as military applications. This activity, however, is not restricted to these applications. Early in the process of industrialization, for example, England restricted the export of textile manufacturing machinery. For developing countries, however, the principal type of export

Table 3.1
Components of the International Trading System

Component	Implementation Mechanism
National regulations on trade	Tariffs; Quotas; Voluntary Export Restraints (VERs); Orderly Marketing Arrangements (OMAs); Nontariff Barriers (NTBs)
Multilateral trading organization	World Trade Organization (WTO) -- formerly the General Agreement on Tariffs and Trade (GATT)
Nonreciprocal trading regimes	Lome IV; Caribbean Basin Initiative (CBI); Caribbean-Canada (CARIBCAN); Generalized System of Preferences (GSP)
Developing country response to international trading system	United Nations Center on Trade and Development (UNCTAD); New International Economic Order (NIEO)

controls are those associated with efforts to influence world market prices for particular products, such as petroleum and agricultural commodities, or controls on the export of scarce natural resources or products of cultural significance. In general, a discussion of trade regulation, particularly in the context of the developing world, revolves around import barriers.

Import barriers are of two fundamental types: those barriers whose first-order effect is on the price at which imported goods are sold domestically, and those barriers that primarily affect the quantity of imported goods available for sale. The principal price-related import barrier is the tariff. Tariffs represent taxes, or duties, applied by governments on the c.i.f. value (i.e., the value inclusive of cost, insurance, and freight) of imported goods, normally presented as a percentage of that value.

There are other types of import barriers, several of which are becoming more significant than tariffs. In general, import barriers other than tariffs influence the quantity of incoming imports. These barriers include import quotas that specify the quantity of goods that can be imported. These quotas are particularly popular in industrialized countries in sectors such as agriculture, garments, footwear, and automobiles. Indeed, some of the quota systems that have been established are quite complex, and one in particular—the Multifiber Arrangement (MFA)—has become an integral part of the system of multilateral trading.

Two more recent forms of import barriers that mirror the quota are the voluntary export restraint (VER) and the orderly marketing arrangement (OMA). Both forms of barriers represent the outcome of bilateral negotiations between importer and exporter in which the importer negotiates "voluntary" restraint on the part of the exporter in order to ensure that imports are reduced or that they increase only gradually and in an "orderly" manner. The most visible examples of VERs were in the arrangements negotiated between the U.S. government and the Japanese automobile industry in the mid-1980s. OMAs are also used in efforts to increase the level of imports entering a country, as was seen in the 1986 United States–Japan semiconductor agreement that called for U.S. firms to obtain a 20-percent share of Japan's semiconductor market by 1991.

In theory, all trade barriers other than tariffs could be classified as nontariff barriers (NTBs). In practice, however, this designation has been reserved for particular types of trade barriers that are not formally established as trade barriers but, rather, block imports in unconventional, opaque, and subtle ways. Popular measures are lengthy inspections, stringent health and safety standards, government procurement programs that operate in favor of national firms, and cumbersome distribution systems. In October 1982, for example, the French government stipulated that all imported video recorders (imported mainly from Japan) must clear customs at Poitiers, a small city in the interior of France, rather than at Le Havre, the main port of Paris. Similarly, on arrival in Japan, U.S.-made baseballs must be unwrapped, inspected, and rewrapped. These measures constitute NTBs to the extent that they place importers at a competitive disadvantage relative to domestic suppliers of equivalent goods.

The scope of national regulations on trade is best demonstrated through an examination of the trade laws of one country. Since, for many managers in developing countries, the most important market is the U.S. market, it is worthwhile to examine the trade laws and policies of the United States.

The Trade Laws of the United States

The trade laws of the United States address four types of trade-related problems: rapid increases in imports, unacceptable trade barriers in foreign countries, the inequity of export subsidies provided by foreign governments, and import prices that are lower than fair market prices. The laws provide protection in various forms for firms threatened with substantial or material injury because of increases in imports. The various injury provisions are elaborated on in trade legislation. For example, increased imports cause substantial injury if these imports are no less important than other factors in causing serious injury to a petitioning firm.

This "injury test," established for the first time in the 1974 trade law, was a relaxation of the injury test of the 1962 trade law. That law only allowed relief for petitioning firms if imports were a "major cause" of serious injury. A major cause was defined to be a factor more important than all other factors that could have caused serious injury. The Trade Act of 1974 set out the following criteria that U.S. authorities (U.S. International Trade Commission [ITC]) had to use in determining whether the industry had suffered serious injury: a decline in sales; a higher and growing inventory; and a downward trend in production, profit, wages, or employment in the particular industry.

Countervailing and antidumping laws used even weaker injury tests. These laws allowed the implementation of duties if the actions of the foreign firm or government were causing or threatened to cause material injury. The threat of material injury might be indicated by increases in production capacity, rapid increases in U.S. market penetration, or substantial increases in U.S. inventories.

The penalties for the laws were various. The escape clause led to penalties in the form of duties or quotas applied against the relevant imports. As an alternative to import relief, under the U.S. trade laws beginning with the provisions of the 1962 act, the ITC could recommend that trade-adjustment assistance be provided to the workers and firms suffering from import competition. This assistance could take the form of financial, technical, or retraining assistance. The laws designed to ameliorate the effects of unfair trade practices by foreign governments allowed the Executive Branch of the U.S. government to retaliate against countries felt to have unacceptably high trade barriers or to be engaged in unfair trade practices. Last, the countervailing and antidumping laws permit the assignment of offsetting duties against the exports of firms that have benefited from subsidies from their home governments (countervailing) and against firms that are believed to be pricing their goods below fair market values in the United States (antidumping). Table 3.2 provides a summary of the applicable laws.

The Rationale for Trade Barriers

Countries erect barriers to imports for a variety of reasons. The classic case for import restrictions is the infant industry argument. According to that argument, especially as formalized in several of the new models of trade, certain industries need protection from imports in their infancy in order to allow them to develop so that they can compete internationally in the future. This argument in its purest form agrees with the general principles of comparative advantage trade theory but supports protection for particular types of infant industries because of two fundamental assumptions of that theory that—as pointed out in Chapter 2—do not, in reality, hold true.

One of these assumptions is that firms operate according to constant rather than increasing returns to scale. The second is that firms do not climb a learn-

Table 3.2
Summary of U.S. Trade Law

	Escape Clause	Retaliation	Countervailing Duty	Antidumping Duty
Problems Addressed	Increasing Import competition	Foreign Trade Barriers	Government Export Subsidies	Unfair Import Price
U.S. Laws	Sec. 201 of 1974 Trade Act (as modified)	Sec. 301 of 1974 Trade Act (as modified)	Sec. 303 of 1930 Trade Act (as modified)	Sec. 731 of 1930 Trade Act (as modified)
Rules	Increased imports found to cause "substantial injury" to petitioning firms	Barriers restrict U.S. commerce	Firm receives export subsidy which causes "material injury" to U.S. firm	Firm is found to have priced below "fair market causing "material injury" to U.S. firm
Penalties	Duties, Quotas, OMAs, VERs	Any import restraint at President's discretion	Countervaling duties applied	Antidumping duties applied

Source: Adapted from Alvin G. Wint and David B. Yoffie, "United States Trade Law," in *International Trade and Competition: Cases and Notes in Strategy and Management,* edited by David B. Yoffie (New York: McGraw Hill, 1990).

ing curve; that is, the unit costs of production a firm faces do not decline with experience in production or delivery of the good or service. Consequently, there is a rationale for governments to protect firms in their countries that have solid prospects of internationally competitive operations but need protection from imports until they reach a scale of production and a level of experience that will allow them to compete with their foreign rivals.

Continuing this line of argument, trade policy is presumed to be able to help individual firms to internalize the externalities associated with their own activities. Externalities represent those benefits of a firm's industrial activities that cannot be completely captured by the firm. The firm's technical skills or other attributes, for example, might be easily diffused throughout the broader economy and lead to improvements in the operations of other entities. The firm might operate in an industry that creates spillover effects, or backward or forward linkages, to the rest of the economy that are particularly beneficial. If so, there may be a rationale to ensure that such a firm is protected for the benefit of the broader economy. Industries of this type are often described as strategic industries. Such industries are presumed to be more critical to a country's development than others. Efforts should be made to ensure that these industries remain local.

The critical problem governments face, of course, is in deciding which firms have the prospects for internationally competitive operations and which firms are actually strategic. Most governments have discovered that protection—a political good—once given, is difficult to take away. Of course, the firms continue to make a solid case for the need for protection from their foreign rivals because they often do not mature into adults. In another form of protection, it is less important for governments to identify potentially competitive firms because protection is applied across an entire economy. This is true of the protection applied in a strategy of import-substitution industrialization as discussed in Chapters 1 and 2.

Another rationale for protection, particularly observed in developed countries, is the desire to avoid unemployment in the context of industries that are in decline. There are economic and political aspects to this form of protection. From an economic perspective, advocates of protection to avoid unemployment would, like those advocates of the infant-industry argument, point to the deficiencies of classical trade theory. This theory, they argue, assumes that it is costless and easy to move workers from industries that are in decline and are losing their competitive advantage to industries that are in ascendance within the economy. In reality, the argument goes, this is exceedingly difficult to accomplish in many cases; and so, governments should protect such industries to avoid increases in the ranks of the unemployed.

However, political considerations and the lobbying efforts of local interest groups and unionized workers are the dominant drivers in this type of protection. Were the issue an economic one, then the protection should apply to the worker and not to the job. Thus, workers could be protected with unemployment benefits and retraining programs rather than protecting jobs. If the route of protecting the job rather than the worker is taken, under the political conditions that apply in most countries, once firms gain the benefit of government largesse in the form of import protection that allows them to sell goods at prices higher than those that prevail in world markets, they will never give up that protection without promising to levy (and levying) a political cost on the perpetrators of any policy of import liberalization.

Examples of Protection

From the perspective of developing countries, the textile and agricultural industries in developed countries have been probably the most protected industries. The textile industry is of particular concern because, given the labor intensity of this industry and the relative simplicity of the technology employed, it represents the industry that most labor-rich developing countries seek to enter or expand when they aim to increase manufactured exports. It is interesting also that this industry has featured critically and early in the development drive of England, the United States, Japan, and the newly industrializing countries (NICs) of East Asia.

Developed countries, despite a loss of comparative advantage in this industry, literally refuse to move out of the industry, largely because of political considerations. In the early 1950s, U.S. textile manufacturers, under pressure from Japanese imports, lobbied for protection from the U.S. government. Even though Japanese penetration was no more than 2 percent of the 1956 U.S. market, the political leverage generated by the industry's 2.5 million workers assured that the request for protection would be viewed positively by the U.S. administration.

At that time, however, given its free-trade position, the U.S. government was unwilling to impose a quota. It chose instead to negotiate a "voluntary" export restraint with Japan. In 1961, the United States sought to institutionalize protection for the textile sector by negotiating with other developed countries a Short-Term Cotton Textile Arrangement (STA) that legitimized protection for the textile industries of these countries under the GATT because the arrangement established the right of importing nations to act unilaterally to restrict certain classes of imports, such as textiles. The STA, and subsequently the LTA (Long-Term Cotton Textile Arrangement) and the MFA are negotiated exceptions to GATT rules. The 1961 STA was followed by the signing of an LTA in 1962 that continued the extant protectionist policy. Neither the STA nor the LTA covered imports of textile products made of wool or human-made fibers. Consequently, in the aftermath of the LTA, imports of products made with these fibers increased rapidly.

To rectify this omission, a more comprehensive protectionist agreement— the MFA—that continued the policy but expanded the types of textile products that could be protected was negotiated in 1974. The MFA followed closely after bilateral negotiations between the United States and Japan, Hong Kong, Korea, and Taiwan that restricted imports of products made with wool and human-made fibers from these countries. Article III of the MFA allows an importing country to control imports unilaterally from countries with which it does not have a bilateral agreement. Under the auspices of the MFA, the United States and other developed countries currently have an intricate system of quotas for textile and related products that restrict market access in these industries. The U.S. quotas are triggered when a country's exports reach 1 percent of the U.S. market in any single product category.

Another highly protected industry around the world is agriculture. Most industrialized countries, especially the countries of Europe, North America, and Japan, protect their domestic agriculture industries. The aggressive protection of agriculture is reflected in the symbolism of Japan allowing no imports of rice into the country, to the extent that the Japanese government removed rice products on display in an exhibition. Similarly, in 1992, French farmers blocked roads in France with tractors in opposition to the Blair Accord. This was an agreement between the United States and the European Community (EC) that called for cuts in agricultural subsidies to European farmers. This series of events represents another vivid example of the pervasiveness of agricultural protection and the difficulties associated with dismantling such protection once it has taken root.

The extent of protection received by European farmers is reflected in statistics drawn from the mid-1980s. At that time, it cost European farmers on average \$235 to produce a ton of wheat at a time when the world price of wheat was \$75 per ton. Despite such a draconian imbalance, the Europeans exported 20 million tons of wheat per year, including some in the form of flour. This was made possible by huge subsidies to European farmers and flour millers from the EC. Indeed, the extent of these subsidies is measured by the fact that the EC's Common Agricultural Policy, from whence these subsidies emerged, consumed the bulk of the EC's operating budget at that time.

Protection of agricultural products, in the manner described previously, results largely from another rationale for protection, that is, protecting local industry from imports because of nationalistic reasons or security concerns. The argument put forth by proponents of this form of protection is that economic concerns are not the only ones upon which countries should focus when they set policies. Even if there is an argument for free trade on the grounds of economic efficiency, other factors may dictate a need to protect a country's domestic industries. This form of protection is reflected in statements such as that of a Japanese politician toward the end of the Cold War to the effect that Japan could single-handedly alter the global military balance of power by selling semiconductor chips to the former Soviet Union rather than to the United States.

Statements such as this lend fodder to those who would argue that a country needs to maintain strategic domestic industries for military reasons. In such discussions, the definition of *strategic* can become quite broad. Thus, the U.S. footwear industry is reputed to have sought protection on national security grounds on the basis that if the industry were to die there would be no domestic production of military boots. Domestic production of military boots, the industry maintained, is critical to national security.

In sum, there are various reasons that countries around the world have outlined in support for their policies of protecting a range of domestic industries. In industrialized countries, the most notable industries that have gained government largesse in the form of protection are textiles, footwear, agriculture, automobiles, and steel. In developing countries, the range of industries protected by governments has been very wide, since much of the protection took place in the context of a strategy of import substitution. This protection has occurred despite the fact that many of these governments, particularly governments of industrialized countries, support the principles of free trade as enshrined in the primary multilateral trading institution, the World Trade Organization.

THE WORLD TRADE ORGANIZATION

The World Trade Organization is the world's principal multilateral trading organization devoted to the principles of free trade. It came into being on January 1, 1995, following ratification by the world's principal trading countries during 1994 and, in particular, by the U.S. Congress in December 1994. The WTO is the successor organization to the GATT and was born out of the eighth round of GATT negotiations, the Uruguay Round. Unlike the GATT, which is a trading code, the WTO is a trading organization.

The GATT was one of three multilateral entities created in the aftermath of World War II (the others to be discussed in Chapter 4 being the International Monetary Fund and the International Bank for Reconstruction and Development [The World Bank]). These three entities were supposed to be the glue that would hold the world economy together for the foreseeable future. While the IMF and the World Bank were to provide financial stability to the world economy and financing for reconstruction of war-torn economies, infrastructure development, and balance of payments support, the GATT was supposed to ensure that the world never again resorted to the beggar-thy-neighbor trade policies of the 1930s. In that period, the rest of the world matched the very high American tariff increases of the 1930 trade act (the Smoot–Hawley legislation), leading to a worldwide trade war and a significant reduction in world trade.

As the victors of World War II met in Bretton Woods to carve out a new system of finance for the world, the principal intellectual force in that group, John Maynard Keynes, advocated the creation of a powerful institution, the International Trade Organization (ITO), that would monitor world trade and ensure the removal of trade restrictions. This organization never came into being, primarily because of the resistance of the U.S. Congress to the creation of such an entity. Instead, the more amorphous and less powerful GATT code was created by the signing of the GATT legislation on October 30, 1947, by the representatives of twenty-three countries in Geneva. The creation of the

WTO in 1995 is largely a reflection of the fact that John Maynard Keynes may have been correct and that, despite the activities—and many would say successes—of the GATT, there is a need for a more powerful trading institution rather than a trading code.

The key operating provision of the GATT in its role as a multilateral trading entity was the most-favored-nation (MFN) principle. That principle stated that any trading concession that one GATT member bestows on another GATT member had to be extended to all other members of GATT. More specifically, Article I of the GATT text stated:

> With respect to customs duties and charges of any kind imposed on or in connection with importation or exportation or imposed on the international transfer of payments for imports and exports, and with respect to the method of levying such duties and charges . . . any advantage, favour, privilege or immunity granted by an contracting party to any product originating in or destined for any other country shall be accorded immediately and unconditionally to the like product originating in or destined for the territories of all other contracting parties.

The idea, of course, was to ensure that bilateral deals were eschewed in favor of multilateral deals since bilateral deals would have to be extended to other GATT members anyway. The reader will recognize either that virtually every country in the world has been in contravention of GATT rules or that there are exceptions to the MFN provision. There are indeed exceptions to this provision, of which two are particularly prominent. The first is in respect of countries that have made formal attempts to integrate their economies. In most cases, these are geographically proximate countries that form themselves into free-trade areas or one of the other forms of economic integration; but the lack of geographic proximity has not stopped some countries from claiming this exception. In 1985, for example, the United States and Israel entered into a free-trade agreement, using this exception to the MFN principle.

The second major exception was with respect to industrialized countries which choose to allow preferential access to goods (especially manufactured goods) emanating from developing countries (in some cases, their former colonies), such as the Caribbean Basin Initiative (CBI) and the Lome Conventions to be discussed later in this chapter.

The GATT, even though it focused on removing trade barriers, also allowed countries to retaliate to some particular trade-related actions of other countries—a form of action that is enshrined in U.S. law, as shown in Table 3.2. If countries could prove that their trading partners had been engaged in dumping products—that is, selling goods below the costs of production—in their country, they were allowed under GATT legislation to retaliate by instituting antidumping (AD) duties. These AD duties would be designed to recalibrate the prices of the imported product to reflect the price of similar products in the exporting firm's home market or in a third-country market. Similarly, the GATT allowed countries to retaliate against the exports of firms that have benefited from subsidies from the firms' home governments. In cases where firms benefit from such subsidies, countries were allowed to impose countervailing duties (CVDs) on imports from the offending country that are equal in amount to the subsidy that was granted to the firm.

The GATT actually operated through a series of negotiating rounds. Every few years, representatives from each GATT member country met to negotiate reductions in trade barriers. Eight such negotiating rounds had been completed up to 1995: Geneva in 1947, Annecy in 1949, Torquay in 1950–1951, Geneva in 1956, Dillon in 1960-1962, Kennedy in 1964–1967, Tokyo in 1974–1979, and Uruguay in 1986–1993. The reader will note that the trade negotiations became more complicated with the passage of time as demonstrated by the increasing length of each round of negotiations, culminating with the seven-year marathon session otherwise known as the Uruguay Round. This increased difficulty reflected both a gradual increase in the number of GATT members sitting at the negotiating table and also a movement toward more difficult issues in the area of trade liberalization. Given the increasing length of these negotiating rounds, it was almost inevitable that the GATT acronym came to be expanded as the "General Agreement to Talk and Talk."

The GATT negotiations, while time-consuming and arduous, were clearly effective in their goal of reducing tariffs. Whereas average tariffs among industrialized countries were about 45 percent in 1945, they were less than 3.5 percent in 1993. The Kennedy Round of negotiations, in particular, was very successful in reducing tariffs. In that round, the major industrialized countries agreed upon a weighted average 35-percent cut in tariffs. As tariffs were cut, however, countries began to introduce NTBs to restrict trade. These restrictions were, in many respects, more difficult to deal with because of their amorphous, often unquantifiable nature. A country could, and countries did, declare that it was reducing tariffs while it actually substituted NTBs for these tariffs.

It was to this issue of NTBs that the GATT negotiations turned during the Tokyo Round of trade negotiations between 1974 and 1979. This was the first time that NTBs had ever been systematically discussed during GATT negotiations. There was some progress in agreements to reduce these barriers, but the GATT negotiations continued to avoid making hard decisions about reducing trade restrictions in several very sensitive industries. It was this task that was to be the center of the round of trade negotiations that began in Punta del Este, Uruguay, in 1986.

The Uruguay Round of trade negotiations focused principally on four sectors: agriculture, textiles and apparel, trade in services, and the protection of intellectual property. The round of negotiations was long and complicated because of the sensitive nature of the sectors the negotiations were seeking to liberalize. The round of negotiations separated countries into different groups. On the one hand was a division between agricultural exporters, notably the Cairns Group of agricultural-exporting countries, including countries such as Argentina, the United States, and Australia, and countries such as Japan and the countries of the EC that opposed wide-sweeping trade liberalization in the agricultural industry.

The round also divided developing countries and developed countries. In general, developing countries were eager for liberalization in textiles and apparel, an industry in which they had a competitive advantage but one that was heavily protected by developed countries. On the other hand, developed countries argued for liberalization of trade in services and protection of intellectual property that would allow additional trade in creative products once the owners' investment in the intellectual property that was central to these products could be protected. Developing countries were concerned about the impact of liberalized trade in services and had been reluctant to enforce intellectual property protection because such protection increased the cost of intellectual goods for developing countries.

The Uruguay Round of negotiations was eventually brought to a conclusion on December 15, 1993. This date represented a deadline of sorts because the U.S. Congress had provided the Executive until that date to negotiate an agreement that would be voted either up or down—the so-called fast-track provision. After that date, Congress would seek to adjust any negotiated agreement, which would, of course, essentially have meant that an agreement would probably not take place given that there were more than 100 sovereign nations involved in negotiating the terms of the agreement. The new agreement was actually signed by the contracting parties on April 15, 1994. With the signing of this agreement, the GATT presided over its demise and ushered in the WTO.

The WTO was given the mandate of deepening and broadening the trade liberalization process of the GATT. It would do so by continuing the movement begun during the Uruguay Round of the liberalization of trade in services, agriculture, textiles, and the elimination of NTBs in addition to tariffs.

Developing countries have concerns that they may have achieved little during the Uruguay negotiations. There were compromises by developed countries in the areas of agriculture and textiles, but they were also significant demands for the developing countries to open their service industries to international trade and to increase significantly the vigilance with which they protected intellectual property.

NONRECIPROCAL TRADING ARRANGEMENTS

As pointed out earlier, one of the exceptions enshrined in the GATT's MFN provision was bilateral trade between industrialized countries and developing countries. Several such arrangements have been negotiated over the years. The most wide-sweeping of these programs is the generalized system of preferences (GSP). The GSP represents a collection of schemes presented by individual industrialized countries that allow trade preferences to be granted nonreciprocally to developing countries.

Many developing countries benefit under the GSP by being able to export some of their manufactured goods, semimanufactured goods, and processed and semiprocessed agricultural products at preferential duty rates into industrialized countries. These schemes, however, tend to exclude the most popular manufactures of developing countries, such as textiles and leather goods. The countries of the European Union (EU), Australia, Japan, Canada, and the United States all have GSP programs. Of these countries, the United States was the last to implement a GSP program. The U.S. program came into being in 1975 during the Ford administration.

Other such programs include the Lome Convention. The Lome Convention was first negotiated in 1975 between the EC and a group of developing countries from the regions of Africa, the Caribbean, and the Pacific—the so-called ACP group of countries. The impetus for the Lome Convention came primarily from the effort to protect the preferential trade arrangements various European countries had established with their former colonies in the wake of the entry of these countries, in particular, Britain, into the EC. This agreement has been renewed three times since its original negotiation. The most recent of these was the Lome IV Convention negotiated in 1989 for a ten-year period.

Other nonreciprocal trading arrangements include the CBI negotiated between the United States and many of the countries that border the Caribbean Sea. The CBI provides preferential access to the U.S. market for agricultural and industrial goods produced in these countries, with very important exceptions. These exceptions include apparel and footwear and certain types of agricultural goods (e.g., sugar). The Caribbean also benefits from a nonreciprocal trade arrangement with Canada called CARIBCAN that also allows preferential access for exports from the Caribbean that enter the Canadian market. Despite the existence of these nonreciprocal trading arrangements, however, developing countries still believe that industrialization and development will evade them in the existing international trading system, thus the emergence of efforts over the years to change the rules of the international trading game for developing countries.

DEVELOPING COUNTRY RESPONSES TO THE INTERNATIONAL TRADING SYSTEM

Although for many years developing countries were concerned about their ability to benefit from the international trading system, it was not until the 1960s that these concerns could be pursued collectively and formally. In 1964, under the auspices of UNCTAD, 119 nations came together to debate the existing international trade and financial system and how developing countries fit into this system. As a result of this conference, UNCTAD was established as a permanent agency of the United Nations, with the mission to work to change the international trading system so that it became more responsive to the needs of developing countries.

From the start, UNCTAD has held regular conferences. Through these conferences, the principal nonreciprocal trade regime between developed and developing countries discussed earlier, the GSP, was developed and enshrined in GATT legislation.

The developing countries had a more ambitious agenda. Developing from the work of Prebisch and others, and with the backdrop of colonialism and the view that the world's trading system was developed at the behest and for the benefit of former colonial powers, there was concern that the only hope for developing countries was a change in the entire system of international commerce. It was out of this concern that, under the auspices of UNCTAD, developing countries during the 1970s called for the emergence of a New International Economic Order (NIEO). The NIEO was a constantly evolving idea; but its primary principles, from the perspectives of its adherents, involved political management of the world economy that would ensure that the terms of trade between developed and developing countries were more nearly "equal" and that would guarantee access to technology for the world's poorer nations.

To this end, the developing countries tried to negotiate buffer financing facilities to which industrialized countries would contribute. These facilities, it was argued, would serve to smooth out fluctuations in the world market prices for commodities exported from developing countries. The hope was that this would insulate developing countries from the devastating effects of gyrations in world market prices of raw materials. The NIEO also included a code for technology transfer and a code of conduct to be followed by multinational corporations. An important principle behind the idea of the NIEO was that governments of countries should become more involved in assessing and adjusting for the impact of unfettered world markets on the economies of developing countries.

Other than the introduction of the GSP, UNCTAD and the NIEO have experienced very little success. Industrialized countries have been unwilling to accede to the requests of developing countries for changes in the world trading and financial system. Increasingly, leaders of developing countries have recognized the futility of negotiating arrangements in which they enter negotiations from positions of weakness. Jamaica's former prime minister, Michael Manley, indicates how his own views on the subject of North–South cooperation of this form have changed over time:

The New International Economic Order was formally buried at the supposed moment of its birth at the North–South Summit at Cancun, Mexico in 1981. Ronald Reagan, who had just been elected, killed it with a smile. He smiled at Julius Nyerere. He smiled at all of us and just said no. In two days, 20 years of international struggle went up in a smoke. Everyone packed up and left Cancun confessed of their powerlessness, admonished and discharged with a smile. . . . During the 1980s, I turned my ideas on their head. There is no reality to grand plans aimed at equalising North and South. There are only states doing their small part in a decentralised fashion to hook up with a dispersed global economy.

Many developing countries today agree with Michael Manley. There is a recognition that developing countries must forge their own way in the world and that there can be no dependence on nonreciprocal free trade or on arrangements based on concessions from industrialized countries because there is no sense of permanence in any such concessions. This lack of permanence in nonreciprocal free trade was demonstrated for the ACP countries during 1993 and 1994. These countries, since the first Lome Convention, had preferential access to the EC banana market. In 1993 and 1994, however, based on pressure from Germany, the EU (successor to the EC) began a process of reducing the preferential access provisions that have helped these ACP countries but that, by doing so, have hurt the export prospects of more competitive banana producers in Central America.

In the context of these changing views, the institutions that fall under the umbrella of the United Nations have adjusted their focus. Thus, the U.N. organ that was dedicated to creating a code of conduct for multinational corporations, the United Nations Center on Transnational Corporations (UNCTC) was disbanded in the early 1990s. This organization had, for many years, shifted its focus from developing a code of conduct to providing policy advice to developing countries on how they might best improve the investment climates of their countries. Similarly, an important part of UNCTAD became the International Trade Center that was involved in generating material for countries in their export-development and -promotion activities.

Developing countries have also responded, however, by exploring the possibilities for economic integration, both regionally among each other in a form of south–south cooperation and by seeking to join the dominant markets of industrialized countries on the basis of reciprocal free trade. It is these efforts at economic integration that are examined in Chapter 4.

FURTHER READING

Bhagwati, Jagdish. *The World Trading System at Risk.* Princeton: Princeton University Press, 1991.

General Agreement on Tariffs and Trade (GATT). *Text of the General Agreement.* Geneva: GATT, 1969.

Girling, Robert Henriques. *Multinational Institutions and the Third World: Management, Debt and Trade Conflicts in the International Economic Order.* New York: Praeger, 1985.

Manley, Michael. "Killed by a Smile." *Jamaican Sunday Gleaner,* 17 May 1992, p. 15.

Rodrick, Dani. "Conceptual Issues in the Design of a Trade Policy for Industrialization." *World Development* 20 (3; 1992): 309–320.

Wint, Alvin G., and David B. Yoffie. "United States Trade Law." In *International Trade and Competition: Cases and Notes in Strategy and Management,* edited by David B. Yoffie. New York: McGraw Hill, 1990.

Chapter 4

Regional Economic Integration

For several decades, developing countries have viewed regional integration efforts as a possible solution to their development problems. Regional economic integration has also been on the policy agenda of several industrialized countries. The pace of integration has varied across regions. The pace of integration can be assessed through an examination of where an integration effort falls among the various types of integration.

TYPES OF REGIONAL ECONOMIC INTEGRATION

Regional economic integration might be viewed as a continuum with discrete points at which countries can either stop the integration process or pause prior to integrating further. These points are a free-trade area, a customs union, a common market, and an economic union. The extent of integration deepens as countries move sequentially from a free-trade area to an economic union.

Free-Trade Areas

Countries might choose to remove trade restrictions in particular sectors of an economy. An example of such a sectoral free trade is the United States–Canada automobile pact created in 1965 that created free movement of automobiles and automotive components between the United States and Canada.

In general, however, free-trade areas are more ambitious. They typically include a movement to a free market for a wide range of goods and services that originate from and are traded to one of the member countries of the regional trade area. The objective is that all types of restrictions on trade should be removed. Recall that such restrictions include tariffs; quantitative restrictions such as quotas, licensing procedures, and various NTBs such as excessive regulation of imported goods; and government procurement policies that favor products that emanate from local firms. In so doing, however, member countries retain the right to set their own rules with respect to trade with non-member countries.

Although most regional integration efforts begin as free-trade areas, this does not mean that an area where trade among countries is truly free is easily established. In the Single Europe Act of 1992, one of the world's most effective regional integration efforts was still trying to create a region where trade among countries is truly free some thirty-five years after the signing of the Treaty of Rome that initiated this regional integration effort.

There are several free-trade areas around the world. In 1960 the European Free Trade Association (EFTA) was formed by seven European nations: Austria, Denmark, Norway, Portugal, Sweden, Switzerland, and the United Kingdom. This group was later joined by Finland and Iceland, while Portugal, Denmark, and the United Kingdom left EFTA to join the European Community, leaving six countries in EFTA. EFTA was, in fact, a response to the development of the EC. The nations that joined did so because they were not interested in joining the EC. EFTA abolished tariffs and other restrictions on intraassociation trade. In 1993, EFTA—which has always been the largest trading partner of the EC—joined with the EC to create a European-wide free-trade area (European Economic Area).

In 1994, the North American Free Trade Agreement (NAFTA), incorporating the United States, Mexico, and Canada, came into being. Other free-trade areas have come and gone. Thus, for example, a Latin American Free Trade Association (LAFTA) was formed in 1960, and a Caribbean Free Trade Association (CARIFTA) was formed in 1965. Neither of these associations survived. They were replaced by other forms of integration.

The Association of South East Asian Nations (ASEAN) represents an attempt at regional integration that has not agreed to full free trade but has sought to engage in other forms of regional cooperation. It was formed in 1967 by Singapore, Thailand, Indonesia, Malaysia, and the Philippines. Brunei joined this group in 1984 on gaining its independence. ASEAN has adopted preferential tariffs for member countries in some areas, in addition to other forms of regional collaboration. Similarly, the Latin American countries of Brazil, Argentina, Paraguay, and Uruguay have negotiated a free-trade agreement, MERCOSUR, that calls for an end to tariffs among these countries by 1995. Other free trades are planned for the future. In December 1994, for example, at a Summit of the Americas at which the thirty-four democratic nations in the Western Hemisphere were in attendance, an agreement was reached on the creation of a free-trade area of the Americas by the year 2005.

Customs Unions

The customs union differs from the free-trade area in that it adds to the removal of trade barriers among member countries the requirement that member countries agree on a common set of restrictions with respect to trade with nonmember countries. Such an agreement might, for example, be reflected in an external tariff that is common to member countries.

The Caribbean Common Market (CARICOM) is a good example of a customs union incorporating the Caribbean countries of Antigua and Barbuda, Bahamas, Barbados, Belize, Dominica, Grenada, Guyana, Jamaica, Montserrat, St. Christopher (St. Kitts) and Nevis, St. Lucia, St. Vincent, and Trinidad and Tobago. Since the early 1990s, this group of thirteen countries has made concerted efforts to establish a common external tariff (CET) that creates common trade restrictions to imports from non-CARICOM countries.

Another example of a customs union that comes from the same region of the world is the Andean Group. The Andean Group originally comprised six South American countries: Bolivia, Chile, Colombia, Ecuador, Peru, and Venezuela. The first five countries joined in 1969; Venezuela joined the group in 1973. The integrative effort went beyond free trade to include the creation of a CET. This group also sought closely to regulate flows of foreign-direct investment (the Andean Pact) in an effort to attract only investment that is thought to be in the national interests of the country. These restrictions, in particular, forced Chile to withdraw from the customs union in 1976 as it sought to attract investment to accelerate its development. All members of the group relaxed investment restrictions in 1987 in keeping with the acceleration in the movement of capital around the world.

Common Market

Common markets continue the process of integration. They extend integration beyond customs unions by allowing the free movement of factors of production among member countries. Since land is relatively immobile and capital has become freely mobile around the world with only a few exceptions, the principal factor of production whose mobility is enhanced in a common market is labor. Regional groups forming common markets seek to allow citizens of one member country to live, work, and vote in any member country of their choosing.

The EC provides an example of a common market since the latter half of the 1980s. The citizens of the twelve European countries are viewed as citizens of the EC; and since the late 1980s, all citizens of member countries have been eligible to carry EC passports. Further, provisions have been made that allow citizens of nation states to vote across the region and to work in different countries within the region without restrictions. These provisions became formal and fully comprehensive as the EC signed the Maastricht Treaty and formally became an Economic Union. This treaty *guaranteed* the citizens freedom of movement and residence within the union.

Economic Unions

The fourth discrete point on the regional integration continuum is the economic union. Here, member countries agree—in addition to eliminating trade barriers, creating common restrictions to imports from the rest of the world, and allowing the free movement of workers—to harmonize their economic policies. The objective is for convergence among the primary economic policy variables, such as inflation, interest rates, and exchange rates. In some cases, countries share a common currency as the ultimate technique for creating convergence among inflation, interest rates, and exchange rates. Such a common currency might well be monitored by a common central bank.

Several small groups of countries have created economic unions, often within broader regional integration efforts. Thus, the Organization of Eastern Caribbean States (OECS) share a common currency, the Eastern Caribbean dollar, and a common central bank within the broader ambit of CARICOM. Similarly, a group of countries within the EC—Belgium, Netherlands, and Luxembourg (the BENELUX countries)—have also formed an economic union. The West African Monetary Union represents another example of an economic union with a group of West African countries (Mali, Benin, Burkina Faso, Côte d'Ivoire, Niger, Senegal, and Togo) sharing a common currency and a common central bank.

Again, however, it is the EC itself that represents the boldest attempt to form an economic union. The first traces of such a union began in 1979 with the creation of the European Monetary System (EMS) that included the creation of an exchange rate mechanism (ERM) that would tie the currencies of the various countries together within a band, and a European Currency Unit (ECU) that, as a basket of the main European currencies, would represent the first step toward a common European currency. The primary legislation for economic union, however, came several years later in the Maastricht Treaty that was proposed in 1991 and finally ratified by all twelve member countries in 1993. This treaty, among other things, proposed a timetable for convergence of the economies of the member countries.

Although the integration continuum is presented linearly and sequentially, countries actually move toward further integration in fits and starts. They may actually be at different points along the integration continuum simultaneously. Thus, while the EC was making plans to form an economic union in the early 1990s, it was also still in the process of completing its free-trade area begun in 1957 in the context of the creation of the single market of 1992. What is also clear is that the farther a region moves down the continuum, the greater the extent to which each country must give up powers of government to political institutions that will be created at the regional center.

Thus, a free-trade area requires little in the way of regional political structures and in the area of devolution of power to the center. Free-trade areas are possible with the creation only of negotiating and dispute-settlement bodies. By the time a region gets to the point of economic union, however, the political structures at the center will have become formidable and, in fact, most economic decisions will now reside with the political and economic institutions of the center. This is why some would include a political union as the final stage of economic integration, the argument being that by the time a region has formed a truly functional economic union it will have created so many common political institutions and each nation state will have devolved sufficient power to these institutions that the region would, in fact, be close to political union. Table 4.1 summarizes the different types of integration areas.

Table 4.1
Types of Economic Integration

Type of Integration	Principal Features
Sectoral Free-Trade Area	Elimination of tariff and nontariff barriers among member countries in particular sectors.
Free-Trade Area	Elimination of trade barriers among member countries throughout the entire economy.
Customs Union	Elimination of trade barriers plus the development of common barriers to imports from the rest of the world.
Common Market	Elimination of trade barriers plus the development of common external barriers and the free movement of factors of production among member countries.
Economic Union	Elimination of trade barriers plus the development of common external barriers plus the free movement of factors of production and the harmonization of economic policies.
Political Union	Elimination of trade barriers plus the development of common external barriers plus the free movement of factors of production, the harmonization of economic policies, and common political institutions and governance procedures.

THE RATIONALE FOR INTEGRATION EFFORTS

The rationale for integration efforts across both developing and developed countries derives from a desire to take advantage of the following benefits that are believed to result from economic integration.

Access to Larger Domestic Markets

One of the benefits expected from regional integration is the creation of a larger domestic market for firms throughout the region. Of course, as is true of all notions of free trade, widening the domestic market creates dislocation for some firms. In the context of the creation of regional integration among countries, one would expect that some firms, possibly in several countries, are going to be displaced by the activities of more efficient competitors from other countries in the integrated area. Notwithstanding this dislocation, countries might still be brought together out of a belief that specialization will ensure that the losses suffered by some firms within the integrated area are more than offset by the benefits to consumers and to other more competitive companies within the region.

Assistance from a Stronger Economy

Even countries that are concerned about the prospects for their firms in competition with others within the region might still be interested in entering a regionally defined economic area. One rationale often espoused by such countries is the desire to be assisted in their economic development efforts by the activities and resources of a more powerful neighbor. Such assistance might include the fiscal discipline associated with integration with a strong economy that has a stable currency, low inflation rates, and a government that is not profligate in its spending. Investment by firms from the richer economy into the poorer economy is often contemplated. Such investment should ensure that the poorer country is able to benefit from its relative advantages (e.g., labor cost advantages) vis-à-vis the richer country.

Avoidance of Hostility

Another motivation for the formation of an economically integrated region is the desire of erstwhile enemies to intertwine their economies in such a way that hostilities between them would become extremely unlikely. The most powerful example of economic integration to achieve such a purpose is widely viewed to be the regional integration effort among several European countries that began with the formation of the European Economic Community (EEC), which was created with the signing of the Treaty of Rome in 1957. The key linchpin in European integration has been the alliance between France and Germany, two countries that stood on opposite sides in World Wars I and II.

Fear of Extraregional Competition

Another motivation associated with the formation of an integrated economic region is the fear of extraregional competition. As other countries or regions of the world become more powerful, countries outside of the areas of economic ascendancy are concerned about a reduction of their competitiveness. Indeed, in some cases, these countries begin to actually fear that they will be marginalized. Such concerns often galvanize these countries into the formation of their own regional efforts to restore some balance to global competition.

The recent efforts at both European and North American integration seem to have their origin, at least partly, in concerns about the balance of global competition. When the European effort at integration began in 1957, the United States had become the world's dominant economy, consequent upon the decimation of the European and Japanese economies during World War II. The various European countries felt that there was no possibility of regaining economic parity with the United States as individual countries. Thus, integrating their economies became the logical route to regaining economic parity.

As some of the European economies and Japan have experienced more rapid rates of growth than the United States in recent decades, the tables have, to some extent, been turned. Thus, one reason for the efforts of the United States to form a North American regional economic area beginning in the late 1980s was to counter the economic might of Europe and a booming Pacific Rim centered around Japan and other rapidly growing East Asian economies. During the vociferous debate on the inclusion of Mexico in this regional area, for example, much was made of the fact that with Mexico's inclusion, the North American Free Trade Agreement would comprise the world's largest economy with some 360 million consumers, compared with the 320 million consumers of the EC.

Despite this catalog of reasons supporting the formation of regionally integrated economic areas, very few such efforts at integration have actually been successful. The obstacles to the formation of these regions and to their success, once formed, are quite formidable.

OBSTACLES TO THE FORMATION AND SUCCESS OF REGIONAL ECONOMIC AREAS

There are two fundamental dilemmas that make economic integration difficult for countries: the dilemma of difference and the dilemma of governance.

The Dilemma of Difference

Typically, the greater the differences among countries—whether along the lines of economic development, culture, race, language, religion, size, or history—the more difficult it becomes to create and sustain a regional economic area. The most critical difference is that in the degree of economic development. If this gap is too wide, the richer countries are concerned about the gains to be achieved with access to the poorer countries' markets, while the poorer countries are concerned about the ability of any of their firms to survive in the face of competitive markets, notwithstanding their understanding of comparative advantage that suggests that their firms should be competitive in some sector.

Richer countries, of course, have no interest in integrating with countries whose primary activity will be to perform the role of neighborly supplicant. The early efforts at integration among the English-speaking nations of the Caribbean point to the problems associated with integration among economies of different levels of development and size. Although all small developing countries, the countries of Trinidad and Tobago and Jamaica in 1961 viewed themselves as richer and bigger than the eight smaller economies of the Caribbean that would be their partners in this regional federation. Consequently, on hearing that Jamaica had voted against federation in a national referendum, the leader of Trinidad and Tobago, Dr. Eric Williams, declared that 1 from 10 left 0.

The dilemma of difference, however, extends beyond issues of differences in size and level of economic development. Often added to such differences are variations along racial, cultural, historical, political, linguistic, and religious lines. Under such circumstances, countries find it particularly difficult to integrate their economies. Indeed, given the extent to which these cultural, linguistic, political, and racial differences are splintering existing nation states, it is not surprising that they make it difficult to create new integrated areas.

This is not to suggest that countries cannot overcome their differences and come together if the impetus is sufficiently powerful. Many are still astounded, for example, that a linguistically and culturally disparate Europe has been able to integrate economically. One feels compelled to point out, however, that despite the extent to which the countries of the EU have integrated, it has taken more than thirty years with many starts and stops and that, although different, the countries that have integrated are of predominantly the same race and religion. Although they have a history of animosity, there are also strong historical links. Recall, for example, that at one point the royal families of England and Germany were related. Further, the six countries that signed the Treaty of Rome were at relatively similar levels of development. The poorer countries of the group, particularly Spain, Portugal, and Greece, were added as the EC felt that it could accept them. Yet, each of these three countries, though currently poor by European standards, has a history of democratic and political institutions and a record of industry and ambitions that extend well beyond current capabilities. When the focus shifts to allowing regular membership for countries such as Turkey that are in or on the border of the Middle East and North Africa, the dilemma of difference becomes even more acute.

The evolution of North American integration provides yet another example of this dilemma. The negotiations surrounding the integration of the United States and Canada in 1989 were not easy, especially from the Canadian perspective. Canada, of course, with the majority of its population of 27 million living in close proximity to the United States, has long been concerned about economic and cultural domination by the behemoth to its south. Consequently, there was a vocal group within Canada that raised concerns about the impact of the United States–Canada Free Trade Area, created by a treaty that was ratified with scarcely any publicity in the United States. Yet the dilemma of difference is illustrated by the fact that the ripple of concern in Canada associated with the United States–Canada Free Trade Agreement paled in comparison to the tidal wave of rhetoric in the United States associated with extending regional integration to Mexico in the form of NAFTA, which was ratified by the U.S. Congress in 1993.

The dilemma of difference takes an interesting twist when one turns to the issue of the likely success of integration efforts. Although similar countries may find it easier to agree to integrate, these same countries, particularly if they are also developing countries, find that similarity is a disadvantage when one turns to the prospects for success of the effort.

The example of the English-speaking Caribbean countries illustrates this dilemma well. By 1973, all these small countries had recognized that, given their size, they might be best served by integrating their economies. It was in this spirit that the Treaty of Chagaraumas was signed in 1973, creating CARICOM. The eventual debate over the initiation of integration efforts was not strident. The thirteen Caribbean countries that comprise CARICOM are very similar. They are small islands, with the exception of Guyana and Belize. They speak a common language, share a common culture and history, are of predominantly the same race, generally practice the same religion, and share relatively similar political systems.

Because of the similarity of their factor endowments and market characteristics, however, these countries find it difficult to gain significant advantages from economic integration. They produce similar goods and thus find it difficult to specialize. The sectors that have sustained these economies are minerals; traditional agriculture products, in particular, sugar and bananas; and tourism. Economic activity of this type does not lead to a climate for intraregional trade. Consequently, trade within CARICOM has been in the range of 5 to 8 percent of the overall trade of any single member country. Indeed, only Trinidad, with the most developed manufacturing base among the group, has been able to have as high a ratio of 8 percent of its total exports directed toward CARICOM member countries.

Economic integration efforts in developing countries, in particular, tend to suffer because of limited complementarity among the countries in the integrated area.

Dilemma of Governance

Another dilemma that affects the ability of an integrated area to succeed surrounds the issue of national sovereignty—the dilemma of governance. The issue is that, although these efforts are described as attempts at economic integration, they represent much more than economic areas. These areas are, in truth, combinations of economic and political coordination. Many countries have concerns about willingly giving up their ability to govern themselves. This resistance is couched in the form of maintaining national sovereignty—the independence of governance that essentially defines the modern nation state. This issue is of particular concern because most countries have engaged in desperate struggles to preserve their ability to govern themselves, whether in the context of military confrontation or in the independence struggles that many developing countries initiated in the second half of the twentieth century.

The dilemma of governance has been most obvious in the context of the efforts at European integration. In that context, Britain in particular—with its long and storied tradition of nationhood, its legacy of political institutions such as the "old lady of Threadneedle Street" (the Bank of England), and its reminisces of an era when it stood proud in the world—has had the most difficulty with the notion of relinquishing governance to regional powers. To be sure, issues of national sovereignty, while present at all levels of integration, become more acute as regions are successful in moving along the road of integration.

REGIONAL INTEGRATION
AMONG DEVELOPING COUNTRIES

Developing countries have been active in seeking to integrate their economies, operating principally on the premise that these integration efforts would lead to larger domestic markets. Table 4.2 indicates the various integration efforts of developing countries that span all the developing regions of the world.

An effective regional free-trade area, which is the foundation for any successful integrative effort, should be able to accomplish two goals. The first is that it should be able to *divert* trade from an extraregional to an intraregional basis. More important, however, this increase in intraregional trade and by extension production should serve to *create* additional trade as increased intraregional production leads to increased intraregional consumption and extraregional exports. Yet, most developing countries that lie in the same region have competitive and noncomplementary economies. Consequently, as demonstrated in Table 4.3, they have found it difficult to develop integrated areas in which there is a significant proportion of intraregional trade. Table 4.3 indicates the contrast between intraregional trade in the EC and intraregional trade in various developing countries' integration efforts.

Partly because of historical (often colonial) trade practices and partly because of natural endowments, these countries tend to produce many of the same commodities—whether agricultural, mineral, or service oriented (such

Table 4.2
Economic Integration among Developing Countries

Association	Countries	Date Formed	Type of Association
Andean Common Market (Andean Pact)	Bolivia, Peru, Colombia, Ecuador, Venezuela, Chile	Formed in 1969; Chile left in 1976	Customs Union
Association of South East Asian Nations (ASEAN)	Indonesia, Malaysia, Philippines, Singapore, Thailand, Brunei	Formed in 1967; Brunei joined in 1981.	
Caribbean Community (CARICOM)	Antigua & Barbuda, Bahamas, Barbados, Belize, Dominica, Grenada, Guyana, Jamaica, Montserrat, St Kitts & Nevis, St Lucia, St. Vincent, Trinidad & Tobago	Formed as Caribbean Free-Trade Area (CARIFTA) in 1968; became CARICOM in	CARICOM is a Customs Union; CARIFTA was a
Central American Common Market (CACM)	Costa Rica, El Salvador, Guatemala, Honduras, Nicaragua	Formed in 1960	Formed as a Customs Union
Latin American Integration Association (LAIA)	Argentina, Chile, Bolivia, Colombia, Ecuador, Mexico, Paraguay, Peru, Uruguay, Venezuela	Created in 1960 as Latin American Free-Trade Area. Disbanded in 1980, replaced with LAIA.	Formed as a Free-Trade Area
East African Community	Kenya, Tanzania, Uganda	Created in 1967. Disbanded in 1977.	Free-Trade Area
Economic Community of African States (ECOWAS)	Benin, Gambia, Ghana, Guinea, Cote d'Ivoire, Mali, Mauritania, Niger, Nigeria, Rwanda, Senegal, Togo, Upper Volta	Created in 1965	Created as a Free-Trade Area. Adjusted to a Customs Union
Organization of Eastern Caribbean States (OECS)	Anguilla, Antigua, Dominica, Greneda, Monsterrat, St. Kitts, St. Lucia, St. Vincent	Created in 1976	Economic Union
MERCOSUR	Brazil, Argentina, Paraguay, Uraguay	Created in 1993: to take effect in 1995.	Free-Trade Area
West African Monetary Union	Mali, Benin, Burkina Faso, Cote d'Ivoire, Niger, Senegal, Togo	Created in 1960	Monetary Union

Note: ASEAN did not conform to any of the types of regional integration efforts discussed previously.

Table 4.3
Intraregional Trade as a Percentage of Total Exports, 1960–1987

Economic Group	1960	1970	1976	1980	1983	1987
EC	34.6	48.9	NA	52.8	52.4	58.8
CACM	7.5	26.8	21.6	22.0	21.8	11.9
CARICOM	4.5	7.3	6.7	6.4	9.3	6.3
LAFTA/LAIA	7.7	10.2	12.8	13.5	10.2	11.3
Andean Group	0.7	2.3	4.2	3.5	4.3	3.2
ECOWAS	1.2	2.1	3.1	3.9	4.1	5.5

NA: Information not available.

as tourism)—for export to world markets. It is difficult, therefore, for them to engage in the trade diversion that is the first-order task required to create an effective free-trade area. This is why the Caribbean and Latin American integration efforts, for example, found it difficult to increase intraregional trade as a percentage of trade with the world into the double-digit levels. This failure occurred even during a period of import substitution when tariffs for the rest of the world were extremely high in order to encourage the formation of local regional manufacturing industries. Since they are unable to gain the trade diversion that can increase intraregional production, these countries have found it difficult to create trade through regional integrative efforts. Even in the presence of CARICOM, for example, the vast majority of Jamaica's trade increases during the 1980s, principally in the areas of tourism, apparel, and nontraditional agriculture, represented extraregional trade.

Complementarity among regional countries seems easier to accomplish if these countries have an assortment of manufacturing industries for which differentiated products and heterogenous tastes ensure reciprocal demand, complemented by agricultural, mineral, and service sectors. This is not the situation in which most developing economies find themselves. It appears that regional integration efforts among themselves will not easily take them to that point, although one might point out that the larger developing countries have a greater chance of success in this regard than the small microstates.

The developed countries have been much more successful at achieving gains from the integration process. Developed-country integration efforts are of interest to the manager in a developing country, whether in the public or private sector, because they clarify the benefits and costs of integration. These efforts are also of interest because they have a bearing on the access developing countries have to the markets of individual developed countries after integration. The issues of access have been quite important in the two major developed-country integration efforts: those of the European and North American regions.

REGIONAL ECONOMIC INTEGRATION
IN DEVELOPED COUNTRIES

The issue of regional economic integration in the developed world has focused on the integrative efforts of two regions: Europe and North America. The European example has figured prominently in this chapter; however, it is worth continuing to examine this example in detail because this integration effort has lessons for the developing countries of the world with respect to the depth of integration achieved, the length of the experiment in integration, and the pitfalls that have been encountered along the way. The example of North American integration is interesting to the developing countries for other reasons. Principal among these is that it represents the first example of a regional integration effort that will involve developed countries integrating with a developing country.

European Integration

The efforts of countries of Europe to integrate their economies actually began in 1951 with the signing of the Treaty of Paris. With this treaty, six European countries—France, Germany, Italy, Belgium, Luxembourg, and the Netherlands—created the European Coal and Steel Community. This represented an agreement among member countries to eliminate barriers to trade in the sectors of coal and steel. It is interesting to note that, at this time, those two sectors were viewed as strategic sectors in the industrialization process. They are possibly akin to the strategic role played by the semiconductor industry in the late twentieth century.

This was followed by the signing of the Treaties of Rome by these same six countries creating the EEC and the European Atomic Energy Community (Euroatom) in 1957. The EEC was to allow for the integration of the entire economies of these countries. Euroatom was dedicated to the peaceful use and development of nuclear energy. The creation of this latter community indicated the extent to which concerns about avoiding another devastating world war motivated the entire integration effort. The three communities were run by joint institutions, so one could describe the integrative effort up until 1993 as one European Community.

In 1973, the original six countries were joined by Denmark, Britain, and Ireland. This represented a watershed period in the growth of the EC because

Britain, due to historical circumstances, has had a greater influence on world affairs than the country's geographical (or late twentieth-century economic) size would predict. The accession of Greece in 1981 and Portugal and Spain in 1986 brought the membership to twelve countries. As pointed out earlier in this chapter, the EC was also linked by a free-trade agreement to the six Scandinavian countries that form EFTA.

In 1987, the EC developed the Single European Act that was to come into effect by 1992. This act would create a completely free-trade area by eliminating remaining restrictions on trade such as those in the area of government procurement, product standards, transportation procedures, and financial services. This proposal was followed by the development of the Maastricht Treaty of Economic Union in 1991. This treaty sought to create enabling legislation for further integration. It created a common economic policy, social policy, and competition policy for the countries of the EC and laid out a timetable for a common EC currency and an EC central bank to be in place by the end of the century.

For the Maastricht Treaty to go into effect, it required unanimous ratification by all twelve member countries. As it turned out, the treaty created significant debate within the EC. This debate came to a head in June 1992 when Danish voters rejected the treaty in a national referendum. After modifications, soul searching, and EC pressure, the Danes eventually ratified the treaty as did all the other member countries, albeit with very narrow votes in some countries such as France. Nevertheless, the treaty came into effect in 1993. At that point, the EC was formally renamed, becoming the *European Union,* reflecting the movement to an economic union.

As integration progressed, political structures were created and expanded. The regional group was governed by a commission, consisting of seventeen commissioners; a parliament, comprising 518 parliamentarians; a council of ministers, with one minister from each country; and a court of justice, which was analogous to a supreme court on which sat a justice from each country. The principal programs have been an agricultural program (common agricultural policy) by which regional farmers are supported with subsidies (ostensibly in order to allow them to modernize), a social policy, regional policy, transport policy, competition policy, and trade policy. A financial policy which comprised the ECU and the ERM has been critical in the integration process.

One interesting issue from the example of European integration is the extent to which the dilemma of governance becomes more pronounced as integration progresses. In an effort to skirt this dilemma, the Europeans developed a new concept—that of subsidiarity. This meant that all decisions of governance should be taken at the lowest possible level of government. Britain, in particular, concerned about compromising national sovereignty, has been strident in its demands for continued national autonomy. The Danish vote on Maastricht was also viewed as a desire to preserve national autonomy from the encroaches of "Eurocrats" in Brussels.

The speed of European integration was also slowed in September 1992 with the currency problems of Britain and other countries. The ERM had joined the currencies of the member countries together in a currency band whose outer limits were tied to the weighted average of member countries' currencies. An individual currency could only deviate by a negotiated prespecified amount from this weighted average. (Negotiations actually revolved around only two limits—one of 2.25 percent, and another of 6 percent.) Britain, after opting out of the ERM since its inception in 1979, finally joined in 1991. By September 1992, however, speculative pressure on the British pound forced Britain to withdraw the pound from the ERM. Over the next year, all other countries within Europe—except Germany and the BENELUX countries—faced pressures on their currencies. The factor that precipitated this currency crisis was a strong German Deutsche mark that appreciated as Germany engaged in a high interest rate policy in order to acquire capital to finance higher-than-expected costs in its efforts to reunite and modernize Eastern Germany. Germany refused to reduce its interest rates to take the pressure off the currencies of other countries, intervening in currency markets to help only France when it appeared that its critical partner in European integration was also going to be forced to withdraw from the ERM.

Notwithstanding the problems of continuing the integration process into the 1990s and the length of the period of the European integration experiment, integration in Europe appears to have been a success. The countries of Europe have developed complementary economies such that the trade of each country in the group is predominantly European trade, as is demonstrated in Table 4.3, which showed that European trade was almost 60 percent of the total trade of member countries in 1987. Further, the countries of Europe have been able to benefit from the antiinflationary posture of Europe's strongest economy, Western (formerly West) Germany. Many European governments, for example, believed that the ERM would force them to the type of fiscal discipline that might have been difficult to achieve in the absence of ERM-derived constraints. The integration effort has tried to deal with the dilemma of difference by providing transfers from richer member countries to poorer member countries such as Ireland, Portugal, Spain, and Greece.

North American Integration

The dilemma of difference becomes stark in the context of North American integration. The North American analogue to European integration is not nearly as comprehensive in scope. The origins of North American integration do, however, go back to the 1960s. In 1965, the United States negotiated a free-trade pact with Canada in the automotive sector. In that same year, it negotiated with Mexico an agreement whereby American firms could set up assembly plants along the U.S.–Mexican border. Firms established along the border were allowed to import raw materials into Mexico duty free and reexport the finished goods to the United States also on a duty-free basis. This program came to be known as the Maquiladora program.

These programs were the only formal elements of integration among the three economies until 1987. In that year, the United States and Canada began negotiating a free-trade agreement between both countries. This agreement went into effect in 1989. In 1990, George Bush of the United States and Carlos Salinas of Mexico began negotiations toward a United States–Mexico trade agreement. Canada joined these negotiations shortly thereafter, and the initial outlines of a North American Free Trade Agreement began to emerge. The discussions toward this end were completed in 1992. Bill Clinton's administration endorsed this agreement in 1993 with adjustments to appease the U.S. labor and environmental lobbies, and the agreement was ratified by the U.S. Congress in the same year.

After ratification by all three governments, NAFTA went into effect in 1994. A key feature of the agreement, particularly from the perspective of other Latin American countries, is that other countries may be permitted to enter NAFTA. Indeed, contemporaneously with the decision to negotiate a NAFTA agreement, U.S. President George Bush, in his 1991 State of the Union address, spoke of an Enterprise of the Americas Initiative (EAI) that would eventually involve the creation of a hemispheric free-trade area, extending throughout Central, South, and North America. NAFTA would be just the beginning of such an arrangement.

NAFTA will eliminate trade barriers among all products produced by the three countries within a five-, ten-, or fifteen-year period, depending upon the sensitivity of the product. It also will eliminate restrictions on intraarea investments, provide adequate protection for intellectual property, and create dispute-settlement procedures. The agreement does allow for temporary safeguard protection for an industry hurt by imports within the first fifteen years of the agreement. It also opens government procurement to North American firms and implements MFN treatment for NAFTA service providers. The principal institution created by the agreement is a trade commission comprising ministers or cabinet-level officials chosen by each country. The agreement establishes a secretariat to serve the commission.

Unlike the European integration effort, North American integration has a much less storied history. The Maquiladora program has received very mixed reviews. It has clearly created employment for Mexicans, but there has been very little in the form of linkages within the rest of the Mexican economy. Also, there are continued criticisms of environmental damage as a result of the program. Similarly, the automotive pact between the United States and Canada has not had a profound impact on the economies of either country.

NAFTA did, however, generate considerable debate. Most of this debate occurred within the United States around the issue of whether such an agreement would result in a significant loss of American jobs to Mexico and whether it would lead to further deterioration of the environment in Mexico because firms would move to Mexico to take advantage of what were viewed as less stringent environmental regulations in that country. Fundamentally, however, and often unvoiced, the debate was also about the wisdom of the United States and Canada entering into a free-trade arrangement with a developing country like Mexico that, among other things, had only recently (in 1986) joined the GATT and indicated any intention or ability to engage in free trade with the rest of the world. The debate, especially as it emerged from 1992 U.S. presidential candidate, Ross Perot, focused on the question of whether integrating with a developing country might not impede the development prospects of an industrialized country such as the United States.

PROSPECTS FOR DEVELOPMENT
THROUGH REGIONAL ECONOMIC INTEGRATION

As developing countries examine the processes of economic integration in the context of their concerns about the existing nature of the world economy, as reflected in the discussion of Chapter 3, many contend that south–south cooperation through integrating economies is a possible route out of the underdevelopment morass. Others, particularly with the precedent of NAFTA, see economic integration's best case for assisting the development process coming from developing countries integrating with developed "Northern" economies.

Regional Integration between
Developed and Developing Countries

What becomes of the prospects for development through integration between the developed countries and developing countries? Prior to NAFTA, there was no example of integration in the form of reciprocal free trade between developed and developing countries. (There is some debate on this point revolving around how to classify European countries such as Ireland and Portugal. In addition, the United States–Israel free-trade area created in 1985 might represent an exception to this statement.) There is, nevertheless, empirical evidence on one side of this issue. Developing countries have enjoyed nonreciprocal preferential trading arrangements with developed countries. The GSP which many developing countries were able to access; the Lome Convention providing preferential access to the European market for exports from a group of African, Pacific, and Caribbean states; and the preferential trade arrangements provided by Canada and the United States to exports from the Caribbean (CARIBCAN and CBI, respectively) are a few such nonreciprocal preferential trade arrangements.

With the ratification of NAFTA, one might anticipate that the rules of the game are about to change and that nonreciprocal free-trade agreements between developed and developing countries are likely to wane and be replaced by reciprocal free-trade agreements. Countries from South America, Central America, and the Caribbean are eager to apply for membership to NAFTA for this principal reason. These countries recognize that even if they currently have nonreciprocal preferential access to the U.S. market, this is likely to be a short-lived relationship. They also recognize that the only way to guarantee continued access to that market is in the form of membership in a North American Free Trade Agreement. The Caribbean countries, in particular, with their preferential access to the North American market through the CBI and CARIBCAN programs, are negotiating for continued access to this market on the same terms as Mexico until their applications for membership to NAFTA can be considered.

What about the impact of such a reciprocal free-trade regime on development in developing countries? It would seem reasonable to anticipate that a reciprocal trading arrangement is likely to be no more effective in spurring the development process than these nonreciprocal arrangements have been. The only caveat one might attach to the foregoing statement is that a reciprocal trading arrangement might be more generous in its access to developed country markets than has been true of these nonreciprocal trading arrangements. Most of the latter arrangements have tended to exclude various sectors (e.g., textiles, footwear, and certain agricultural products) in which the developing countries were most likely to generate the largest quantity of exports.

However, the increased exports from this enlarged access will face the countervailing effect of the short-term dislocation associated with the developing country providing equivalent access to imports from the developed country. The net effect is probably indeterminate before the fact, but it is not at all obvious why integration between developed and developing countries will, in and of itself, spur economic growth and development in developing countries. After all, global free trade in the nineteenth century did not create development in the developing countries of that era (most of which are the same "places" [the names and governments have changed] seeking development today). Developing countries may be forced to enter these agreements in order to keep the markets that they currently have. This is not, however, equivalent to a prediction that such arrangements will be precursors to the development of these countries.

FURTHER READING

Beckford, George, and Norman Girvan, eds. *Development in Suspense*. Kingston, Jamaica: Friedrich Ebert Stiftung, 1989.
World Bank. *World Development Report, 1991*. New York: Oxford University Press, 1991.

Chapter 5

International Financial and Monetary Systems

The manager in a developing country is concerned not only with the movement of goods and services across countries but also with the international monetary system that allows these goods and services to move efficiently across national borders. Indeed, the international monetary system performs a role for the international economy that is directly analogous to the role a national monetary system provides in lubricating intranational trade in goods and services. To continue the analogy, a national monetary system includes the following three principal types of institutions: commercial banks that accept deposits and lend funds at market interest rates; development banks that lend funds at below market interest rates or to particular groups of customers for specific activities favored by the governments that provide their capital base; and a central bank that issues money, acts as a banker to the commercial banks, and is responsible for regulating the country's monetary system.

This is not to suggest that there are not other financial institutions that operate within a national economy. Brokerage firms, investment banks, and others clearly play an important role in national financial systems. However, the role of the commercial banks and the central banks are clearly more important, with the development banks playing an interesting, if often controversial, role in the context of developing countries.

Within the international monetary system, there exists a similar collection of institutions. Many commercial banks around the world operate internationally. Operating internationally means that these banks accept deposits and grant loans in currencies other than that of the country in which they reside. The international monetary system also has its own development banks. These include, most prominently, the International Bank for Reconstruction and

Development (IBRD), a part of the World Bank Group. The IBRD is a truly international institution whose activities span the globe. There are also, however, many development banks that confine the bulk of their financial activities to a collection of countries within a particular region of the world.

The analogy between national and international monetary systems holds least at the level of corresponding central institutions that regulate and monitor the monetary system. Even here, however, there are two analogues at the international level to the national central banks. One of these is the Bank for International Settlements (BIS), headquartered in Basel, Switzerland. This institution serves as a banker to the central banks. In particular, it facilitates currency transactions among the central banks of the major industrialized countries. The other is the IMF. This institution began its life as a regulator of the entire monetary system. Today, however, its activities focus primarily on regulation of the monetary systems of those countries that comprise the developing world. Table 5.1 summarizes the structure of the international monetary system.

INTERNATIONAL DEVELOPMENT BANKS

While all elements of the international monetary system are important, the institutions within that system that have a mandate to enhance the competitiveness of their client or member countries are the international development financial institutions. The principal institution in this regard is the World Bank

Table 5.1
Comparing the Structure of National and International Monetary Systems

National Monetary System	International Monetary System
Commercial banking activity	International financial operations of commercial banks
Development banking activity	World Bank Group
	Regional development banks: Inter-American Development Bank, African Development Bank, Caribbean Development Bank, Asian Development Bank, European Investment Bank, European Bank for Reconstruction and Development
Central banking activity	Bank for International Settlements (BIS), International Monetary Fund (IMF)

Group. There are also many regional development banks that conduct similar functions on a less global scale.

The World Bank

The World Bank is a publicly owned financial intermediary, a bank owned by national governments. The brainchild of John Maynard Keynes, it was formed as the IBRD by the forty-four delegates to the U.N. Monetary and Financial Conference in Bretton Woods, New Hampshire, in 1944. The delegates at this conference agreed to create an international monetary system for the post–World War II period. The three institutions to govern this system were the GATT, the IBRD, and the IMF.

The WB's shareholders are member governments, currently over 150, that have paid capital into the WB in rough proportion to their economic strength. The United States has the largest share of paid-in capital (about 20 percent) and is, as a consequence, the largest shareholder of the WB. The IBRD focused initially on providing funding for the reconstruction of war-torn Europe. The U.S. Marshall Plan for rebuilding Europe, however, quickly pushed the IBRD into the second element of its role—development.

The IBRD sought to fulfill its developmental role by borrowing money on international markets and lending these funds to developing countries. Although it borrowed at market rates and on-lent the funds, the developing countries that turned to the IBRD for funds got them at cheaper rates than they would be able to obtain independently. This is because with its AAA credit rating, the IBRD borrowed at the lowest possible rates. Essentially, the IBRD loans allow nonprime borrowers to get loans at close-to-prime rates. Although the IBRD's loans represent the best rate to which developing countries have access, this lending is also quite profitable from the IBRD's perspective. There is, for example, no recorded case of a country defaulting on an IBRD loan.

Possibly as a consequence of this irony of profitable loans in the context of a development institution, another type of WB lending was initiated in 1960. In that year, the WB created the International Development Association (IDA). This was not a new entity but, rather, a new type of lending; that is, existing IBRD staff administered these new IDA loans. IDA lending is available only to the world's poorest countries. Rather than through commercial markets, IDA funds are generated through the capital contributions of the WB's member countries and allocations from the income of the WB. They are lent to the poorest developing countries on concessionary repayment terms. Most such loans are for periods of fifty years at interest rates of less than 1 percent per year. Currently, about twice as much has been lent in the form of IBRD loans relative to IDA loans. Table 5.2 provides data on the WB loan program in Latin America and the Caribbean over the 1983–1992 period.

The lending program of the WB has changed over time. Prior to the 1980s, most lending, whether IBRD or IDA, was project lending. The WB's lend-

ing program financed infrastructure projects such as dams for irrigation purposes, school building programs, roads, and other such projects. Since the
1980s, however, noting that the projects it financed seemed to do better in
particular macroeconomic climates, the WB began financing reform of a
country's macroeconomic climate through structural adjustment loans (SALs).
These loans, described in WB parlance also as nonproject loans, were provided to governments under the condition that they initiated particular reforms. Table 5.3 provides an example of the data used by the WB in arriving
at the conclusion that projects were more profitable in the context of particular macroeconomic climates.

The reforms recommended by the WB tended to be a part of standard neoclassical economic tradition: reducing budget deficits; privatizing state-owned
enterprises; liberalizing trade by reducing tariffs and other barriers to trade;
reforming tax systems to increase incentives for productive activity while also
increasing tax collections; allowing prices to adjust to market-determined
levels by eliminating government subsidies and removing price controls; and
allowing the most important price in an economy, the exchange rate, to adjust to market-determined levels by floating that rate. SALs were complemented by SECALs (sector adjustment loans) that supported economic reform
in particular economic sectors (e.g., agriculture, finance).

In addition to its bank lending, the WB has several other affiliates. Collectively, these entities comprise the World Bank Group. In 1956, the International Finance Corporation (IFC) was formed with a mandate to promote the
development of private institutions in developing countries. Thus, unlike the
WB whose loans are made directly to governments and backed by government guarantee, the IFC lends to and purchases equity in private firms in
developing countries. The IFC operates relatively independent of the WB. It
has its own staff, although its activities are overseen by the WB's Executive
Board; and the president of the WB is also the president of the IFC.

The IFC does not seek to be the primary financier to a firm in a developing
country. Rather, it views its role as catalytic. In addition to its financial commitment to a project, it will often help the firm to generate financing from
other financial institutions. The IFC does not participate in the management
of the companies to which it provides financial assistance, even in circumstances where it participates in equity financing. The IFC's articles of agreement also include a mandate for the corporation to help developing countries
create an climate that is conducive to private investment. The IFC finances
far fewer projects, in much smaller quantities, than its senior affiliate.

In 1988, another WB affiliate was created—the Multilateral Investment
Guarantee Agency (MIGA). This entity has the mission of promoting economic development by encouraging the flow of foreign-direct investment to
developing countries. MIGA accomplishes this objective through its insurance and policy advice services. It insures investment against loss resulting
from noncommercial, primarily political, risks such as expropriation, blocked

currency transfers, breach of contract, war, revolution, and insurrection. It also provides advice and consultative services to member countries to enhance the investment climate and promote specific investment opportunities.

Since its formation, MIGA has delegated some elements of its advisory mission to another WB affiliate that was spawned by the IFC's Development Department in 1986. This entity, the Foreign Investment Advisory Service (FIAS), is a joint venture of the WB, the IFC, and MIGA. FIAS provides policy advice to developing country governments interested in attracting foreign investment. It provides advice in the areas of legal reform, investment policies, investment promotion programs, linkages between foreign and private investment, and institutional design. Since its formation, FIAS has worked in some seventy developing countries providing advice in these areas. Collectively, the WB with its IBRD and IDA loans, the IFC, MIGA, and FIAS comprise the World Bank Group.

The Regional Development Banks

In addition to the WB, various regional development banks exist around the world dedicated to the economic development of their regions. The typical structure of these banks is that their membership consists of countries within the region with extraregional members usually being developed countries that are donors to the regional bank. These banks include the European Investment Bank, formed in 1957 by the Treaty of Rome to promote European development; the Inter-American Development Bank, formed in 1959 to promote social and economic development in Latin America; the African Development Bank, formed in 1963 to promote economic development in Africa; the Caribbean Development Bank, formed in 1970 to assist in the development of the countries of the Caribbean region; the Asian Development Bank, formed in 1966 to foster economic development in Asia; and the European Bank for Reconstruction and Development, formed in 1991 to promote development in Eastern Europe.

THE ROLE OF THE
INTERNATIONAL MONETARY FUND

National monetary systems are regulated and controlled by a central bank that monitors the commercial banks, works with the development banks, issues currencies, and operates as the lender of last resort within the economy. In the international monetary system, these functions are, to some extent, carried out by the BIS and the IMF. Of these two institutions, the IMF has had the greatest impact on financial operations in developing countries. This institution was created with the intention that it would serve to regulate and monitor the international monetary system and be a banker to the world's central banks.

Table 5.2

World Bank Loans to Latin America and the Caribbean by Sector (US$ Millions)

Sector	1983 - 1987 Annual Average	1988	1989	1990	1991	1992
Agriculture	1,095.8	1,404.8	161.8	855.7	941.5	1,569.6
Development Finance	402.0	970.0	1,164.3	471.7	844.5	577.0
Education	83.7	88.3	140.0	-	595.3	786.1
Energy and Power	626.7	423.0	830.0	897.5	260.0	110.1
Industry	74.6	1,065.0	860.0	_	200.0	300.0
Nonproject	460.1	250.0	692.0	1,378.0	422.3	593.8
Population and Health	39.4	109.0	99.0	389.2	337.3	47.5
Public Sector	-	-	500.0	350.0	604.0	325.0
Small Enterprise	278.6	-	155.0	77.5	-	-
Technical Assistance	22.4	-	50.7	59.0	68.8	48.2
Telecommunications	6.0	-	45.0	-	-	-
Transport	455.1	210.6	149.3	1,029.0	114.0	438.2
Urban Development	205.8	491.0	675.0	450.0	364.0	616.0
Water	171.1	252.3	320.0	7.7	485.0	250.0
Total	*4,021.3*	*5,264.0*	*5,842.1*	*5,964.7*	*5,236.7*	*5,661.5*
IBRD	3,949.2	5,152.0	5,703.7	5,726.7	5,067.2	5,256.5
IDA	72.1	112.0	138.4	238.0	169.5	405.0
Number of operations	44	37	43	41	44	45

Source: World Bank, *World Bank Annual Report, 1992* (New York: Oxford University Press, 1992).

Table 5.3
Economic Rates of Return for Projects Financed by the World Bank, 1968–1989

			Percentage Return			
Policy Index	All Projects	All Public Projects	Public Projects in Agriculture	Public Industrial Projects	Public Projects in Nontradeable Sector	All Private Projects
Trade Restrictions						
High	13.2	13.6	12.1	NA	14.6	9.5
Moderate	15.0	15.4	15.4	NA	16.0	10.7
Low	19.0	19.3	14.3	NA	24.3	17.1
Foreign Exchange Premium						
High (> 200%)	8.2	7.2	3.2	NA	11.5	NA
Moderate (20 - 200%)	14.4	14.9	11.9	13.7	17.2	10.3
Low (0 - 20%)	17.7	18.0	16.6	16.6	19.3	15.2
Real Interest Rate						
Negative	15.0	15.4	12.7	17.9	17.9	11.0
Positive	17.3	17.5	17.0	17.8	17.9	15.6
Fiscal Deficit as a Percentage of GDP						
High (> 8%)	13.4	13.7	11.7	10.3	16.6	10.7
Moderate (4 - 8%)	14.8	15.1	12.2	21.0	16.8	12.2
Low (< 4%)	17.8	18.1	18.6	14.1	18.2	14.3

Source: World Bank, *World Development Report, 1991* (New York: Oxford University Press, 1991).

NA: Information not available.

The IMF and the international monetary system it was designed to police arrived together with the formation of the WB and GATT at the 1944 Bretton Woods Conference. The conference participants were most concerned about rebuilding the world's trade and financial system in the hope of averting another world war. The new monetary system was to be built around a regime of fixed exchange rates. Each country's exchange rate would be fixed at a parity level linked to gold. The U.S. dollar became the preeminent currency under this new system as the U.S. government guaranteed that it would be willing and ready to buy or sell unlimited quantities of gold at US$35 per ounce.

Under this system, a country would be able to run an external deficit or surplus with other countries. The idea, however, was that countries running deficits should be able to borrow from the IMF to finance their deficits and not have to reduce trade because of a temporary deficit. Similarly, countries running surpluses would be able, if they so chose, to lend their surplus reserves. The banking activities of the IMF revolved around the subscriptions in gold and foreign currencies that each member country had to supply to the IMF. These subscriptions provided the basis for the IMF's loans.

If, however, a country had a fundamental deficit that was chronic and long term in nature, it would have to adjust to that deficit. Adjustment could take place by reducing domestic demand, changing the value of the country's currency if allowed, or imposing trade restrictions. The new monetary system argued that a country should adjust to its deficit primarily by reducing demand. The IMF would also examine the situation; and if it believed a devaluation was necessary, the country would be allowed to devalue. Countries would not be allowed to devalue at will because the new system sought to avoid the competitive devaluations that had taken place in the interwar years.

The exchange rate system established at Bretton Woods lasted until the 1970s. It came apart in 1971. During the 1960s, the United States had been running a significant external deficit with the rest of the world. Central banks from countries around the world accepted dollars in payment for exports to the United States because of the strength of the U.S. economy and the commitment to exchange dollars for gold. Many countries preferred holding dollars because these holdings attracted interest, whereas gold bullion did not. As these dollar reserves accumulated in central banks around the world, however, it soon became clear that if these governments sought to exchange their dollars for gold, the United States would not be able to honor its obligation.

In fact, this is what happened in 1971. The United States, after a decade of external deficits and recent expansive monetary policies that increased the supply of dollars, faced a run on the dollar. On August 15, 1971, President Richard Nixon suspended the convertibility of dollars into gold. With this suspension, the entire system of fixed exchange rates broke down. Developed countries, in particular, no longer defined their currencies with respect to a parity with gold or with the U.S. dollar. Increasingly, these countries allowed their exchange rates to be determined by market forces.

Many developing countries, on the other hand, continued to peg their currencies to the currency of a major developed country trading partner. In the meetings of the IMF held in Jamaica in 1974 (the Jamaica Accord), the IMF's members agreed to legalize the movement to floating exchange rates that began in 1971. Superstitious Jamaicans might, in retrospect, wonder if Jamaica's hosting of the meeting that legalized a floating exchange rate system was not an omen, given the extent to which the Jamaican currency has "floated" downward since 1974.

With the change in the international monetary system from one of fixed exchange rates to floating exchange rates, there was also a change in the function of the IMF. Since countries no longer had fixed exchange rates, the IMF no longer needed to monitor exchange rate parities and decide whether countries should be allowed to devalue. Instead, the IMF increasingly became involved in another of the functions assigned to it by its Bretton Woods creators: lender of last resort to those countries suffering from deficits in their balance of payments.

The IMF's Lending Program

Rather than decline in significance with the loss of its principal regulatory function, the IMF became more influential, but primarily within the developing countries of the world. Developed countries running external deficits found that they could finance these deficits from private international capital markets. The case of the United States was again exceptional. During the 1980s, especially, the United States had been able to finance its deficit through foreign holdings of U.S. dollars and foreign acquisition of U.S. assets.

Developing countries, however, have experienced severe and prolonged external deficits. This has been particularly true since the oil price increases (induced by the Organization of Petroleum Exporting Countries [OPEC]) of the 1970s, which were coupled with decreases in the prices of many other raw materials produced by these countries. Most countries found that they were unable to finance these deficits through private capital markets. Also, the deficits were sufficiently large that domestic adjustment via reduced imports and expanded exports would have been very difficult in the short term. Thus, these countries turned to their banker of last resort—the IMF—for assistance.

The amount a country can borrow from the IMF is related to its quota, that is, its original subscription with the IMF. Members have complete access to the reserve tranche since that comprises amounts held at the fund from the country's own reserves. Each member country thereafter has access to four credit tranches, each equivalent to 25 percent of its quota. The first such tranche is easily obtained. The succeeding tranches become increasingly more difficult. As countries seek to gain access to these higher credit tranches, the IMF imposes progressively more stringent conditions on the loans.

Over time, the IMF has engaged in different forms of lending. In the 1960s, it created a compensatory financing facility that allowed member countries to borrow to make up for sudden shortfalls in exports earnings. In the 1970s, it created a special oil facility to assist countries in their efforts to deal with the effects of the oil crisis. During this same period, it also created an extended fund facility that offered countries a five- to ten-year repayment period rather than the three- to five-year period that had been typical of most of the IMF's loans.

These then are the principal functions of the IMF. It currently is most involved in lending money to developing countries. In making these loans, it spends significant effort monitoring the economies to which it lends and ensuring that the conditions associated with its loans are met. Many developing countries believe that the conditions that the IMF insists upon, such as currency depreciation, reduction of government budget deficits, and elimination of government subsidy programs, are too stringent and impinge upon the sovereignty of the country. It is in this respect that the IMF has come to be viewed as a villain by many developing countries. Increasingly, the question is asked as to whether the two Bretton Woods Institutions that face each other across Nineteenth Street in Washington, D.C., contribute to the development of the developing economies.

INTERNATIONAL OPERATIONS OF COMMERCIAL BANKS

The final critical element of the international monetary system is the commercial banks that operate internationally by engaging in banking transactions in currencies other than the currency of the country of which the bank is a resident. As far back as the beginning of the twentieth century, European banks were engaging in these types of international financial banking transactions; but a significant expansion in this type of activity took place in the 1970s to the extent that a new term was coined to describe this financial activity—*euromarkets*. Euromarkets consist of eurocurrencies, eurobonds, and euroequities.

Eurocurrencies are broadly defined as currencies on deposit in or borrowed from a country other than the country that issued the currency. Thus, U.S. dollars on deposit in a bank in London are Eurodollars, and Japanese yen on deposit at the same London bank would be Euroyen. Note, however, that the prefix euro is a historical vestige only. Thus, Japanese yen on deposit in Singapore would also be Euroyen. Also, the nationality of the bank that engages in these financial transactions is irrelevant. Thus, eurocurrency transactions are not the province only of multinational banks. Any bank can participate in euromarket transactions.

The eurocurrency market became popular as recently as the 1970s. One version of the origin of this market suggests that it stemmed from the desire of Soviet bloc countries and several Arab oil-producing countries to keep the U.S. dollars they earned from mineral sales outside the territorial control of the United States. Both sets of countries were concerned that in the event of disputes with the United States their dollar assets might be frozen if they were held on U.S. territory. Once the supply of U.S. dollars was in place, the other factor that led to the rapid expansion of the market was the absence of government regulation of this supply. U.S. dollars on deposit in London are outside the regulatory jurisdiction of the U.S. Federal Reserve, but they are also outside the jurisdiction of the Bank of England.

Since these deposits were virtually unregulated, banks were in a position to lend euromarket funds at lower interest rates than the rates that applied to loans of the same magnitude borrowed in the country from which the currency originated. This possibility of lower interest rate loans spawned a demand for eurocurrencies. Interest rates in the eurocurrency market have tended to be linked with the London Interbank Offer Rate (LIBOR), which is an interbank interest rate.

By the 1990s, eurocurrencies dominated international financial transactions. Indeed, with the liberalization of banking systems and the movement away from exchange control in many developing countries, eurocurrencies are no longer novel. In the early 1990s, for example, both Jamaica and Trinidad eliminated exchange controls and allowed nationals to hold funds in foreign-currency accounts in local banks. In both countries banks immediately began offering foreign-currency accounts and making foreign-currency loans. Although not eurocurrency transactions in the sense in which the market is usually described, with an emphasis on multimillion-dollar transactions, these transactions qualified as eurocurrency transactions on all other dimensions.

The emergence of foreign-currency activities in developing countries offers challenges and opportunities. The challenges in the financial arena correspond to those in the arena of trade in other types of goods and services. As the world becomes more integrated and economic borders collapse, it becomes more difficult for any form of uncompetitive economic activity to survive. To the extent that firms and individuals in developing countries can increasingly scan the globe for investment and banking opportunities, it creates additional pressure on banks that operate in these countries to offer competitive options and services. The opportunities for local banks lie in their newly created abilities to work with locally based firms in penetrating overseas markets by being able to provide foreign-currency loans to these firms. Ultimately, for developing countries, as has been true in many developed countries, the competitiveness of the financial sector will be closely intertwined with the competitiveness of other sectors of the economy.

THE IMPACT OF THE PROGRAMS OF THE FUND AND THE BANK ON DEVELOPMENT

From the perspective of developing countries, the focus of the international monetary system is typically on the programs of the "Fund" and the "Bank." Most developing-country governments have gained an astonishing familiarity with negotiating teams from these institutions. The first point one might make in assessing the effect of these institutions on development is that while the WB and the other regional development banks are development institutions, the IMF is a club. It makes no claim to be a development institution but, rather, a financial institution that exists to lubricate the world's system of commerce by ensuring that trade is not reduced because countries have short-term payment problems.

As pointed out earlier in the chapter, even though the WB is a development institution, most of its loans are commercial loans; and the WB makes a profit from the distribution of these loans. In fact, the WB has made a profit every year since 1948. The point is that both institutions play a role that is partly development; but at the same time, both are commercially viable entities.

The criticisms of the operations of these institutions, however, take their starting point from the position that they should be interested in helping the development of developing countries rather than in being principally concerned about creating stability in the international monetary system. The institutions are criticized for applying identical remedies to countries regardless of each country's particular situation and of applying these remedies—essentially a market philosophy—in a doctrinaire way. They are also criticized for imposing austerity and being insufficiently concerned about the impact of their prescriptions on the poor.

Also, the institutions are criticized for colluding in their actions against developing countries and for duplicating functions and otherwise operating in an inefficient manner. These criticisms are voiced in the context of the profitability of the institutions. Critics point out that some governments are taking loans from the WB to pay off the IMF so that funds are essentially just crossing Nineteenth Street. Given this situation, observers in developing countries ask how these institutions can be assisting in the development process.

Some of the criticisms are credible. The institutions do have an agenda for reform that is quite similar from country to country. Conditionalities on loans, for example, bear a marked resemblance from country to country. Yet, it is interesting to note that much of the Bank–Fund orthodoxy is now being pursued by many developing countries in the absence of pressure from the multilateral institutions. Many in the Fund and the Bank see this as a vindication of the legitimacy of their past prescriptions.

The conditions stipulated by the institutions do impose austerity on the countries in question. However, that particular criticism to some extent misses the point of the IMF's role in particular. Recall that the entire idea of IMF lending is to provide a country with breathing space while it makes the adjustment to fundamental external deficits. This adjustment will typically come through a combination of austerity programs that reduce demand and programs that increase the supply of tradeable goods. Thus, in seeking to ensure that its loans will be repaid, the IMF is supposed to impose austerity. The WB as a development institution should theoretically be more concerned about the impact of its programs on the poor. Historically, this has not been the case. In recent years, however, there has been additional effort on the part of the WB to ensure that its lending programs help the poorest groups in developing countries. This new approach recognizes the accuracy of criticisms that the Bretton Woods Institutions have focused insufficiently on the devastating conditions of the poor in developing countries.

The debate about collusion and duplication between the Fund and the Bank has become more pronounced in recent years. The Bank and the Fund at times like to suggest that they represent independent operations; yet, to many developing-country governments, this has always seemed very shallow. They see institutions that sit across from each other in Washington, D.C. They note further that these institutions share an annual meeting and at times participate in joint missions. Efforts at indicating their independence might continue, but these efforts will never carry much weight in the developing world.

Of more concern in recent years has been the notion that each institution is duplicating the other's function. The implication, of course, is that there might be savings associated with the rationalization of these institutions. The duplication of function has become an issue especially since the 1980s, when the WB began engaging in structural adjustment lending, which came with macropolicy conditions attached to the loans. Historically, the IMF had been the institution involved in macropolicy issues. At the same time, the IMF was increasing its extended fund financing loans and thereby moving gradually into the area of long-term financing. The Bank had historically been the long-term financier, with the IMF providing financing of a short-term nature only. The operations of these institutions clearly overlap, but it is not clear how important that issue is to developing countries. There may, at some point, be a merger of the Bretton Woods organizations; but that merger would do little to assist in the development prospects of the developing countries.

Possibly a more fundamental criticism that might be offered by the student of international business is that these multilateral institutions operate from the assumption that the principal constraint upon development is an absence of capital and inappropriate macroeconomic policy. The focus on the capital constraint to development is entirely understandable when one again considers the context in which the multilateral institutions were formed and the fact that they are, first and foremost, financial institutions. Contextually, the institutions were created at the same time as the Marshall Plan, which transferred significant resources from the United States to Europe. The WB similarly saw its role as transferring capital to developing countries to fuel development.

The intellectual environment that prevailed during the formative years of these institutions further contributed to their assumptions about the development process. The multilateral institutions were probably influenced by the Harrod–Domar Growth model. As pointed out in Chapter 1, this model of economic growth suggested that the growth rate of national income is directly and positively related to the savings (local and foreign) available to the country. Rostow's linear stages theory of economic growth followed this line of inquiry by focusing on the conditions necessary for a country to "take off" into a pattern of self-sustaining growth. In fact, Rostow defined the savings condition quite specifically. Countries that had access to savings (their own or the savings of other countries) equivalent to 15 to 20 percent of their GNP could take off on a trajectory of rapid growth that would also be self-sustaining.

The IMF with its focus on macroeconomic policy was also heavily influenced by the contextual environment within which it was formed. Many economists placed much of the blame for the Great Depression, and even World War II, on the protectionist trade policies, the competitive devaluations, and the general macroeconomic instability of the interwar years. It seemed obvious, therefore, that an institution wedded to maintaining international macroeconomic stability was essential. The IMF has been engaged in that task since its formation. As indicated earlier, the WB joined the IMF in this task with the 1980s move to SALs and SECALs.

Thus, based on the evidence of the past in the context of the success of the Marshall Plan in the resuscitation of Europe, for example, and the evidence of the present (as shown in Table 5.3), the multilateral institutions have operated on the fundamental assumption that the path to economic growth and development is paved by adequate supplies of capital and a stable macroeconomy whose prices are undistorted.

Since the 1980s, in particular, the multilateral institutions have sought to solve both perceived obstacles to development simultaneously. They have provided capital under the general condition that the borrowing country restructure its economy, or sectors within that economy, along lines that will promote macroeconomic stability and the removal of price distortions. In large part, as indicated in Table 5.4, the borrowing countries have tried to reform their economies along the lines mandated by these institutions. In a 1988 study, the WB examined the extent to which conditions were complied with in fifty-one SALs and SECALs in fifteen countries. On average, 63 percent of the countries surveyed complied with the conditions attached to the loans.

Despite the degree of compliance with the conditions of the multilateral institutions, this has not translated into growth and development for developing countries. For low- and middle-income economies (i.e., most developing countries), average growth rates of GDP during the 1980s—the period of massive experimentation with structural adjustment lending—was 3.8 percent, compared to an average growth rate for the same group of countries of 5.3 percent during the 1970s. As is well known, the 1980s were a period of particularly slow growth for the Latin American and Caribbean region. These countries recorded growth of 1.6 percent per annum over the period of 1980 to 1989. Of course, in the absence of counterfactual evidence, it is not possible to state the impact of adjustment programs on economic growth.

Table 5.4
Compliance with Loan Conditions by a Sample of Countries

Conditions	Percentage of Countries Complying with Loan Conditions
Exchange Rate	100
Trade Policies	59
Import Quota Restraints	59
Import Duties	77
Import/Export Finance	0
Export Incentives	62
Other Trade Policies	0
Fiscal Policy	64
Tax Policy	40
Budget/Public Spending	71
Public-Enterprise Reforms	78
Financial Sector	79
Industrial Policy	80
Energy Policy	90
Energy Pricing	88
Agricultural Policy	56
Agricultural Pricing	60

Source: World Bank, "Adjustment Lending: An Evaluation of Ten Years of Experience" (Washington, D.C.: World Bank, Policy and Research Series No. 1, 1988).

One might argue, however, that the growth results are, at least in part, a result of the fact that the assumptions of the multilateral institutions with respect to the development process are incomplete at best. While macroeconomic stability and adequate supplies of capital may be *necessary* conditions for development, they are not *sufficient* conditions for growth and development. This may not have been true about the resuscitation of Europe and Japan in the aftermath of World War II. The countries of Europe and Japan had developed modern systems and institutions and had mature, competitive firms before the war. Japan may not have penetrated world markets in a manner similar to their penetration of these markets in later years, but Japanese fighter planes held their own during World War II when compared with planes from the United States.

The developing countries of the world, almost uniformly, have no such history. For them, the development dilemma is, in fact, considerably more complicated. A modern Marshall Plan, were it feasible by the standards of international politics, would not alone lead to growth and development. For the developing countries of the world, the road to development must be paved with the generation of ideas as much as it is with the creation and attraction of capital.

Consequently, more attention in the development process needs to be placed upon the mechanisms through which firms in developing countries—the principal agents of economic activity—can generate new ideas. In particular, for small developing countries, these firms must generate ideas that lead to internationally competitive operations. Clearly, the activities of these firms are affected by issues of macroeconomic stability, other elements of government policy, issues of social stability, and international politics. However, it is the activities of these firms that undergird the development process. It is their competitive operations, the interlinkages among them, and the diffusion of the results from their competitive operations throughout the society that represent the sufficient condition for growth and development.

The implication of this perspective on development is that, to be successful in the promotion of development, the multilateral financial institutions must take a more micro-orientation to the understanding of the development process. This is not instead of their orientation toward macroeconomic policy, but it is in addition to this orientation.

Indeed, since the establishment of the IFC as a subsidiary of the WB in 1956, cognizance has been taken of the need to conduct analyses and provide assistance at the level of the individual firm; but the IFC's current position in the Caribbean region also illustrates how much farther this perspective needs to be taken. As Table 5.5 indicates, the IFC's total commitments (i.e., outstanding cumulative positions from both loans and equity) to the CARICOM countries as of June 1993 represent about half of the funds received by one such country (Jamaica) from the WB in 1991 alone. Accordingly, despite the movements in this direction over the last few years by the multilateral financial community, additional efforts in the direction of a more microfocused development strategy are necessary.

Were the multilateral institutions to adopt a more microperspective, seeking to understand the nature of the competitive advantages of countries down to the level of particular sectors and even firms, it would require them to place more emphasis on understanding specific national situations and to be more flexible to national peculiarities. This would mark a change in orientation for institutions that have historically operated on the basis not only of common principles but also of standard prescriptions.

To some extent, the criticisms of the multilateral institutions raised earlier in this chapter are better understood in the context of the perspective they place upon the process of development. To the extent that the multilateral institutions provide generic advice of a macropolicy nature only, standard prescriptions are often appropriate. Universally, countries seeking to promote export industries will find that overvalued exchange rates are an impediment to export success. Profligate governments everywhere will find that their profligacy leads to a vicious cycle of inflation and currency instability or currency flight. In general, countries will find that privatization policies that force governments to turn over to the private-sector enterprises that have been incurring losses will assist in the process of curing government profligacy.

Table 5.5
International Finance Corporation Commitments in CARICOM, June 30, 1993 (US$ Millions)

Country	Company	Loans	Equity	Total Commitment
Barbados	Caribbean Financial Services		0.3	0.3
	Town and Commercial Properties Limited	1.0		1.0
Jamaica	Caribbean Cement Company	8.0		8.0
	Citizens Bank Limited	2.0		2.0
	Mutual Security	1.3		1.3
	St. Mary Banana Estates	2.6	1.2	3.8
	The Falcon Fund Limited	0.3		0.3
St. Lucia	Club St. Lucia	3.4		3.4
Trinidad and Tobago	Development Finance Limited		0.6	0.6
	Home Mortgage Bank		0.4	0.4
	Trinidad Nitrogen Company	18.8		18.8
		37.4	2.5	39.9

Source: International Finance Corporation, *IFC Annual Report, 1993* (Washington, D.C.: International Finance Corporation, 1993).

At the more microlevel, there is a need for creative solutions that show greater variation from country to country. Again, it is at this level that competitive advantage is increasingly going to be derived. Currently, for example, according to the standards of WB and IMF advice, what recommendations would these institutions have for the poor developing country that is fiscally prudent, has liberalized its markets, and has privatized its entities; for one can make a strong argument that such a country having "successfully" undertaken these reforms could easily still be poor?

As a final point, one might well ask whether the task of making recommendations to the multilateral financial institutions is not, in fact, best conducted by the nationals of the developing countries themselves. Ultimately, this will need to be the case. The governments of developing countries and the institutions that suggest that they are in the business of assisting them develop must recognize the importance of moving toward a structure in which individuals within developing countries understand and seek solutions to their own development problems; particularly to the extent that these problems are increasingly less driven by a paucity of capital and more driven by a paucity of ideas. While the process of moving to national-led development strategies continues to gather momentum, the most effective way in which the multilateral institutions can assist in the development process is by extending their analyses in the manner described in this chapter.

Ultimately, it is important also to remember that the WB and the IMF—but particularly the IMF—are financial institutions as much as development institutions. In addressing the issue of the impact of these institutions on development, it is useful to return to the analogy that began this chapter. The development banks around the world, for example, assist in the development process in much the same way as a nation's development banks might—no more or no less. Where funding from these institutions is used to enhance the productive capabilities of the country, that funding will have contributed to the process of development. Where it has not been so used, the implications are obvious. One final consideration that continues the analogy and should occupy the minds of technocrats in developing countries is that banks—whether national or international—make profits by lending money and that bank officers are evaluated based not only on the quality of their loans but also on the quantity of such loans.

FURTHER READING

Girling, Robert Henriques. *Multilateral Institutions and the Third World.* New York: Praeger, 1985.

"The IMF and the World Bank." *The Economist* (12 October 1991).

International Finance Corporation. *IFC Annual Report, 1993.* Washington, D.C.: International Finance Corporation, 1993.

World Bank. "Adjustment Lending: An Evaluation of Ten Years of Experience." Washington, D.C.: World Bank, Policy and Research Series No. 1, 1988.

World Bank. *World Bank Annual Report, 1991.* New York: Oxford University Press, 1991.

World Bank. *World Bank Annual Report, 1992.* New York: Oxford University Press, 1992.

World Bank. *World Development Report, 1991.* New York: Oxford University Press, 1991.

Worrel, Delisle, et al., eds. *Financing Development in the Commonwealth Caribbean.* London: Macmillan Education, 1991.

Chapter 6

Managing Foreign Exchange

Clearly, the factor that has the greatest influence on the transfer of funds among countries is the reality that almost all countries issue their own currencies. The fact that most nations today have a national currency creates a plethora of foreign currencies around the world and a market for the exchange of these currencies. For managers and analysts in developing countries, it is important to consider carefully how foreign exchange markets operate and how exchange rates are determined in the particular context of the developing country environment. Similarly, public policymakers must consider carefully how exchange rate policies of developing country governments affect the competitiveness of the economies they manage.

THE FUNCTIONING OF EXCHANGE RATE MARKETS

In conducting foreign exchange transactions, whether they involve the exchange of Mauritiani Ouguiyas into Japanese yen, Vietnamese dong into French francs, Ghanian cedis into British pounds, or Honduran Lempiras into U.S. dollars, managers will utilize foreign exchange traders who will usually quote two numbers: a price at which he or she is willing to buy, the bid price, and a price at which he or she is willing to sell a given currency, the offer or ask price.

Foreign exchange quotations are either direct or indirect. A direct quote represents the price in the home country's currency of one unit of foreign exchange. Thus, in Singapore, S$1.63/US$ is a direct quote for the U.S. dollar. An indirect quote, on the other hand, is the reciprocal of a direct quote and is the price of foreign currency in one unit of the country's home currency. Thus, an indirect quote for the U.S. dollar in Singapore is S$/US$0.61.

As managers are well aware, there are two principal types of exchange rates. *Spot exchange* rates are those rates which relate to transactions in foreign exchange which involve immediate delivery and acceptance of the exchange proceeds. This is the type of exchange transaction most popular in developing countries, although a few developing countries have developed markets for the alternate type of exchange transaction—the forward transaction. *Forward exchange* markets allow the purchase and sale of foreign exchange for delivery at some point in the future, usually within a few months.

It is important to note that banks in some developing countries that are said to be using forward markets may not be using these markets in their formal sense. In conditions of scarcity of foreign exchange, customers are known to buy foreign exchange forward at predetermined rates; but this transaction, if it is primarily a mechanism for obtaining scarce foreign exchange, is not equivalent to the normal forward contract. The principal difference lies in the legal sanctity of the arrangement. Such arrangements often represent verbal commitments or written commitments that do not have the force of a contract.

Forward rates are often linked to spot rates through the calculation of a forward premium or discount. This is an annualized percentage difference between the spot rate and the forward rate. It is useful in comparing differences in spot and forward rates with differences in interest rates. The precise calculation of this difference differs slightly based on whether indirect or direct quotes are used. Assuming that indirect quotes are used:

$$\text{Forward premium or discount} = \frac{(\text{Spot} - \text{Forward})}{\text{Forward}} \times \frac{12}{n} \times 100$$

Assuming that direct quotes are used:

$$\text{Forward premium or discount} = \frac{(\text{Forward} - \text{Spot})}{\text{Spot}} \times \frac{12}{n} \times 100$$

In both calculations, n = the number of months remaining on the forward contract.

DETERMINATION OF EXCHANGE RATES

The manner in which exchange rates are determined is not unlike price determination in other contexts. As the price of currency, an exchange rate simply represents the interaction between the demand and supply of that currency, with one caveat; that is, while changes in exchange rates since the movement to floating exchange rates in 1973 can be explained by interactions in demand and supply, the pre-1973 exchange rates were not set by market forces. Thus, the fact that in 1994 the pound/dollar exchange rate was UK£1 = US$1.5 does not suggest that there is greater demand for the U.K. pound than for the U.S. dollar.

During the era of fixed exchange rates, these countries chose to peg their currencies to different quantities of gold, with the United Kingdom opting for a unit of currency, the pound, that was worth more in gold than the U.S. dollar. The more telling indicator of demand for a country's currency relates to the movement in relative currencies since the global movement to a floating exchange regime. In this regard, the U.S. dollar has appreciated significantly against the pound sterling in the period of floating exchange rates. It is from the change in exchange rates over this period that one can conclude that the demand for the U.S. dollar in the 1973–1993 period has outpaced the demand for the pound sterling.

In an analysis of exchange rates, therefore, the focus is on the movement in rates rather than on absolute rates. A change in the price of German Deutsche marks relative to U.S. dollars, for example, is determined by the interaction of the demand for German marks by holders of U.S. dollars, coupled with the demand for U.S. dollars by holders of German marks. Holders of U.S. dollars who demand Deutsche marks will supply dollars in exchange for these marks. Similarly, holders of Deutsche marks who demand U.S. dollars will supply marks in exchange for these dollars. That is, the factors leading to the supply of U.S. dollars will mirror exactly the factors leading to a demand for German marks; and, correspondingly, the factors leading to a demand for U.S. dollars will mirror the factors leading to the supply of German marks. Table 6.1 illustrates the typical transactions that affect the demand and supply of currencies and thus the price at which these currencies are exchanged.

As indicated in Table 6.1, these factors that have an impact on the exchange rate between two countries include principally trade in goods and services and investment, whether direct investment or portfolio investment. Thus, demand for Deutsche marks relative to U.S. dollars will increase with increases in German exports of goods to the United States and exports of services, such as an increase in the expenditure of U.S. tourists visiting Germany. In both cases, U.S. residents will exchange dollars for Deutsche marks to facilitate their imports from Germany. Demand for Deutsche marks relative to U.S. dollars will also increase as U.S. firms or residents invest in Germany by purchasing German assets.

Last, in terms of investments, demand for Deutsche marks relative to U.S. dollars will also increase as German firms or citizens that have invested in the United States seek to remit profits or repatriate capital from these investments. In both cases, these firms or citizens of Germany will seek to convert the profits they have generated from their U.S. investments or the capital they initially invested in the United States to German Deutsche marks to facilitate the transfer of these funds back to their country of citizenship. Obviously, the same analysis applies in assessing the demand for U.S. dollars relative to German Deutsche marks. This demand is based on exports of U.S. goods and

Table 6.1
Principal Determinants of the Mark/Dollar Exchange Rate

Factors Influencing Demand for German Marks (and supply of U.S. dollars)	Factors Influencing Supply of German Marks (and demand for U.S. dollars)
U.S. importers buying German goods	German importers buying U.S. goods
U.S. direct investors investing in Germany	German direct investors investing in the United States
U.S. portfolio investors investing in Germany	German portfolio investors investing in the United States
U.S. consumers buying German services	German consumers buying U.S. services
German direct investors in the United States repatriating capital or remitting profits	U.S. direct investors in Germany repatriating capital or remitting profits

services to Germany and U.S. investments in Germany relative to German investments in the United States.

This is not to suggest that other factors do not play an important role in the demand and supply of currencies and thus the price of these currencies. Governments can and do intervene to influence the price of their currency or the currency of another country. Exchange rates can also be influenced by speculative activity. In such circumstances, individuals affect the demand and supply of currencies for none of the purposes already identified. Government intervention and speculative activity, however, tend not to be the underlying forces that affect changes in exchange rates. Rather, in the context of developed countries, in particular, the factors outlined in Table 6.1 tend to be the most critical in their impact on exchange rates over the long term.

THE DEVELOPING COUNTRY DIFFERENCE

The process of exchange rate determination based on the demand and supply for particular currencies also holds true in the context of exchange rates between currencies of developed and developing countries, yet there are differences. One fundamental difference relates to the convertibility of a country's currency. When a firm or individual accepts a foreign currency in payment for goods and services, the presumption is that, at some point in the future, that foreign currency can be exchanged for another currency of choice at no loss or can be used to purchase goods and services of acceptable quality and price from the country of issue. The greater the probability of redemption for internationally acceptable goods and services, the greater the likelihood that the currency can be exchanged without loss to the holder. Currencies that are easily exchanged for other currencies are described as convertible or "hard" currencies. Those currencies that are not easily exchanged are viewed as nonconvertible or "soft" currencies.

The currencies of most developing countries are not easily exchanged for other currencies. Consequently, exporters from these countries will, instead of demanding payment in their home currencies for the goods and services they export, accept payment in one of the world's hard currencies. These exporters want to be sure that the hard work of exporting that they engage in is rewarded by gaining access to a currency that they can then use to engage in international business transactions of their choosing. Accepting payment in the soft currencies of their own countries would not constitute such a reward. This applies to exporters of goods and of services. A Colombian exporter of goods to the United States will accept—indeed, will demand—payment in U.S. dollars, as will a Kenyan hotelier. This has implications for the determination of prices of developing country currencies. Thus, the price of the Kenyan shilling relative to the U.S. dollar is principally a function of the demand for U.S. dollars relative to the supply of U.S. dollars.

The impact of the demand and supply of Kenyan shillings on this price is more muted than would be true were the Kenyan shilling a convertible currency. Unlike the situation when analyzing price changes among convertible currencies, the supply of U.S. dollars is not the mirror image of the demand for Kenyan shillings; and the supply of Kenyan shillings is not the mirror image of the demand for U.S. dollars. Thus, to return to the Colombian exporter, the export activity increased the supply of U.S. dollars; but it may not have significantly increased the demand for Colombian pesos, since it is quite possible that most of the proceeds from the export sale would remain in a hard currency. The Colombian exporter might only convert the portion of the proceeds necessary to continue his economic activity. By the same token, however, when that exporter needs to import goods and services, he will draw down from reserves in foreign currencies. Thus, in the Colombian case, an increase in demand for U.S. dollars will not be matched by an increase in the supply of Colombian pesos in the foreign exchange system in the manner that would prevail between two countries with convertible currencies.

This is not to suggest that, for developing countries, exchange rates are completely exogenously determined and, therefore, entirely outside the control of the government of the developing country. These governments can, of course, influence the demand for and supply of foreign currencies. An increase in the supply of the currency of the developing country, for example, is likely to have an impact on the exchange rate through its influence on inflation. However, for developing countries, the greatest impact on exchange rates between their currencies and those convertible currencies of their developed-country trading partners will be the interaction between the demand and supply of those convertible currencies.

The analysis thus far, however, while identifying the factors that might lead to an increase in the demand and supply of particular currencies, has stopped short of uncovering the fundamental economic relationships that help to determine exchange rates among national currencies. The following section on theories of exchange rate determination seeks to uncover these relationships.

THEORIES OF EXCHANGE RATE DETERMINATION

Movements in exchange rates are determined by the relative demand and supply of the currencies in question. The demand and supply of these currencies are, in turn, influenced by relative trade and investment patterns between the countries in question. One might go one step back and ask what factors determine these relative trade and investment patterns. The typical response to this question, posed in its usual manner as a backdrop to an analysis of international business transactions among industrialized countries, focuses on two economic indicators: inflation and interest rates. Inflation, it is argued, determines movements in interest rates as reflected in the theory of purchasing power parity. Interest rates have their own impact on exchange rate movements, as identified by the concept of the Fisher Effect and the International Fisher Effect.

Purchasing Power Parity

The theory of purchasing power parity is deceptively simple. It argues that, other things being equal, changes in the differential rate of inflation between two countries should lead to equal but opposite changes in the spot exchange rate. Thus, for example, if the United States and the United Kingdom have inflation levels such that in 1992 inflation in the United States is 9 percent and inflation in the United Kingdom is 20 percent, then this should lead to a 10-percent depreciation of the British pound relative to the U.S. dollar. This is because the differential inflation between both countries is 10 percent, given by the following formula for calculating the differential inflation in Country X relative to Country Y:

$$\frac{[(1 + \text{Inflation Rate in Country X}) - (1 + \text{Inflation Rate in Country Y})]}{(1 + \text{Inflation Rate in Country Y})} \times 100$$

If the exchange rate at the beginning of 1992, quoted on a direct basis, was £0.50/US$1, then the exchange rate at the end of the year according to purchasing power parity should be £0.55/US$1 given by the following equation for calculating percentage changes in spot exchange rates quoted on a direct basis:

$$\text{Percentage change} = \frac{(\text{Ending Rate} - \text{Beginning Rate})}{\text{Beginnning Rate}} \times 100$$

The rationale is that U.K. inflation that is 10 percent higher than the corresponding U.S. version will price U.K. tradeable goods 10 percent above their U.S. counterparts. This price increase will lead to a reduction in demand for U.K. goods relative to U.S. goods. This reduction in demand for goods will lead to a reduction in the demand for pounds sterling relative to U.S. dollars.

At the same time, the higher inflation in the United Kingdom compared to the United States will lead to a greater increase in purchasing power in the United Kingdom relative to the United States. This increased purchasing power will allow U.K. citizens to demand more foreign goods and services (as well as local goods and services). This increase in imports will increase the demand for U.S. dollars relative to U.K. pounds and thus reduce the value of the pound relative to the dollar. Equilibrium will be restored when the price of the pound sterling relative to the U.S. dollar has declined in proportion to the differential increase in U.K. inflation relative to U.S. inflation.

Like most economic theories, purchasing power parity is rife with a variety of assumptions. The theory assumes, among other things, that recorded inflation rates apply with equal weight to the tradeable segment of the economy as they do to the basket of goods used to record price changes, that exporters increase prices proportionally to increases in domestic costs, and that the elasticity of demand across a country's tradeable sectors is unitary (i.e., demand changes proportionally with changes in prices). In addition, it relies on the ceteris paribus assumption that no other factor affecting exchange rates has changed. Given these assumptions, purchasing power parity is best regarded as one potential indicator of the direction in which one might anticipate that an exchange rate would move.

To this extent, purchasing power parity as a general conceptual tool in anticipating exchange rate movements is as useful in analyzing the exchange rate movements of developing country currencies as it is when analyzing the movements of developed country currencies. In fact, given that differential inflation rates are often substantially higher between a developed country and a developing country than among developed countries, it is potentially even more useful in the developing country environment. Thus, where differential inflation rates between two countries are in the order of 70 percent, as they were between Jamaica and the United States during 1991 with Jamaica experiencing about 75 percent inflation and the United States about 3 percent, it would be very strange if there were no depreciation of the Jamaican dollar against the U.S. dollar.

Although strange, it would be possible for there to be no depreciation of the Jamaican dollar. Many other factors could change. Jamaica could have experienced a highly successful year in which it identified new export markets, thus offsetting export losses due to higher local prices. U.S. firms could have invested in the country by purchasing productive assets, thereby increasing the available supply of foreign exchange. Jamaican wage earners might have saved the increases they were able to negotiate in an inflationary year, even if this meant a reduction in their consumption, instead of spending some portion on imported foods, cars, or consumer durables. The government of Jamaica could have negotiated with the banking sector to artificially restrict foreign exchange in an effort to stabilize the exchange rate.

There is no guarantee that any of these events would take place. The effects from the theory of purchasing power parity, on the other hand, take on a certain automaticity in the context of floating exchange rates. Returning to the earlier example, for instance, the actual depreciation of the Jamaican dollar relative to the U.S. dollar was 89 percent in the year in which inflation rates in Jamaica were 70 percent higher than were U.S. inflation rates. Tables 6.2 and 6.3 present data on average annual inflation rates and average annual changes in exchange rates between the currencies of a sample of developing countries and the United States over the period of 1980 to 1991. Table 6.2 examines countries in which the average annual inflation rate was less than 10 percent. Table 6.3 examines countries in which the average annual inflation rate over the same period was in excess of 10 percent.

The data lend considerable support to the validity of purchasing power parity concepts in the context of developing countries. The average difference, in absolute terms, between annual inflation rates and annual rates of exchange rate change in low-inflation countries was 2.90 percentage points, with a range of 0.03 to 7.70 percentage points. For high-inflation countries, the mean absolute difference was 9.54 percentage points, with a range of 2.18 to 20.35 percentage points. With the exception of three countries—Barbados, Antigua, and Singapore—all other countries in the sample experienced a depreciation in the value of their currencies relative to the U.S. dollar over the period. In both sets of countries, the extent of the depreciation in currency values tended to be less than proportionate to the changes in inflation.

Although the data seem to lend support to purchasing power parity models, this type of analysis clearly does not allow one to suggest the direction of causality. According to purchasing power parity, although differences in differential inflation rates leads to changes in relative exchange rates, it is also true that exchange rate changes lead to differences in relative inflation rates. Such effects might operate through a number of different channels. The worker, for example, that sees a depreciating exchange rate causing imported goods to increase in price may push for wage increases to meet these higher living costs. If such wage increases are granted without proportionate increases in the productivity of these workers, then inflation of the cost-push variety is likely to be the result. Inflation can also be caused by other factors such as inflationary government monetary and fiscal policies.

Other Parity Models

Apart from purchasing power parity, there are other important parity relationships that are deemed to hold true in an economy, particularly developed economies. Table 6.4 indicates these parity models.

The *Fisher Effect* suggests that nominal interest rates are a combination of a real rate of return and an allowance for anticipated inflation. If nominal interest rates do not adjust to changes in inflation such that real interest rates become negative, there is a transfer of real income from creditors to debtors. In such a situation, saving is discouraged with a range of problems likely to arise therefrom. Consequently, it is reasonable to anticipate that nominal rates will adjust to changes in inflation.

Interest Rate Parity indicates that differential interest rates between securities denominated in two currencies should correspond to the differential between the spot rate for these currencies and the forward rate. The differential between the spot rate and the forward rate for a currency is denoted as the premium or discount on the forward market, as outlined earlier in the chapter. In cases where the forward rate for a currency is less than the spot rate, the currency is said to be priced at a discount on the forward market. Where the forward rate is higher than the spot rate, the currency is priced at a premium on the forward market.

According to the interest rate parity model, if interest rate differentials between securities of equal risk and maturity in different currencies do not correspond to the premium or discount on the forward market for these currencies, then arbitrage opportunities will be created. In taking advantage of these arbitrage opportunities, through a process called covered interest arbitrage, the model suggests an eventual convergence between the interest rate differentials and the differentials between the spot and forward rates for the currencies in question.

The *Forward Rate as an Unbiased Predictor of the Future Spot Rate* suggests that the best information the market has about the future spot market is currently embodied in the forward market. If the market anticipates that a currency is likely to depreciate relative to another currency, then the forward rate for that currency will be at a discount relative to the current spot rate, and vice versa.

The *International Fisher Effect,* which is largely derivative, draws upon the above parity models in arriving at the conclusion that current interest rate differentials between securities of the same risk and maturity in different countries are an effective predictor of exchange rate changes. The spot exchange rate should change in response to differential interest rates. This relationship is also sometimes referred to as Fisher Open. The underlining premise behind the parity models is that economies will adjust to obvious disequilibria in financial and exchange markets. Consequently, the most effective way of understanding the parity relationships is through a numerical example. One technique that is very useful in this regard is that of covered interest arbitrage.

Covered Interest Arbitrage. Assume an initial situation in which one-year interest rates on risk-free government securities of 5 percent in the United States and 7.5 percent in the United Kingdom, and spot and forward rates of US$2 = UK£1. This situation provides an opportunity for an arbitrageur to

Table 6.2
Inflation and Exchange Rate Comparisons in Low-Inflation Countries

Country/ Currency	Average Differential Inflation 1980-1991*	1980 Exchange Rate Relative to U.S.$	1991 Exchange Rate Relative to U.S.$	Average Annual Change in Exchange Rate (Percentage)	Difference between Differential Inflation and Annual Change in Exchange Rate
Nepal/Rupees	4.70	13.20	42.70	11.30	-6.60
Bangladesh/Taka	4.90	19.85	38.58	6.30	-1.40
Rwanda/Francs	-0.10	92.80	125.10	2.75	-2.76
Congo/ CFA Francs	-3.40	225.80	259.00	1.25	-4.65
Mauritius/Rupees	3.70	10.30	14.80	3.35	0.35
Niger/ CFA Francs	-1.60	225.80	259.00	1.25	-2.85
Kenya/Shillings	4.90	7.60	28.07	12.60	-7.70
Benin/ CFA Francs	-2.50	225.80	259.00	1.25	-3.75
Central African Republic/ CFA Francs	0.90	225.80	259.00	1.25	-0.35
Mauritiania/ Ouguiyas	4.20	46.00	77.80	4.90	-0.70
Honduras/Lempiras	2.50	1.96	5.40	9.65	-7.15
Indonesia/Rupiah	4.10	627.00	1,950.00	10.90	-6.80
Antigua/EC$	2.60	2.70	2.70	0.00	2.60
Barbados/B$	0.95	2.01	2.01	0.00	0.95
Morocco/Dirhams	2.80	4.33	8.10	5.86	3.06
Thailand/Baht	-0.50	20.60	25.30	1.88	-2.38
Malaysia/M$	-2.40	2.20	2.70	1.88	0.52
Trinidad/TTS	2.10	2.40	4.25	5.33	-3.23
South Korea/Won	1.40	660.00	760.00	1.30	0.10
Singapore/S$	-2.20	2.09	1.63	-2.23	-0.03

Sources: World Bank, *World Development Report, 1993* (New York: Oxford University Press, 1993); International Monetary Fund, *International Financial Statistics,* various issues.

*The data in this column represent average differential inflation between each country and the United States over the period 1980–1991. The average differential inflation for the United States over this period was 4.2 percent. The differentials are calculated using the standard formula for calculating differential inflation discussed previously in the chapter.

earn risk-free arbitrage profits. Consider a U.S. investor with an investment of US$1 million. This investor could convert his investment pool into pounds on the spot market, invest in one-year U.K. government securities at an interest rate of 7.5 percent, and simultaneously sell the pounds to be received on the forward market. This transaction would result in interest earnings of US$75,000, or US$25,000 in excess of the possible earnings from the investor's alternate investment opportunity in the United States.

Table 6.3
Inflation and Exchange Rate Comparisons in High-Inflation Countries

Country/ Currency	Average Differential Inflation 1980-1991*	1980 Exchange Rate Relative to U.S.$	1991 Exchange Rate Relative to U.S.$	Average Annual Change in Exchange Rate (Percentage)	Difference between Differential Inflation and Annual Change in Exchange Rate
Tanzania/ Shillings	20.60	8.30	234.00	35.50	-14.90
Sierra Leone/ Leones	52.60	0.8639	434.80	71.40	-19.20
Malawi/Kwach	10.30	0.8258	2.80	11.74	-1.44
Nigeria/Naira	13.40	0.54	9.90	30.30	-16.90
Sri Lanka/ Rupees	6.70	18.00	42.50	8.12	-1.42
Lesotho/Loti	9.20	1.34	0.365	-11.15	20.35
Egypt/Pound	8.00	0.92	3.33	12.40	-4.40
Philippines/ Peso	9.90	7.60	26.65	12.08	-2.18
Ecuador/Sucres	32.50	25.00	1,270.00	42.90	-10.40
Peru/Soles	275.80	507.00	NA	NA	NA
Colombia/ Pesos	20.00	50.90	706.00	27.00	-7.00
Jamaica/J$	14.80	1.78	21.50	25.40	-10.60
Costa Rica/ Colones	17.90	8.60	135.00	28.40	-6.50
Chile/Pesos	15.60	39.00	375.00	22.80	-7.20
Venezuela/ Bolivaires	16.30	4.30	61.50	27.40	-11.10
Argentina/ Peso	400.00	.199	NA	NA	NA
Uruguay	57.80	10.025	NA	NA	NA

Sources: World Bank, *World Development Report, 1993* (New York: Oxford University Press, 1993); International Monetary Fund, *International Financial Statistics,* various issues.

*The data in this column represent average differential inflation between each country and the United States over the period 1980–1991. The average differential inflation for the United States over this period was 4.2 percent. The differentials are calculated using the standard formula for calculating differential inflation discussed previously in the chapter.

NA: Data for these countries were not available because they changed their currencies between 1980 and 1991.

The model suggests that such a situation is unstable—a nonequilibrium situation. Equilibrium will be regained with adjustments of the following types in the exchange markets. The spot rate of the pound relative to the dollar will change in such a way that the pound appreciates relative to the dollar reflecting the increasing demand for pounds that results from this lack of parity in interest rates. The extent of the adjustment in the spot market would be an

Table 6.4
Parity Models

Model	Explanation
Purchasing Power Parity	Spot exchange rates change in proportion to the differential inflation between two economies.
Fisher Effect	Nominal interest rates in a country are a combination of a real interest rate plus an allowance for anticipated inflation.
Interest Rate Parity	Differences in national interest rates in two countries for securities of equal risk and maturity will be equal to the forward discount or premium.
Forward Rate as an Unbiased Predictor of Future Spot Rates	The current forward rate for a currency captures the market's best information about the likely future spot rate for that currency, and is the best indicator of future spot rates.
International Fisher Effect	Spot exchange rates change in proportion to differences in interest rates on securities of equal risk and maturity in two countries.

appreciation of 2.38 percent of the pound relative to the dollar corresponding to the differential interest rate of 2.38 percent (1.075/1.05) of the pound relative to the dollar. An appreciation of this magnitude would lead to a new spot market rate of £1 = $2.0476.

The full adjustment could also take place in the forward market. If the adjustment takes place in the forward market, it will result in an appreciation of the dollar relative to the pound as the demand for dollars in the forward market increases; that is, to take advantage of the lack of parity across currencies, arbitrageurs will be buying dollars on the forward market. The amount of the appreciation in the forward rate for the dollar that can be expected under such conditions is 2.325 percent, corresponding to the differential interest rates of the dollar relative to the pound (1.05/1.075). If the full adjustment took place in the forward market, the forward rate would change from £1 = $2 to £1 = $1.953. Of course, adjustments could also take place in both spot and forward markets.

If interest rate differentials between financial instruments denominated in different currencies are resolved in the forward exchange market, as the covered interest arbitrage example demonstrates, these interest rate differentials also become resolved in the spot market. This conclusion can be derived from the concept that the forward market is an unbiased predictor of future spot markets. It is this final link that leads to the prescriptions of the International Fisher Effect.

Theoretically, an economy in equilibrium will find the Fisher Effect, interest rate parity, purchasing power parity, forward parity, and the International Fisher Effect all operating in tandem. Under such circumstances, if the United States has inflation that is 15 percent above Germany, this should lead to a nominal interest differential for U.S. risk-free securities that is 15 percent above German rates for securities of similar risk (Fisher Effect), a forward discount of the U.S. dollar relative to the German Deutsche mark of 15 percent (interest rate parity), and an expected depreciation of the spot market value of the U.S. dollar relative to the Deutsche mark of 15 percent (forward parity). Cumulatively, these parity relations lead to the International Fisher Effect.

A Developing-Country Perspective on the Fisher Effect

From a developing-country perspective, however, the disjuncture between theory and practice is quite pronounced in the context of the International Fisher Effect. The financial model discussed previously assumes the existence of a forward market for foreign currencies. For many developing countries, no such market exists. However, that is not the fundamental problem this line of analysis poses in its ability to explain foreign exchange rate determination in developing countries. Rather, it is the notion that one can identify financial instruments that investors perceive to be of similar risk across developing and developed countries and that investors are able to convert the proceeds from the sale of these financial instruments to the currency of their choice in a timely and low-cost manner.

The issues of risk perception and convertibility problems, in fact, become merged. One of the reasons foreign investors are unlikely to view securities issued in developing countries and by developing-country governments (government securities certainly being a principal form of risk-free security elsewhere) as offering the same risk profile as a security issued by a government in an industrialized country that boasts a convertible currency is the fact that they impute to such securities the risk of nonconvertibility. This issue of nonconvertibility is a profound one. One might argue that it should be possible for a government in a developing country to increase interest rates to a level that would compensate for nonconvertibility risks.

Two things mitigate against the probability of such an occurrence. The first is that, for many portfolio investors around the world, most developing countries do not even appear on the map of investment prospects. This is changing, and stock markets in some of the faster growing developing countries are booming. Nevertheless, this has been the dominant situation in the past.

The second problem associated with this reticence on the part of investors is the impact of a high interest policy on inflation; economic growth; and correspondingly, changes in the currency. Many investors view the exchange risk associated with developing-country securities to be unacceptably high. Financial theory might suggest that they ascribe to high interest rates such high levels of anticipated inflation and currency depreciation that virtually no interest rates will generate an investment response.

The risk that investors impute to the securities of many developing countries is illustrated not only by the fact that government securities do not attract an overseas market, except a secondary market at very significant discounts, but also by the reticence of the country's residents to invest, even in hard currency investment options. In recent years, for example, some developing countries such as Jamaica and Trinidad and Tobago moved to liberalize their foreign exchange systems, eliminate exchange controls, and allow residents to open foreign currency accounts. Even here and given the attraction of interest rates on U.S. dollar accounts that exceeded similar accounts in the United States, residents of these countries have been slow to transfer their U.S. dollar deposits from U.S. banks and offshore financial centers to banks in Jamaica and in Trinidad and Tobago.

One concern of residents with larger deposits has been the issue of confidentiality and concern about investigation into the source of the funds and the tax implications. For many others, however, the concern has been that, at some point in time, access to their own foreign currency accounts will be restricted because of national circumstances. In an environment where perceptions of risk run as high as they do, even real interest rate differentials play a relatively muted role in exchange rate determination.

The situation in Jamaica in 1994 illustrated this situation. The interest rate differential between risk-free securities in Jamaica and the United States for much of the year was in the order of 44 percentage points, with Jamaican Government Treasury Bills offered at rates of 50 percent, compared with rates of 4 percent in the United States. The gap was sufficiently wide that interest arbitrage activities did occur, leading to an increase in foreign exchange inflows into Jamaica. While these inflows helped to stabilize the value of the Jamaican dollar relative to the U.S. dollar, these flows did not lead to an appreciation of the Jamaican dollar relative to the U.S. dollar.

EXCHANGE RATE DETERMINATION
IN DEVELOPING COUNTRIES

Rather than interest rate differentials, three sets of variables have a critical impact on movements in exchange rates for developing countries. Fundamental to such movement, or its counterpoint of stability, is the ability of the country to generate foreign exchange relative to its demand for foreign exchange. The depreciation in the currencies of many developing countries has followed declining foreign exchange earnings as traditional exports have floundered on international markets. The fundamental earning capability of a country, however, does not explain the movement of the Ghanian cedi from 3.5 cedis to the U.S. dollar in 1982 to 350 cedis to the U.S. dollar by 1989. Ghana's earning capability did not decline by a factor of 100.

In recent years, many developing countries have moved away from fixed exchange rate systems to floating rate systems determined by market forces. The fixed exchange rates tended to be highly overvalued; that is, despite changing economic circumstances that would have dictated a downward movement in the exchange rate, governments kept exchange rates fixed, primarily by stifling demand for foreign exchange and utilizing foreign currency reserves to support the fixed exchange rate. In these circumstances, parallel markets that operated outside of the official system and in which foreign currencies were bought and sold at rates considerably in excess of those rates that prevailed in the official banking system tended to emerge. As governments moved to market-determined exchange rates, the rates depreciated considerably relative to the existing official rate but not as significantly relative to the parallel market rate that prevailed prior to the movement to a market-determined exchange rate.

As countries moved to floating exchange rates, they have also had to focus on the problem of speculation. Individuals speculated against currencies in some countries. Speculating against a currency can quite easily become a self-fulfilling prophesy. It is rare that a government has the resources to avoid speculative activity, as the United Kingdom discovered to its chagrin as it tried to bolster the pound when it came under speculative attack within the EU's ERM in 1992. The efforts of the U.K. government were not successful, and sterling was required to drop out of the ERM, a mechanism that it had joined only one year earlier.

The other important factor that has contributed to depreciating exchange rates has been the high inflation levels in many developing countries, as indicated in Table 6.3. This has been particularly true in Latin America where the significant depreciation in exchange rates can be largely placed at the door of Latin America's extremely high inflation rates, along the lines of the purchasing power parity theory discussed earlier.

EXCHANGE RATE POLICIES IN DEVELOPING COUNTRIES

Issues associated with exchange rates are quite emotive in developing countries. In many quarters, they are viewed as indicative of a country's national competitiveness. While this is not true, there is good reason for concern about exchange rates and exchange rate policy. During the 1970s and the early 1980s, the multilateral institutions pushed developing countries to devalue their exchange rates to reflect market realities. The argument that prevailed was that the exchange rate was the most important price in the economy. If that price was distorted, all other prices would be distorted and economic activity would suffer because of confused price signals. This decline in economic activity—so the argument went—would be particularly severe in the area of export activity, since exporters would be at a disadvantage relative to their competitors from countries with realistic exchange rates, which were thus able to offer to world markets lower-priced goods and services. Developing countries, influenced by IMF and WB conditionalities and by what the WB describes as the emergence of a market-friendly consensus toward development, have followed this advice. This has created the widespread movement toward liberalization of exchange rate regimes.

With this liberalization, though, all is not suddenly well on the exchange rate policy front in many developing countries. This is because as several developing countries have moved to more liberal exchange rate regimes, they have experienced a rapidly depreciating exchange rate. Such an exchange rate can create a vicious circle of unproductive economic activity. This is especially true of developing countries in which trade comprises a significant proportion of economic activity. In such countries, as exchange rates depreciate, the country experiences inflation as citizens try to maintain their living standards and prices of goods and services are raised even higher than real movements in cost would dictate. These high levels of inflation, created also by loose monetary policy and profligate government spending, in turn, create additional depreciation of the currency along purchasing power parity lines— and so the circle continues.

Inflation has two fundamental consequences. It tends to skew the distribution of income toward the existing affluent. Pensioners, civil servants, and the unemployed tend to lose while capital-rich citizens who can hedge against inflation through real estate, foreign currency, and stock market activities tend to gain during an inflationary spiral. For developing countries that began their inflationary spirals with income distributions that are already skewed as pointed out in Chapter 1, further inequality is likely to lead to social unrest. The other consequence of high inflation levels is that the signals that high inflation generate skew economic activity away from productive activity and toward distribution and financial manipulation of existing assets.

The challenge for developing countries in these circumstances is how to break the vicious cycle and create, instead, a virtuous cycle of low inflation, a stable exchange rate, and an environment in which productive economic activity can be spawned. The answer is probably not to be found in the past. In prior years, developing countries instituted exchange controls, set fixed exchange rates, and stringently conserved foreign exchange in an effort to husband exchange reserves and stabilize exchange rates. As noted, the principal outcome of such a strategy was a vibrant unofficial market for foreign exchange coupled with extremely high levels of capital flight.

A favored response in developing countries today is that exchange rate stabilization must come from an increase in the supply of foreign exchange. This is the environment in which export-oriented productive activity is held up as the solution to the exchange rate stabilization policy. The argument offered is that inflows of foreign exchange associated with this new national strategy will ensure that sufficient supplies exist to maintain a stable exchange rate. This response, however, simply begs the question of how this export drive is to succeed in economies that have an inflationary environment that is not conducive to productive activity. Other responses attack the demand side of the foreign exchange equation. They focus on a policy of high interest rates to "mop up liquidity" so that residents will be unable to use their excess liquidity to chase foreign currencies. These same high interest rates, however, do not provide the environment for productive activity that is the ultimate goal of the liquidity mopping-up exercise.

For most countries, breaking the cycle will involve tackling domestic inflation in a coordinated way. Some countries, for example, tighten monetary policy without ensuring fiscal responsibility on the part of the government, which in most developing countries is responsible for some one-third of the country's spending. A successful fight against inflation involves policy success in the monetary and fiscal areas. Some argue for an independent central bank along the lines of the German Bundesbank to ensure that the principal focus of monetary policy is price stability. It is noteworthy that the developing countries with the lowest inflation and the greatest exchange rate stability have been those with independent central banks, such as the countries of the West African Monetary Union with its Central Bank of West African States, or the countries of the Eastern Caribbean with their Eastern Caribbean Central Bank.

Other suggestions involve developing countries returning to domestic money supplies that are fully backed by foreign exchange reserves to ensure that governments have no ability to expand domestic money supply—particularly around election times—without regard for the effect of such expansion on inflation, exchange rate depreciation, and more inflation.

Regardless of the particular set of solutions pursued, two issues should be clear. The first is that the problem of foreign exchange policy in developing countries is not simple, nor are the solutions straightforward. Indeed, the problem has become as much political as it is economic. The increased fiscal responsibility of governments, which is one of the preconditions of price and exchange stability, also must be accomplished without taking away the safety net provided to the most vulnerable in the society if price and exchange stability are not to be achieved at the expense of social instability. This leads to the second issue, which is that price and exchange rate stability are not ends in themselves. Rather, they are simply a means to the end of developing competitive industries in a country.

FURTHER READING

Lessard, Donald R. *International Financial Management: Theory and Application.*
    New York: John Wiley & Sons, 1985.
Stonehill, Arthur I., and David K. Eiteman. *Multinational Business Finance.* 6th ed.
    Reading, Mass.: Addison-Wesley, 1993.

Chapter 7

Balance of Payments and National Financial Management

As countries seek to improve their competitiveness, there are two critical levels at which competent managerial performance is needed: the national level and the firm level. Managers at both levels need to understand the current financial position of the country and its recent financial performance. In these efforts, both sets of managers do what they would do were they seeking to ascertain the competitive situation of a company: They turn to the financial statements.

In the context of a nation, one particular financial statement occupies a position of prominence. It is termed the *balance of payments.* In a manner analogous to a statement of changes in financial position on a cash basis (sources and uses of funds), a nation's balance of payments records changes in the financial position of the country from one period to another. It does so by summarizing the results of all financial transactions between residents of a country and residents of the rest of the world over a particular period. In essence, a country's balance of payments records all forms of international business activity. It is in that respect that this national financial statement is of critical importance to international business practitioners.

Financial transactions are recorded in the balance of payments through the use of a debit and credit accounting system that, in some ways, is analogous to the system used to record corporate financial transactions. International business transactions that lead to the payment by residents of the country to residents of foreign countries are represented as debit entries and carry negative signs. Conversely, international business transactions that result in payments by residents of other countries to residents of the country for which the statement is generated are represented as credit entries and carry positive signs. As in the system of double-entry bookkeeping employed by a business firm, each transaction (in theory) in the balance of payments is recorded as a debit and a credit. Debits involve imports of goods and services, increases in foreign assets, or reductions in foreign liabilities. Credits are exports of goods and services, increases in foreign liabilities, or reductions in foreign assets. Thus, for example, the import of a good is recorded as a debit (imports of goods and services) and the payment for these goods as a credit (decrease in gold, foreign exchange). Table 7.1 indicates more fully the types of credit and debit transactions.

DIVISIONS IN THE BALANCE OF PAYMENTS

A balance-of-payments statement is divided into several divisions. The current account, the capital account, and the reserve account are the three broadest divisions in the balance of payments. The current account comprises all international business transactions that involve no future obligation or opportunity for either of the transacting parties. The capital account, on the other hand, consists of international business transactions that do carry with them a future obligation to make payments to foreigners or a future opportunity to receive payments from foreigners. Thus, the export of a good or a service is a current account transaction. Once the exchange of the good or service is consummated, neither transacting party has any future obligation or opportunity associated with that transaction. Contrast this with a capital account transaction such as investment by a foreign company or the issuing of a loan by a foreign bank. In both situations, the initial transaction creates an obligation on the part of entities within the country—and thus, by extension, the

Table 7.1
Balance-of-Payments Transactions

Debits	Credits
Imports of goods and services	Exports of goods and services
Interest payments to foreign firms	Interest receipts from foreign firms
Gifts to foreign entities	Gifts received from foreign entities
Increases in claims on foreign entities	Decreases in claims on foreign entities
Decreases in foreign claims on local entities	Increases in foreign claims on local entities
Increases in gold, foreign exchange	Decreases in gold, foreign exchange

country—to repay the loan in the future and pay interest until the loan is re-paid or to repatriate the capital invested in the future and remit dividends until the capital is repatriated. Similarly, these initial actions create opportunities on the part of the capital suppliers to receive income and an eventual return of the capital flows.

Beyond a division into current and capital accounts, the balance of payments separates these two accounts into smaller subdivisions. A comprehensive analysis of the various components of the balance of payments is best conducted within the framework of an actual set of accounts. To this end, Table 7.2 presents the balance-of-payments statistics for Jamaica between 1986 and 1992.

The Jamaican statistics indicate that the current account of the balance of payments includes merchandise exports and imports. These are typically set off against each other to provide a balance on merchandise trade. Export balances are usually recorded free on board (fob); that is, net of freight and insurance charges. Import balances are usually recorded to include cost, insurance, and freight (c.i.f.). The current account section of the balance of payments also includes receipts and expenses associated with services such as tourism, information, or any other form of tradeable service.

Also included in the current account is a section on income. This section accounts for transactions involving the payment of income on assets to foreign residents or the receipt of income on assets from such residents. This is the section that would, for example, record interest payments on debt owed to foreigners and dividends remitted to foreign entities that have engaged in capital investments in the country. The final section of the current account deals with unrequited transfers (i.e., transfers that are not reciprocated by the recipient). These transfers can be private or official. Private unrequited transfers involve primarily remittances from or to residents of other countries. Official unrequited transfers involve grants to or from foreign governments.

Public- and private-sector managers, particularly in developing countries, tend to focus on two balances in the current account section of the balance sheet: the merchandise trade balance and the overall current account balance. The merchandise trade balance compares the import of goods with the export of goods. The balance on goods and services compares exports of goods and services with imports of goods and services. The other measure is the overall current account on the balance of payments. For many developing countries, a significant component of economic activity is in the form of services, such as tourism, for example. For these countries, the balance of trade in goods and services and the overall current account balance may occupy more attention than the balance on merchandise trade.

The capital account of the balance of payments consists of direct foreign investment, portfolio investment, and other forms of capital. These other forms of capital include government-to-government loans, loans from multilateral institutions to governments, and loans from private banks. The category

Table 7.2
Jamaican Balance-of-Payments Statistics (US$ Millions)

	1986	1987	1988	1989	1990	1991	1992
Current Account							
Merchandise Exports (fob)	589	709	883	1,000	1,158	1,145	1,053
Merchandise Imports (fob)	-837	-1,061	-1,240	-1,606	-1,680	-1,551	-1,457
Merchandise Trade Balance	-248	-352	-357	-606	-522	-406	-404
Services: Credit	735	841	766	891	1,045	1,043	1,182
Services: Debit	-366	-420	-519	-662	-643	-637	-693
Income: Credit	87	84	122	118	122	74	84
Income: Debit	-394	-466	-487	-525	-605	-537	-392
Private Unrequited Transfers	112	117	436	299	159	161	248
Official Unrequited Transfers	35	59	92	194	123	113	92
Balance on Current Account	-40	-137	54	-291	-321	-191	117
Capital Account							
Direct Investment	-5	53	-12	57	138	127	87
Portfolio Investment	-	-	-	-	-	-	-
Other Capital							
Resident Official Sector	-156	211	35	192	64	11	-66
Deposit Money Banks	8	4	-5	-2	-17	-38	-35
Other Sectors	47	92	69	-149	219	128	204
Balance on Capital Account	-106	360	87	98	404	228	190
Net Errors and Omissions	80	79	-69	4	22	14	-2
Overall Balance	-66	302	72	-189	105	51	305
Reserve Account							
Reserves and Related Items	66	-302	-72	189	-105	-51	-305

Source: International Monetary Fund, *International Financial Statistics,* various issues.

of net errors and omissions represents a balancing item. It is the amount necessary to reconcile the credits and debits within the balance of payments. It arises because balance-of-payments information is taken from different sources, such as returns from questionnaires and records from customs. Thus, although in theory the debits should equal the credits, they rarely do in practice. The net errors and omissions ensures that the credits and debits are equal.

One final balance that is quite important is the basic balance. It is a combination of the balance on current account and the balance on long-term capital. It is considered a useful measure of the real position of a country because it eliminates short-term capital flows. These short-term flows are possibly of a temporary nature and are not necessarily related to the fundamental economic position of the country.

The ultimate reconciliation of the balance of payments occurs through the reserve account. This account serves as an offset to the overall balance in the balance of payments. The net result of a country taking in more foreign exchange than it has sent out (through trade, transfers, and capital movements) must be offset by an increase in that country's reserves of foreign exchange. Similarly, the net effect of a country sending out more foreign exchange than it has taken in (again through trade, transfers, and capital movements) must also be offset by a decrease in that country's reserves of foreign exchange.

BALANCE-OF-PAYMENTS SURPLUSES AND DEFICITS

Despite the fact that a country's balance of payments, by definition, must balance, one often hears about countries facing surpluses or deficits on their balance of payments. Such statements often refer to an imbalance between a particular category within the balance of payments. Thus, countries facing an imbalance in merchandise trade would be regarded as having a surplus or deficit on merchandise trade. The same would be true of countries with imbalances in their current or capital accounts. Further, a country could have a surplus or deficit on its overall balance, even though this surplus or deficit would be offset by changes in the reserve account.

What are the implications of these surpluses and deficits? For developing countries, the typical situation in recent years has been that these countries face deficits on merchandise trade and on their current accounts. In the Jamaican example, the country has experienced a deficit on merchandise trade in every year between 1986 and 1992. This trade deficit has been coupled with a net surplus in the service account largely as a result of tourism receipts; a net debit in the income account primarily because of the cost of servicing debts incurred in earlier years; and net credits in both private and official unrequited transfers, reflecting remittances from Jamaicans living overseas and aid from foreign governments. The net result of all these transactions on the country's current account has been that deficits have still prevailed in most years. The deficit on merchandise trade and income accounts has not been adequately offset by surpluses in services and unrequited transfers.

Deficits on current accounts, which essentially suggest that a country is spending more than it is earning, can be financed in two ways. The first is by a surplus on capital accounts. Such a surplus could be generated through direct investments; portfolio investments; and loans from multilateral institutions, governments, and private banks. Referring again to the Jamaican case, the years 1987 to 1992 saw surpluses on capital accounts. These surpluses derived from a mix of direct investment and loans. The surplus on the capital account was sufficient to offset the deficit on the current account in most years so that the country achieved an overall surplus in its balance of payments in all years except 1986 and 1989.

If a country is not able to offset a deficit on its current account with a surplus on its capital account, then it is forced to offset its overall deficit by using its foreign exchange reserves. Neither strategy for offsetting a current account deficit is sustainable in the long run. The ability to generate a capital surplus, for example, requires that foreign investors be willing to invest in the country or that governments, banks, and multilateral institutions be willing to lend. Both transactions operate on the assumption that, in the future, the country will be able to generate enough foreign exchange out of its current economic activities (reflected in the current account) to pay the income on the capital invested and to support the repayment of this capital. The longer the period of deficit in the current account, the greater the repayment obligations. This will reduce confidence in the international investment and lending community and thus reduce the capital flows a country is likely to receive.

The use of foreign exchange reserves to offset a balance-of-payments deficit is an even less sustainable strategy. Under such circumstances, a country is likely to deplete its reserves of foreign exchange very quickly. This is especially true because nonoil developing countries tend to have low reserves of foreign exchange. Consequently, both current account and overall deficits on a country's balance of payments tend to lead to adjustments to deal with these deficits. Some component of these adjustments may occur automatically, especially in countries with market-driven exchange rates. In some cases, however, the adjustment process is managed by the government or dictated by multilateral institutions.

ADJUSTING TO BALANCE-OF-PAYMENTS DISEQUILIBRIA

For countries with floating, or market-determined, exchange rates, the adjustment process to a deficit in the current account section of the balance of payments or to an overall deficit on the balance of payments should occur relatively automatically. In the more extreme case of an overall deficit on the balance of payments, there must have been within that year some reduction in the country's reserves of foreign exchange. For most countries, that is, those that do not have very large exchange reserves, such a reduction will lead to an increase in the price of foreign exchange to reflect its relative scarcity. An increase in the price of foreign exchange is equivalent to a depreciation in the country's exchange rate relative to its trading partners. This depreciation should lead to some reduction in the volume of imports of goods and services because of their higher price, and some increase in the volume of goods and services because of their lower relative price on world markets. This should reduce the merchandise deficit and thereby reduce the current account deficit and move the overall balance of payments closer to a situation in which the deficit is reduced or a surplus is created.

Adjustments to surpluses in a country's balance of payments should operate in the opposite direction. Increases in supplies of foreign exchange to which a country gains access if it has an overall surplus on its balance of payments should lead to an appreciation of the exchange rate. This appreciation should, in turn, increase imports as their local price falls with the appreciation of the local currency and decrease exports as their international price rises with this appreciation. These trends should couple to reduce or eliminate the trade surplus, which would then, as a consequence, reduce the overall surplus in the balance of payments.

For countries with fixed exchange rates, the adjustment process becomes less automatic. In these circumstances, adjustment requires government intervention. In the case of a country with a chronic balance-of-payments deficit, one form of intervention might be to devalue the currency. Indeed, recall that in the pre-1973 international monetary system, the role of the IMF was to evaluate a country's economic circumstances to see if a change in the parity rate of its currency was warranted, given those circumstances. The objective of the devaluation would be to accomplish the same purposes as the depreciation in the currency described earlier. Another form of government intervention might be to control the supply of foreign exchange by restricting access to the foreign exchange controlled by the government. Another would be to restrict artificially the demand for foreign goods by imposing import controls, whether in the form of requiring that importers obtain licenses or by placing price or quantitative restrictions on imported goods. Last, in this regard, governments might intervene by seeking to expand the supply of exported goods through a variety of export expansion and promotion programs.

In practice, the balance-of-payments disequilibria that developing countries have experienced have resulted in countries resorting to the use of most of the aforementioned techniques in an effort to restore equilibrium, with varying degrees of success. In general, even for the countries with market-determined exchange rates, the automatic adjustment process has not worked as smoothly as theory would predict. The developing countries of the Caribbean provide an illustration of the reasons that practice diverges from theory. The assumption is that changes in the country's exchange rate will lead to a proportional response in trade volumes. In particular, for developing countries, that depreciation of the currency will lead to increased exports and reduced imports. In these particular countries, however, the demand for imported goods tends to be relatively inelastic. These goods consist of staple food products, automobiles, and machinery and raw materials for virtually all productive establishments in the economy. As the prices of these imported goods increase with a depreciation of the currency, demand does not decrease proportionally to the increases in price.

In the other direction, as the currency depreciates, there is not a commensurate increase in the quantity of goods exported. An examination of the productive structure in these countries and many other developing countries illustrates why supply increases are so slow to respond to price increases. In some cases, these countries are producing under quotas that are not being filled prior to the depreciation of the currency because of supply problems. This was true of Jamaica in the early 1990s in the areas of textile and bananas, for example. In some of these cases (e.g., bananas), developing countries throughout the Caribbean had a preferential trade system in which they were not competing on a price basis. In Jamaica's case, for example, in 1993 that country had a quota of 105,000 tons of bananas that it could export to the EU without paying duties; yet Jamaica exported between 70,000 and 80,000 tons of bananas. Depreciation of the currency under those circumstances was likely to have no effect on supply.

For the adjustment responses of countries that experience sustained balance-of-payments surpluses, the classic example comes from Japan. In this country, theoretically, the significant and sustained surpluses should have led to an appreciation of the yen that would automatically reduce these surpluses. This automatic process has not worked, however, as Japanese producers have sacrificed profits and increased efficiency in order to maintain their global market share. Similarly, Japanese consumers have resisted purchasing foreign goods, even with reductions in the price of these goods. Also, the Japanese government has continued to protect local firms in industries in which, absent the protection, there might have been significant imports in response to the more competitive prices of imported goods.

Adjustments that the governments have attempted have also not been successful in many instances. In some cases, the same reasons that applied in the context of the automatic adjustment process prevailed. Thus, for example, currency devaluations have met with only limited success in eliminating balance-of-payments problems for the reasons discussed previously. Efforts to restrict access to foreign exchange have generated vibrant underground foreign exchange markets. Attempts to restrict imports have led to illicit smuggling of goods and to an inability to generate goods for export because of the pernicious effect of import-licensing systems and high protection on the competitiveness of local firms. Export-expansion programs suffer from inadequate funding and a limited capability to deal with the critical export expansion problems of significantly enhancing supply capability and gaining access to critical markets.

What is clear among developing countries today, however, is that the adjustment attempts focus principally on how to deal with the long-run indicators of reduced competitiveness that a deficit on the current account section of the balance of payments suggests. This response is in contrast to that of yesteryear, when developing countries tried to circumvent the issues of fundamentally improving long-term competitiveness and focused instead on gaining capital account surpluses to finance the problems of competitiveness. Today's response is strongly linked to the debt-crisis problems that were created by the stopgap strategy of balancing a current account deficit with a capital account surplus.

THE DEVELOPING COUNTRY DEBT CRISIS AND BEYOND

The debt crisis that developing countries experienced can be traced to a number of elements. The financial condition of most developing countries deteriorated during the 1970s. The debt crises of 1973 and 1979 put a tremendous financial strain on many developing countries. Few countries were able to pay for their increased imports of goods and services out of their exports. Indeed, in some cases, countries were experiencing stagnating markets for their exports at the same time they suffered from the rise in oil prices.

Most developing countries, at the time, operated under fixed rather than market-determined exchange rates so that much of the adjustment process lay in the hands of governments. These governments were reluctant to force a reduction in consumption to meet the changing situation in the world because of the already low levels of consumption that prevailed in many developing countries. Further, the 1970s, in particular, marked a period in which many developing countries were concerned about the impact of foreign investment on their local economies. They did not, therefore, want to generate capital in the form of foreign direct investment. Consequently, the preferred strategy of many countries, particularly in Latin America, was to turn to commercial bank financing for the capital they needed to offset these current account deficits. In Africa and the Caribbean, a greater portion of the lending during this period came from governments rather than from private banks.

On the supply side, many of these private banks were very eager to lend to developing countries. These banks were flush with petrodollars garnered from OPEC countries in the aftermath of the rapid oil increases. Loan markets in the developed world were stagnating. Bank officials had little experience in lending significant sums to developing countries, but the general feeling was that the loans were risk-free because they were guaranteed by governments and governments could not go bankrupt. These governments, so the argument went, would always be in a position to pay their obligations. As a consequence of this spate of lending, the external debts of developing countries increased from less than $100 billion in 1972 to more than $600 billion by 1981.

The entire situation was exacerbated, beginning in the late 1970s, when an inflation-fighting Federal Reserve began the process of reducing U.S. inflation that had reached unprecedented heights during that period. The principal mechanism put in place to accomplish this task was a high-interest-rate regime. These high interest rates, of course, affected most indebted countries because a significant component of world debt and virtually all of Latin American foreign debt was dollar denominated. This confluence of factors led to a rapid rise in loans to developing countries during the late 1970s and early 1980s. This increase came to a halt only on August 12, 1982, when—faced with loan repayments that would completely debilitate its economy—one of the largest borrowers, Mexico, threatened to default on its debts.

The threat of Mexico, followed by other large Latin American countries such as Brazil and Argentina, defaulting on their debts to money center banks in the United States concentrated the minds of the international banking community. Under the auspices of the IMF, the commercial banks were encouraged to continue lending to developing countries to allow them some breathing room in which to adjust their economies. The IMF estimated how much the countries could repay, given their export conditions. The remaining shortfall was to be financed through new loans. This approach, essentially of loan rescheduling, continued through the mid-1980s under an approach sponsored by the U.S. Secretary of the Treasury—the Baker Plan. In general, the rescheduling approach did not work. The weight of loan repayments was much too high. The adjustment process focused on reducing imports; but this reduction crippled domestic industry in these countries, which reduced the country's ability to export to earn foreign exchange. In 1989, the new U.S. Secretary of the Treasury, Nicholas Brady, announced a plan that became known as the Brady Plan, which included debt reduction instead of simply debt rescheduling to deal with the debt crisis.

The model of this program was the 1989 Mexican debt reduction that reduced Mexico's outstanding debt from $107 billion to $92 billion. Support for this debt reduction came from the IMF, the WB, and the Export–Import Bank of Japan. The commercial banks to whom the funds were owed also took a writedown of the outstanding debt. In many respects, the concerted attempts by the international community to respond to the debt crisis have worked. Latin America, in particular, is now growing once again after what is described as the lost decade of the 1980s when debt levels, recession, and inflation levels as high as 2,750 percent in Brazil, 3,080 percent in Argentina, 7,500 percent in Peru, 11,800 percent in Bolivia, and 14,300 percent in Nicaragua created economic malaise throughout the region.

Foreign capital has returned to the region, primarily in the form of direct investment, associated with privatization programs, and portfolio investment; but the larger Latin American countries have also put in place a spate of reforms that have created an environment for growth. These have included many of the traditional neoclassical, monetarist prescriptions for reform: privatization, liberalization of trade and investment, and fiscal reform and conservatism.

The debt crisis is not yet over for countries outside of large Latin American economies that received far less publicity during the 1980s. An examination of countries' debt as a percentage of their exports indicates that many countries continue to face a debt crisis, particularly low-income developing countries in Africa (see Table 7.3). Further, the debt of these countries, and of the island countries of the Caribbean, has primarily been debt owed to governments of industrialized countries and multilateral institutions rather than private banks. As a consequence, many of these countries did not share in the debt reduction programs that helped to reduce the debt of the larger Latin American countries during the 1980s. Many of these countries still face fundamental balance-of-payments disequilibria that must be addressed if economic growth is to take place.

IMPLICATIONS OF BALANCE-OF-PAYMENTS INFORMATION FOR MANAGERS IN DEVELOPING COUNTRIES

The starting point for this discussion of the balance of payments is the important information it provides to managers within the public and private sectors of developing countries. An analysis of a country's balance of payments allows managers to identify the sources of funds to an economy and the areas in which those funds are being used. Conducting such an analysis requires that managers disaggregate the various balance-of-payments categories. This is the only way to understand the true financial situation of a country. Leading up to the debt crisis in the developing countries, much of the funds borrowed were used for maintaining levels of consumption rather than increasing the productive assets of the economy. A close examination of balance-of-payments indices, in collaboration with an examination of the government's fiscal budget, would have provided that information.

The balance-of-payments account also provides information from which managers can forecast future economic events. For example, even though there are lags in the process, deficits are likely to lead to exchange rate depreciation. Managers in both the public and private sectors need to be aware of such relationships.

The fundamental lesson to be learned from the balance-of-payments process and the associated adjustment mechanism, however, is that the interna-

Table 7.3
Debt as a Percentage of Exports

Country	1980	Peak Year	1991
Low-Income Countries			
Burundi	180.1	925.7 (1990)	758.9
Egypt	214.9	547.3 (1987)	280.0
Equatorial Guinea	511.5	618.6 (1991)	618.6
Ethiopia	136.2	635.2 (1991)	635.2
Ghana	108.3	384.5 (1991)	384.5
Guinea-Bissau	927.9	3,463.0 (1986)	3,087.0
Guyana	187.0	831.3 (1990)	831.3
Honduras	152.5	335.9 (1987)	303.6
Kenya	170.4	329.6 (1987)	313.7
Laos	638.6	1,124.0 (1990)	1,124.0
Liberia	111.8	389.4 (1987)	389.4
Madagascar	242.4	853.4 (1988)	795.9
Mali	227.5	508.6 (1986)	473.4
Mauritania	306.7	458.2 (1991)	458.2
Mozambique	1,209.0	1,731.0 (1987)	1,287.0
Myanmar	227.5	1,420.0 (1987)	643.8
Nicaragua	422.3	3,001.0 (1991)	3,001.0
Nigeria	31.9	427.8 (1988)	257.1
Sao Tome	100.7	1,780.0 (1990)	1,780.0
Sierra Leone	153.5	765.7 (1990)	765.7
Somalia	253.5	3,572.0 (1988)	2,595.0
Sudan	504.7	2,743.0 (1991)	2,743.0
Tanzania	370.3	1,119.0 (1990)	1,119.0
Uganda	221.6	1,298.0 (1991)	1,298.0
Zaire	201.0	438.9 (1987)	442.4
Zambia	201.0	773.8 (1986)	503.4
Average	*121.1*	*549.6 (1987)*	*419.1*

tional competitiveness of a country is ultimately accounted for by the international business transactions in which it engages that allow it to earn foreign exchange over a sustained period of time, most notable, export and investment activities. For developing countries, a neomercantilist position that views other forms of activity as a means to the end of enhancing export prospects is probably an appropriate position. This is not to suggest that governments should not seek to attract capital flows, whether via debt or equity, that can assist in achieving enhanced exports. These capital flows must be seen

Table 7.3 *(continued)*

Country	1980	Peak Year	1991
Middle-Income Countries			
Algeria	128.6	313.2 (1987)	199.3
Angola	102.4	242.9 (1991)	242.9
Argentina	242.4	695.5 (1987)	430.0
Bolivia	258.2	875.0 (1987)	432.4
Brazil	304.3	452.6 (1986)	333.7
Bulgaria	34.8	234.8 (1991)	234.8
Congo	163.7	444.5 (1986)	424.4
Cote d'Ivoire	159.4	509.6 (1991)	509.6
Ecuador	203.1	424.0 (1987)	362.7
Jamaica	129.3	299.5 (1985)	188.8
Jordan	79.3	283.4 (1991)	283.4
Mexico	259.2	422.7 (1986)	224.1
Morocco	223.8	400.5 (1985)	255.5
Panama	38.4	137.7 (1988)	108.3
Peru	207.7	481.9 (1988)	479.0
Poland	252.1	294.8 (1987)	281.4
Syria	82.3	690.8 (1987)	301.2
Average	*176.6*	*350.3 (1987)*	*286.7*

Source: World Bank data reported by *The Economist* in "A Survey of Third World Finance,"
  © *The Economist*, London, 25 September 1993, p. 14.

as supportive of the effort to enhance the country's fundamental competitiveness and not as an end in themselves. Foreign direct investment represents a particularly interesting form of capital inflow.

FURTHER READING

Sachs, Jeffrey D., ed. *Developing Country Debt and the World Economy.* Chicago: University of Chicago Press, 1989.
"A Survey of Third World Finance." *The Economist* (25 September 1993): 1–40.
Vernon, Raymond, and Louis T. Wells. *The Manager in the International Economy.* 6th ed. Englewood Cliffs, N.J.: Prentice-Hall, 1991.

Chapter 8

Foreign Direct Investment

Foreign direct investment has figured prominently in the recent economic history of most developing countries. Until the early twentieth century, this investment principally took the form of investment in the extractive, mining, and agricultural industries in these countries. Extractive investment tended to be coupled thereafter with investment in industries in these countries designed to satisfy local demand for particular goods and services, including infrastructure such as electricity and telephone systems. Since the 1980s, foreign investment in developing countries has been directed increasingly at export-oriented projects. While there is a substantial amount of literature on foreign direct investment, there is much less information on the factors that explain the flow of foreign direct investment to developing countries.

Most theories of foreign investment do not address the issue of the direction of foreign direct investment flows. They seek to explain why foreign direct investment takes place rather than why it flows to a particular group of countries. Even those theories that focus only on why foreign direct investment takes place are an important starting point for those seeking to understand why it does or does not flow to developing countries. An important theory of foreign direct investment, in this regard, is the theory of internalization described in the following section.

THEORY OF INTERNALIZATION

Many would argue that foreign direct investment takes place because foreign firms seek access to markets in foreign countries; because they seek access to raw materials or cheap labor; because they are desirous of diversifying the risks associated with operating in a single economy; or, more generally, because they are eager to extend the competitive advantages they have developed at home into foreign markets. These reasons for foreign direct investment, however, do not explain why foreign firms opt for direct investment versus other approaches through which they would be able to accomplish the same objective. These reasons proffered in explanation of foreign direct investment, in fact, are better viewed as reasons that explain why firms engage in international business.

The theory of internalization seeks to extend the reasons firms engage in international business to why they use foreign direct investment as their preferred medium. This theory draws heavily on the more general work of Williamson that explores the conditions under which firms choose a hierarchical approach to engaging in business activities rather than a market-based approach. Williamson argues that where two sets of conditions exist, firms will tend to prefer internal or hierarchical approaches. These conditions include oligopolistic (few sellers) or oligopsonistic (few buyers) market settings and situations of great uncertainty. Oligopolistic or oligopsonistic situations lead to the choice of a hierarchical approach because, in these situations, opportunistic economic agents will make it very difficult for a firm to negotiate an equitable transaction. In situations of uncertainty, the fact that individuals and organizations are limited in their analytical capacity will lead to internal organization because of the difficulty of writing and enforcing long-term contracts that incorporate all the necessary contingencies that arise as a result of an uncertain environment.

Building upon this work, international business theorists suggest that firms that venture overseas either have a particular competitive advantage or seek a competitive advantage. A firm's existing competitive advantage might be its superior technology, its unparalleled management expertise, or its unique brand name. Indeed, these competitive advantages are often intangible assets. Though critical to the firm, they are not identified as fixed assets in the firm's balance sheet.

As pointed out in Table 8.1, the firm has various options it could use to benefit from these competitive advantages. These options span the choice of a market or a hierarchical approach. In particular, the firm could sell or rent these advantages on the international market; that is, a firm could license its superior technology, enter into management contracts in which it rents its management expertise, or allow other firms to use its trademarks by licensing its brand name.

Similar possibilities exist for firms that enter overseas markets to acquire a competitive advantage by gaining access to lower-cost inputs. These inputs could be labor or raw materials. Gaining access to lower-cost inputs is an insufficient explanation for engaging in foreign direct investment because, as pointed out in Table 8.2, the firm also has a range of options with regard to how it might gain access to particular intermediate inputs. The firm could import the raw materials and could gain access to lower-cost labor by importing the good manufactured with this labor, or it could subcontract with a for-

Table 8.1
Options for Exploiting Competitive Advantages (Intangible Assets)

Nature of Competitive Advantage	Market-Based Approach	Hierarchical Approach
Superior technology	Exporting, licensing	Foreign direct investment
Superior marketing skills (brand name)	Exporting, licensing, franchising	Foreign direct investment
Superior construction skills	Build-operate-transfer contracts	Foreign direct investment
Superior management skills	Export management contracts	Foreign direct investment

eign manufacturer to produce a partially finished good. Subcontracting relations could be and are created that leave the foreign subcontractor the task of only packaging the product.

Although firms could use market approaches in their efforts to benefit from their competitive advantages, in many cases they do not. Typically, they do not in circumstances where there are very few players involved in the market. Consider, for example, the firm that has a technology it would be willing to license. It must negotiate with a prospective licensee a fair rental for the technology. It may be difficult, however, to come to an agreement on a fair price without first providing so much information to the prospective licensee that the firm's competitive position is weakened if there is no eventual agreement on a license. This is particularly the case in situations where there are few prospective firms that are interested in licensing the technology. The pro-

Table 8.2
Options for Gaining Access to Inputs

Nature of Input Required	Market-Based Approach	Hierarchical Approach
Raw materials	Importing	Foreign direct investment
Low-cost labor	Importing, subcontracting	Foreign direct investment

spective licensee suffers from a similar problem, particularly when there are only a few prospective licensors.

Such a licensing arrangement, however, also suffers from the prospects of uncertainty. The prospective licensor might be concerned about the likelihood of the licensee becoming a competitor of the firm. It can seek to allay its concerns by writing a licensing contract that does not allow competition, but the threat of competition might be a long-term threat. The licensor might find it difficult to write a long-term contract that effectively deals with the threat of competition or all other possible contingencies that might lead to a weakening of its competitive position.

Similarly, consider the firm that seeks to gain critical raw material supplies from another country by entering into a subcontracting arrangement or by importing instead of by investing in a foreign subsidiary that would supply the necessary raw material to the parent company. Here again, a market with only a few players and problems of uncertainty reduces the extent to which firms opt for the market mechanism over the investment option. In an oligopolistic industry, no firm wants to be caught in a situation where its competitors have captive raw materials while it buys its raw materials on the spot market as needed. Because the market comprises only a few sellers, every time it seeks to buy, it must bargain with prospective sellers about the appropriate price. Indeed, it may find itself in the unpleasant position of bargaining for raw materials with its competitors.

While a spot market situation in which there are few buyers presents the problem of bargaining with opportunistic agents, a subcontracting situation presents the problem of being able to write a long-term supply contract with all the necessary contingencies for dealing with changes due to the uncertain nature of the future. These supplies are likely to be critical to the firm's operations. If these supplies are disrupted or if the variance in quality is wide, this is likely to lead to a significant loss of competitiveness for the firm. Consequently, according to the theory of internalization, firms often choose to engage in international business to provide for them a competitive advantage; but instead of doing so by relying on market mechanisms to exploit existing competitive assets or acquire new competitive advantages, they internalize the market for their intangible assets or their intermediate products.

Of course, firms may not have a full menu of options from which they can choose how best to exploit their competitive advantages. If governments establish trade restrictions, for example, this might lead to increased foreign direct investment because the firm that desires access to a particular market no longer has the option of gaining access to that market through trade. Similarly, restrictions on foreign direct investment may lead to an increase in licensing, since with the restrictions on foreign direct investment, the firm with superior technology that it seeks to profit from now has fewer options that it is able to exercise. However, the theory of internalization is most concerned about identifying the reasons for which foreign direct investment takes place when a firm has its full range of options for gaining a competitive advantage in foreign markets.

This approach to foreign direct investment theory has implications for the types of industries in which one might expect to find significant quantities of foreign direct investment. It would argue, for example, that foreign direct investment should be observed particularly in situations where markets are most uncertain and industry structures feature oligopoly and oligopsony. Two examples might be raw material industries and high technology industries. Many raw material industries are oligopolistic. These industries also tend to be vertically integrated across national boundaries. In seeking vertical integration, these industries move to wherever the necessary raw material supplies are found. In many cases, these supplies are located in developing countries. Thus, there have historically been significant flows of foreign direct investment to developing countries in the raw materials sector.

Another example that is proffered is that of high-technology industries. In these industries, there is significant uncertainty in technology and markets. It is particularly difficult to negotiate arm's-length transactions for licenses because of the rapidity of technological change. There are, indeed, significant flows of cross-border investment in these industries.

THE PRODUCT CYCLE OF TRADE AND INVESTMENT

The theory of internalization deals with the issue of foreign direct investment in developing countries, but only obliquely. Another theory, the product cycle theory, is more explicit about the circumstances under which foreign direct investment, particularly industrial investment, would flow to developing countries. This theory, developed in the work of Vernon and Wells, argued that there was an identifiable process associated with foreign direct investment.

The product cycle theory of trade and investment was driven, at least in part, by the inadequacy of existing trade theory in explaining modern patterns of trade. Recall, for example, that three important drawbacks of comparative advantage trade theory were its assumption that firms did not learn over time, that demand was homogenous across countries, and that firms operated according to constant returns to scale. A quick examination of the reality of business activities, however, suggests that these are particularly unrealistic assumptions. Firms clearly learn over time. The innovating firm has an advantage over its competitors, but these competitors are often able to catch up to the original innovating firm, especially if that firm does not continue to innovate in other areas. Similarly, unit costs of production in most industries decline as output expands, and the nature of demand for particular products clearly differs from country to country.

The product cycle theory contributed to this deficiency by placing its emphasis on the linkages between innovation, demand patterns, trade flows, and investment flows. It argues, first, that innovation takes place in countries with particular characteristics. In the earliest versions of this theory, most new products were being introduced in the United States; and so, as an empirically derived theory, the emphasis was placed on understanding the characteristics of the U.S. market that created the environment for such innovation. The conclusion was that the United States, particularly in the post–World War II period, was the world's largest and most affluent market. In addition, the United States faced high labor costs. This combination, the argument goes, led to the introduction of new products—particularly labor-saving products— in the United States. The large U.S. market reduced the risk of introducing new products. The affluence of U.S. consumers created a group of individuals that could afford to purchase new products, since these products are often priced expensively because production levels tend to be lower early in a product's life.

Since World War II, other industrialized countries have narrowed the income gap between their countries and the United States—in some cases, such as Japan, in dramatic fashion. With the increasing homogeneity of markets in North America, Europe, and Japan, it is not surprising that whereas innovations were, for a while, principally commercialized in the United States, they are now commercialized in any of these three affluent regions of the world. Further, with rising labor costs in all three regions, the principal factor determining the region in which an innovation is commercialized is the nature of the demand within that region. Thus, it is argued, innovations in the area of product miniaturization have been dominated by Japanese companies because of the scarcity of land in Japan which has led to homes far smaller in size than is the case in the United States. Similarly, innovations in energy-efficient equipment and energy-efficient automobiles occurred in Europe and Japan rather than the United States because of the premium placed on energy in the former two energy-poor regions. The product cycle allowed for predictions that went beyond the site of initial commercialization, as shown in Table 8.3.

The argument continued by suggesting that in the early stages of a product's life, production and markets would be concentrated in the innovating country. This is because producers wanted to stay close to their most sophisticated and demanding customers as they refined the product. Thereafter, the products would find markets in other countries at similar levels of development. These foreign markets would be initially served by exports from the producer in the innovating country.

At some point, these foreign markets become sufficiently large that they can support local facilities dedicated to serving them. The increase in size of these markets is also likely to be coupled with a shift toward price competition as the product becomes more standardized. This combination forces initial innovating firms to consider placing production facilities overseas to accommodate larger foreign markets and respond to the imperatives of price competition. These facilities are likely to be located initially in industrialized

Table 8.3
The Product Cycle Theory of Trade and Investment

Stage of Product	Location of Production	Location of Demand
New product	Production is located in innovating country.	Demand for product is in innovating country and other developed countries with niches in developing countries. Demand in markets outside of innovating country is satisfied through exports.
Maturing product	Production continues to be located in innovating country, but also in other developed countries.	Demand continues to grow in innovating country, other developed countries and developing countries. Demand in other developed countries is satisfied by production in these countries. Demand in developing countries continues to be satisfied through exports to these countries.
Standardized product	Production is located in developing countries to take advantage of lower cost production inputs.	Developed country markets are becoming niche markets. Developing country producer exports products back to original innovating country.

Source: Adapted from Raymond Vernon, "International Investment and International Trade in the Product Cycle," *Quarterly Journal of Economics* (May 1966): 190–207.

countries that have spawned the large markets. The role played by developing countries continues to be one of importing the product either from the initial innovating country or from plants in other industrialized countries. The plants in these other industrialized countries could be those of the initial innovating firm or of competitors from that firm's country or from other countries.

Eventually, with increasing standardization of the product, price becomes so important to the ability of a firm to compete for market share and the technology associated with the product becomes so well known that it ceases to provide a competitive advantage. Thus, production shifts to countries that can provide the lowest-cost inputs. For products that use significant quantities of unskilled labor, the most appropriate production location often becomes developing countries with large supplies of unskilled labor. In many instances, one observes a follow-the-leader mentality with this and other forms of foreign direct investment; that is, if one firm producing the particular product that has become standardized moves its production facilities to a developing country to take advantage of lower input costs, other firms from that country and operating within the same industry are likely to follow. These other firms are concerned that if they do not follow, their competitors are likely to gain a competitive advantage.

It is important to note, however, that firms from different countries but operating within the same industry might pursue very different strategies. Consider the example of television. The response of U.S. firms to declining competitiveness in the television industry was to move production to developing countries in which labor cost savings could be realized. Japanese firms, on the other hand, did in this industry what they have sought to do in many others. Instead of rushing to move production to lower-cost labor locations, they upgraded the product—moving early to solid state televisions—and sought to automate the production process. Last, the European television producers protected their producers as they became less competitive, and this protection allowed these producers to continue their operations in Europe.

Nevertheless, the product cycle theory explicitly identifies a role for developing countries with respect to foreign direct investment in industrial sectors that is primarily oriented to producing standardized products for the markets of these countries or for export to world markets. Although the theory has conformed mostly to the strategies of U.S. firms, Japanese firms also found that they were unable to keep particular types of production within Japan indefinitely. Much of the foreign direct investment within Southeast Asia in the late 1980s and early 1990s, for example, involved Japanese investment moving outside of Japan in search of lower-cost production locations.

FOREIGN DIRECT INVESTMENT AND DEVELOPMENT

The debate about the role of foreign direct investment in development has been a relatively intense one. Much has been discussed about the alleged costs and benefits of this investment.

Benefits of Foreign Direct Investment

Advocates of the critical role that foreign investment can play in development point to a series of benefits they suggest emanates from this investment. According to this view, foreign direct investment provides capital. Since many development theorists view a capital gap as an impediment to development—according to the Harrod–Domar model discussed in Chapter 1, for example—then business transactions that lead to capital flows to developing countries should be encouraged. Additionally, foreign direct investment provides technology that can also assist in the development process, access to overseas markets through the business connections of the investing firm, access to "state-of-the-art" management expertise, and employment opportunities for local workers. Further, with these advantages, foreign direct investment is able to assist a country with its export drive and thus enhance the country's balance-of-payments position. Eventually, foreign direct investment could, operating as a catalyst, be the engine of growth for an economy as the management practices, technology, and market connections are diffused from their starting point in particular foreign investments throughout the economy.

Costs of Foreign Direct Investment

This, others claim, is a picture that is not nearly as rosy in practice as it appears in theory. While acknowledging that foreign direct investment will provide capital inflows, they argue that the eventual outflows will exceed this inflow. Of course, such an argument could be made with respect to bank loans, and it would suggest that a rational individual would never take a bank loan. In fact, one must go beyond the outflows and inflows of capital and examine the use to which capital is put within an economy and the fact that a particular quantity of capital can differ in value to a country, depending upon the country's current economic position.

Another criticism relates to the use of the technology brought to the country by foreign investors. Some argue that this technology is rarely diffused to local entities and, in some cases, that it is inappropriate to the local environment in any case. In some instances, the inappropriateness of technology has resulted in the transfer of highly capital-intensive production processes to countries with significant supplies of unemployed labor. The inappropriateness of technology, in these instances, has also reduced considerably the employment benefits of foreign direct investment. Critics would also point to the fact that foreign investors tend to be particularly heavy users of imported inputs. Thus, they can prove to be a drain on a country's exchange reserves not only when they seek to remit profits but also in their ongoing commercial operations.

A more subtle criticism of foreign direct investment in developing countries is that, because of the potential disjuncture between the benefits and costs of a project to a private firm and the social costs and benefits of a project to the nation at large, many projects are initiated in developing countries that create profits for the firm while proving detrimental to the nation at large. This is possibly largely because of distortions in pricing systems so that prices do not accurately reflect the resources used up and because of costs or benefits that accrue to society because of an investment project but that are not captured in the firm's finances. These costs and benefits are described as externalities.

Evaluating Foreign Direct Investment

Since there is this disjuncture between private and social costs and benefits, some effort at reconciliation must be made if governments in developing countries are to have any sense of the impact of foreign investments on the nations they govern. In recent years, approaches have been developed for conducting such a reconciliation. These approaches, often described as social or economic cost–benefit analyses, are imperfect. They simply cannot capture all the nuances of cost and benefit, but they do seek to reconcile those glaring differences that can be quantified.

Conceptually, this process of reconciliation involves several steps that take as their starting point the financial information provided to a host government by a firm seeking to invest. The type of information that might be provided is indicated in Table 8.4. With this type of information in hand, government evaluators can begin to evaluate the benefits associated with such a project by making a series of adjustments to the data provided by the firm. The first necessary adjustment is with respect to the output of the project. In so doing, the analyst will seek to identify the benefits to a nation associated with the production of a particular firm. To this benefit one attaches a cost. The appropriate cost is an opportunity cost. Thus, the government seeks to understand what resources the country would have to give up in order to obtain the benefits to be created by a foreign firm if, instead of using that firm's production facilities, the country were to opt for an alternative. If a firm is producing goods and selling them at world market prices, then the opportunity cost of acquiring these goods elsewhere is likely to be equivalent to the price at which these goods will be sold on the local market.

Adjustments at this level are typically required, therefore, only when a firm is sheltered from international competition (through some form of trade restriction) and is thus able to sell products at higher costs than would prevail on world markets. Alternately, monopolists that do not face stringent regulatory systems might also be able to capture monopoly rents and diverge from world market prices.

The second step is to adjust the cost of the inputs to a project to ensure that these costs represent the value of these inputs to the society. If, for example, a government has chosen to subsidize the cost of energy within an economy, the firm that uses energy will gain the benefit of that subsidy. The energy cost to the nation, of course, has not changed. It is that national cost that should be charged to the project, not the cost that the investor actually pays.

If, on the other hand, a country has substantial levels of unemployment but a legally mandated minimum wage, the wage costs incurred by an investor might exceed the cost of labor to the economy. The cost of labor to an economy is an opportunity cost. It should represent the opportunities the economy loses because the laborer moves to this particular investment project. With large pools of unemployed labor, the economy might not be losing production. Thus, in its extreme version, the cost of labor to the country could actually be zero. From the perspective of evaluating the contribution of an investment project, it is this wage rate—described as the shadow wage rate—that should be used in the analysis. Another typical adjustment revolves around exchange rates. If a country operates an exchange rate, particularly a fixed exchange rate, whose value differs from the rate that represents the true cost of foreign exchange to the country, then adjustments should be made to reflect this true cost in the analysis of costs and benefits.

Table 8.4
Social Cost–Benefit Analysis

	Private Income Statement		Adjusted Social Income Statement
		Taka* (millions)	
Annual sales (200,000 units at 30,000 taka per unit)	6,000	(200,000 x US$400 x 50taka/US$)	4,000
Cost of goods sold			
Labor	(2,000)	(2,000 x 0.60)	(1,200)
Imported raw materials	(1,000)	(1,000 x 1.25)	(1,250)
Local raw materials	(1,500)		(1,500)
Gross profit	1,500		50
Administration and overhead (Including 100 million taka in interest remitted overseas)	(500)	(400 + [100 x 1.25])	(525)
Profits before taxes	1,000		(475)
Corporate taxes at 40%	400		-
Pollution costs	-		(25)
Net Private Profit/(Social Cost)	600		(500)

* Taka is the national currency of Bangladesh.

Note: Assume that this project involves the sale of refrigerators exclusively on the Bangladeshi local market. In addition to being provided with such a pro-forma income statement, government evaluators would be interested in obtaining other forms of information. Such information might include the c.i.f. value of imported refrigerators (assume US$400), the nominal import duties on imported refrigerators (assume 50 percent), the proportion of workers in this project that would be unemployed were the project to be rejected (assume 40 percent), the applicable rate of foreign exchange (assume that the official rate is 40 taka/US$ and the black market rate is 50 taka/US$), and the extent to which the project might contribute to unrecovered pollution costs (assume 25 million takas).

The final step in this analysis is to account for externalities, whether positive or negative. Recall that these are costs or benefits that an economy incurs but that do not accrue to the firm. A firm's production process might be thought to be increasing pollution levels. It may be difficult, however, to tie pollution to the operations of the particular firm and thus charge the firm for the costs of clearing the pollution. This does not alter the fact that, at some point in time, the nation will have to face the costs of such pollution. Alternately, an investment project might create substantial benefits in the area of training workers that migrate to other firms, taking with them particular technological skills. This diffusion of training and technology represents a benefit to the nation that is not captured in the accounts of the private firm. It is thus a positive externality.

Adjusting the information provided in Table 8.4 along the lines indicated would provide a "social profit" quite different from the "private profit." While the private profit associated with the project is estimated at 600 million takas, the social loss is estimated at 500 million takas.

The major disadvantage of this approach is that it is incapable of quantifying all the areas in which private and social costs and benefits diverge from each other. Nevertheless, it at least recognizes the distinction. In that respect, it represents an enlightened approach to evaluating the costs and benefits of foreign direct investment.

Indeed, adopting this approach has provided information on the types of foreign direct investments that typically assist in the development process in developing countries. Based on an analysis of one sample of projects, researchers (Wells and Incarnation) have indicated that foreign investments that take place behind the protection of high tariff walls in developing countries and are oriented toward the domestic markets of these countries are quite likely to be detrimental to the country. Investments oriented toward export markets, on the other hand, are likely to be of benefit to the country that hosts them.

Thus, to return to an assessment of the costs and benefits of foreign direct investment, it is clear that any such analysis should seek to disaggregate foreign direct investment into different forms of investment. Investment for domestic markets is likely to prove costly to the country's economy if tariff protection is high, unless that investment can generate highly positive externalities in the form of diffusion of technology that leads to the creation of other firms that are likely to become competitive on world markets. Investments oriented to export markets, on the other hand, are likely to create net benefits for an economy.

Trends in Foreign Direct Investment in Developing Countries

The conclusion about the differing cost/benefit ratios of various forms of foreign direct investment has not escaped the world's developing countries. It is possibly one of the reasons why there has been renewed interest on the part of developing countries in the investments of foreign firms. Developing countries around the world have been liberalizing their trade regimes and moving away from import-substitution investment regimes to export-promotion development policies. Simultaneously, many firms have been seeking to consolidate their production operations.

Many firms have been moving away from an investment strategy in which they replicated production facilities in each market, a strategy described by scholars as a multidomestic strategy. Instead, they have been placing production facilities in each region to cater to the regional market. Indeed, some firms have gone so far as to completely centralize operations for the firm's entire global market—a strategy described as a global strategy. In these global strategies, companies do not necessarily centralize all elements of their production in one location; rather, they centralize particular elements along the vertical chain of the company's operations in particular locations. Thus, production might be centralized in one location, design in another, research in another, and so forth.

Indeed, in this approach, a firm's operations can become highly specialized. Thus, for example, in the mid-1980s, Ford's European operations had developed a highly specialized strategy surrounding its production operations. Rather than build complete cars in several different markets oriented to those markets, Ford sought to produce a car with European-wide and global appeal and produce different components for that car in the most appropriate locations. Thus, glass and radios would be produced in Canada; valves, wheel nuts, and hydraulic tappets in the United States; tires, radiators, and heater hoses in Austria; fan belts in Denmark; exhaust flanges and tires in Norway; tires, tubes, seat pads, brakes, and trim in Belgium; tires, paints, and hardware in the Netherlands; cylinder heads and carburetors in Italy; and so forth.

In light of these trends in the area of trade liberalization and the associated changes in the investment strategies of firms, much of the investment that has sought entry into developing countries in recent years has been investment oriented toward export markets. The only major exceptions have been in situations where huge markets are opening up for foreign investment (e.g., the markets in Russia, China, and India). Eager to gain some share of these flows of foreign direct investment, developing countries have been competing aggressively to attract foreign investors. This competition to attract foreign investment stands in sharp contrast to earlier eras when developing countries sought to close their economies to foreign investment or impose onerous regulatory conditions on foreign investors that sought entry to their countries.

The typical procedure was for a country to allow investors entry only to a particular set of industry sectors. Prior to admission, those investors interested in the sectors in which the country allowed investment would be subject to a screening process. In this process, the investor's project would be examined by a government agency to determine whether it merited approval for entry. A typical evaluation would focus on the project's financial and technical viability and its likelihood of increasing employment and exports. In some instances, albeit far fewer than one might expect, governments would engage in the type of analysis outlined in the section, "Evaluating Foreign Direct Investment." Once investment projects had been approved, they still faced the task of overcoming a bureaucratic implementation process. Even after implementation, governments often placed performance requirements on these projects. Investors might be advised, for example, that they had to pro-cure a certain portion of their inputs from local sources.

Further, changes in policy over time were not unusual. Thus, investors might be advised to gradually indigenize their work force, that is, ensure that a growing portion of the work force consisted of locals of the country. The entire thrust of the government's relations with foreign investors was regula-tory in nature. The regulations were designed to ensure that the country in-creased the benefits that it received from these investment projects.

Since the 1980s, however, there has been a dramatic shift in the orienta-tion of government's relations with foreign investors. Where governments in developing countries once regulated foreign investment, they now seek to promote their countries as sites for foreign investment. They do so in a num-ber of ways. They change investment policies, regulations, and procedures to make investment easier; although admittedly, investors often find that the rhetoric of government differs from the reality and that, despite liberalization of policy, screening procedures and institutions continue to live on as ves-tiges of former eras.

However, governments do seek to provide incentives to foreign investors, such as tax holidays, reduced tax rates, and rebates on customs duties. Some governments, usually those in developed countries, go so far as to provide for foreign investors cash grants and training allowances. Governments also promote their countries by engaging in active marketing efforts that include advertising and personal selling to prospective investors in the world's major capital markets.

Other developments have also affected the increased demand for foreign direct investment. The debt crisis of the early 1980s and its aftereffects have foreclosed for many developing countries the option of using private financ-ing or government bilateral financing in their efforts to acquire capital for development. The increased movement toward privatization of state-owned enterprises in developing countries has also contributed to a demand for for-eign direct investment.

Despite these trends, the prospects for foreign direct investment playing a critical role in the development process seem no greater than ever before. There are, of course, exceptions. Foreign direct investment has clearly been the engine of growth in the development of the Singaporean economy. The government of this country could legitimately state that "foreign investments have largely been responsible for our rapid progress and modernization" (Re-port of the Economic Committee, *The Singapore Economy: New Directions*). This country began promoting itself as a site for export-oriented investment in the 1960s when most developing countries, many having just gained inde-pendence, were more interested in asserting their economic sovereignty over foreign firms. Singapore has certainly made the most of its "first-mover" advantage.

For other developing countries, the sobering realization is that with the move to consolidation of production operations, most foreign direct investment is flowing to a few countries. The bulk of foreign direct investment continues to be channeled to industrialized countries, the rest is captured by a few rapidly growing developing economies. In 1991, for example, about half of the total foreign direct investment flowing to developing countries went to the countries of Mexico, China, Malaysia, Argentina, and Thailand. Many other countries—most notably, the countries of sub-Saharan Africa but also many Latin American and Caribbean countries and some of the poorer South Asian countries—have realized very little in the way of foreign direct investment in recent years. These countries should not desist from engaging in reforms that make their economies more attractive to both domestic and foreign investors. For many of these economies, however, foreign direct investment is unlikely to be the miracle cure to the critical developmental problems with which they are confronted.

FURTHER READING

Dunning, John H. "Toward an Eclectic Theory of International Production: Some Empirical Tests." *Journal of International Business Studies* (Spring/Summer 1980): 9–25.

Porter, Michael, et al. "How Global Companies Win Out." *Harvard Business Review* (September-October 1982): 15–28.

Vernon, Raymond. "International Investment and International Trade in the Product Cycle." *Quarterly Journal of Economics* (May 1966): 190–207.

Wells, Louis T. *The Product Life Cycle and International Trade.* Boston: Harvard University, Graduate School of Business Administration, Division of Research, 1972.

Wells, Louis T., Jr., and Alvin G. Wint. "Marketing Strategies to Attract Foreign Investment." In *Multinationals in the Global Political Economy,* edited by Lorraine Eden et al. London: Macmillan, 1993.

Williamson, Oliver. *Markets and Hierarchies: Analysis and Antitrust Implications.* New York: Free Press, 1975.

Wint, Alvin G. "Liberalizing Foreign Direct Investment Regimes: The Vestigial Screen." *World Development* 20 (10; 1992): 1515–1529.

World Bank. *World Development Report, 1987.* New York: Oxford University Press, 1987.

Chapter 9

Intermediate Forms of International Business

As firms consider the type of international business activities upon which they will focus they face two extreme choices: (1) international business activities that involve short-term or spot arm's-length transactions between independent entities in different countries (market approach) or (2) transactions that span national boundaries but are wholly internal to and controlled by the firm (hierarchical transactions). For various reasons, identified in Chapter 8, firms seeking to benefit from the markets or resources of a foreign country eschew market-based approaches to achieving their goals and opt for wholly-owned foreign direct investment operations. Between these two points along a continuum in which control by the firm of the relevant market moves from negligible to complete, there are also many other possible types of international business activity. Table 9.1 provides examples of these intermediate forms of international business. They are more than trade among independent parties, but they are less than wholly-owned foreign direct investment.

As indicated in Table 9.1, firms can enter into subcontracting arrangements, licensing activities, turnkey or build-operate-transfer (BOT) contracts, management contracts, and franchising arrangements. Further, they can enter into joint ventures and various forms of strategic alliances. These options involve greater integration between independent entities, but they involve less integration than exhibited among entities of the same organization. It is in this respect that these options are described as intermediate forms of international involvement. They lie between trade among independent contractors and direct investment.

Table 9.1
Forms of International Business

Forms of International Business	Type of Activity
Trade	Export and import of goods and services on spot markets between independent parties.
Intermediate forms of international business	Licensing activities, subcontracting activities, management contracts, franchising arrangements, turnkey or build-operate-transfer contracts, joint ventures, strategic alliances, portfolio investment.
Direct Investment	Wholly-owned foreign direct investment.

INTERNATIONAL SUBCONTRACTING

International subcontracting arrangements involve an agreement between firms in separate countries to enter into a long-term relationship that involves the exchange of goods according to specifications provided by the contractor. The contractor may provide assistance, for example, in the form of technical advice or quality control supervision. The subcontracting arrangement provides for the contractor a relationship in which that firm has greater control of the timing and quality of the supply of needed inputs into the firm's business operation than would be the case if the firm were to rely only on markets. The subcontracting firm, in turn, is able to lock in a market for its products.

The typical arrangement is one in which the contractor purchases either a final or an intermediate good from the subcontractor. In the most extreme cases of international subcontracting, the subcontractor supplies only labor and some management skills. In the rapidly growing garment industry in the Caribbean and Central America, for example, a significant element of this garment industry operates through these contractual arrangements. Under U.S. Tariff Code 807, Caribbean garment producers that produce garments from material that is woven and cut in the United States can export sewn garments to the United States under a particular duty arrangement. The buyer of these garments pays duty only on the value that is added in the foreign location rather than on the entire assembled garment.

Many U.S. garment firms, finding that they cannot compete with low-cost garments from Asia, have entered into arrangements with local firms in the

Caribbean whereby these local firms assemble garments on a contract basis. The foreign firm, in many cases, supplies not only the fabric but also other materials such as zippers, fasteners, clasps, machinery for assembling the garments (e.g., modern hosiery manufacturing machinery), and technical assistance in the use of the machinery.

The arrangement has benefits for both the contractor (the foreign firm) and the subcontractor (the local firm). The contractor gains a dedicated source of supply, since, in cases in which the foreign firm supplies the machinery, it is normal to mandate that the local company can supply no other firm from that dedicated plant. However, the contractor gains this source of supply without engaging in the complications and risks associated with foreign direct investment. The subcontractor, on the other hand, gains a guaranteed market for its product and a source of technical assistance in the production of that product. Indeed, these arrangements simplify considerably the export problem for the typical local firm in a developing country.

INTERNATIONAL LICENSING

Licensing arrangements, with respect to any form of intellectual property, involve the rental of a nonphysical or intangible asset from the licensor to the licensee. The licensee typically pays a royalty. The royalty could be paid at the time of consummation of the contract as a lump-sum payment, as a flat fee at regular intervals during the life of the contract, as a percentage of the licensee's sales or profits during the life of the contract, or as some combination of these payment mechanisms. Through this process, the licensor is able to benefit from the assets that company has developed in a manner other than through exports or foreign direct investment.

This option becomes especially attractive to a company in situations where the company finds a licensee interested in mature technology whose economic value is depreciating, when a firm's managerial resources are constrained, or when the foreign firm is precluded from exporting or establishing investment operations within the country. From the perspective of the licensee, licensing arrangements provide an opportunity to acquire the technology necessary to mount competitive operations or the use of a brand name that has strong customer recognition. The typical licensing arrangement would include a noncompete clause that would prohibit the licensee from competing with the business operations of the licensor for some specified period of time.

Technology is routinely licensed, but so, too, are brand names. The process of licensing is facilitated by the protection that is afforded to these forms of intellectual property. Technology is protected through the application of patents, while brand names tend to be protected through trademarks that are registered by the company that owns the brand. Until quite recently, many developing countries had relatively weak intellectual property legislation; or where the legislation was adequate, the enforcement might be weak. There have been recent changes, however, based on bilateral pressure from developed countries such as the United States, on multilateral pressure emanating from trade accords such as the recently concluded Uruguay Round, and on the recognition by developing countries themselves that this was a mechanism for these countries to protect the intellectual property and creative talent of their own citizenry.

INTERNATIONAL TURNKEY CONTRACTS

Turnkey contracts are popular in situations where major building projects are undertaken. The typical arrangement is that a foreign building contractor or equipment manufacturer undertakes to build a facility and then transfer, that is, "turn the key," over to local interests when the facility is ready for operation. The skills that are offered by foreign companies in turnkey operations are a combination of building, equipment logistics, and project management skills. In a variation on the turnkey contract approach, recent years have seen the emergence of build-operate-transfer contracts. As the name implies, in these arrangements, the foreign contractor would also be involved in operating the facility for some designated period before it is transferred to local interests. Both types of projects are popular in infrastructural industries such as roads and electricity generation. In many cases, the client for these projects is a government entity. Payment on the contract is usually in installments, based on a prearranged schedule.

INTERNATIONAL MANAGEMENT CONTRACTS

Management contracts involve an arrangement between two firms stipulating that the firm receiving the management assistance will pay a management fee, either a flat fee or a percentage of sales, to the firm supplying the management expertise. These contracts are particularly popular in industries in which firms have developed a set of management processes and information systems that provide for them a competitive advantage in the industry. An example of such an industry would be the hospitality industry, in which international hotel firms such as the Hilton have developed a set of management systems they are able to rent to firms in other countries. Since such companies regard these skills as their principal source of competitive advantage, they are more interested in managing hotels under contract than in owning hotels.

INTERNATIONAL FRANCHISING

In some cases, management expertise is supplied in the context of a franchise arrangement. International franchising involves a franchisor renting a package of assets to a franchisee in another country. These typically include a trademark, assistance with management techniques and control systems, operational training, and assistance with equipment and material supply. Of course, not every element from this package is included in every franchise arrangement.

Franchisees normally pay franchisors some combination of a flat fee and a proportion of sales as a royalty. An advantage of franchising from the franchisor's perspective is that it allows for rapid expansion of revenue without a significant capital outlay, since the franchisee incurs the capital costs of developing the stores. For the franchisee, entering such a contract provides the firm with all the ingredients of a business organization—including brand name, technology, and management systems—that have been successful in another location.

The franchisee's principal business challenge is in identifying if such a business is likely to work well in the location it has selected. One of the key issues in international franchising is the degree of standardization across independent franchises. The franchisor would prefer standardization to ensure that its image is not affected by variations in approach from outlet to outlet. Indeed, elements of this standardization are likely to be written into the franchise agreement. The franchisee, on the other hand, may find that some customization of the franchise package is necessary to meet the peculiar needs of the clientele it plans on serving.

Although no investment takes place in the intermediate forms of international business discussed so far, in several of these forms, there is significant interdependence between the firms from different countries. In the two final forms of intermediate involvement, there may—in addition to interdependence—be investment. This investment stops short of wholly-owned foreign direct investment, which represented one end of the spectrum identified earlier in the chapter.

INTERNATIONAL JOINT VENTURES

In international joint ventures, firms from different countries invest jointly in a business venture. From the perspective of the foreign firm, the act of investing jointly with a firm from the host country could be motivated by different conditions. One motivating force might be a desire to reduce the risk associated with a direct investment activity by investing with a local partner that can bring capital, technology, familiarity with the local market and consumers, or familiarity with government policies and procedures to the venture. Another force motivating the formation of joint ventures has been government policy. Many developing countries, particularly prior to the movement toward liberalization of investment regimes in the 1980s and 1990s, developed policies that allowed foreign firms to invest only in joint ventures with local firms. During the 1970s, there were celebrated cases of major multinational firms, notably, Coca-Cola and IBM, leaving India because these companies were unwilling to share ownership of their Indian subsidiaries with indigenous Indian companies.

From the perspective of the local firm in a joint venture (i.e., the firm from the country in which the investment is to be located), the benefits that accrue from a joint venture are typically capital, technology, and management expertise. This is especially true where joint ventures are oriented, as they usually are, toward producing goods for local markets. In joint-venture activity that is geared toward overseas markets, a major benefit a local firm would derive from the foreign partner would be the access to overseas markets that such a partner might provide.

INTERNATIONAL STRATEGIC ALLIANCES

In recent years, a new intermediate form has developed. As risks have apparently increased in many industries and the costs associated with the development of new products escalated, firms are increasingly cooperating in ventures with companies that are their competitors. Increasingly, this cooperation is crossing the boundaries of nation states. It operates in the form of joint research and development arrangements in particular product lines, joint development and upgrading of technology, joint development of new products, and various forms of market-sharing arrangements. The term *strategic alliances* captures the various cooperative arrangements firms have created in their efforts to maintain or enhance existing competitive positions. (Note that this term is also sometimes used to cover all the forms of intermediate involvement described in this chapter.)

The extent to which strategic alliances are growing in popularity is evident from an examination of alliances in one important global industry, the computer industry. Prior to 1980, there were five strategic alliances among computer firms around the world in the form of joint research and development activities. Between 1980 and 1984, there were thirteen such alliances; but over the period of 1985 to 1989, there were twenty-seven such alliances.

In all the intermediate forms of international involvement identified, the motivation for their development was that firms desired to gain benefits from their own intangible assets or gain access to the assets and resources controlled by other firms without relying on trading relations or committing to investment operations.

INTERMEDIATE FORMS AND DEVELOPING COUNTRIES

From the perspective of developing countries, two salient issues might be identified. The first is the extent to which these forms of international involvement are used in developing countries. Most are, in fact, quite heavily utilized. Firms in developing countries tend to be involved as licensees of technology and brand names, as subcontractors in international subcontracting arrangements, and as recipients of management expertise through management contracts. Further, firms in these countries are usually entities to which facilities built under turnkey contracts are transferred.

The form of intermediate involvement in which developing countries are least likely to be involved is that of strategic alliances, as narrowly defined. So far, these alliances, particularly those that involve joint research and development activity, have been the preserve of firms operating in industrialized countries.

The second issue is the extent to which the costs and benefits associated with these intermediate forms of international involvement differ from those associated with international trading activity, on the one hand, and international direct investment activity, on the other. From the perspective of a developing country seeking to gain access to international markets and technology, the choices are usually between intermediate forms and investment.

This is true with the principal exception of capital, for which there is a very well developed international market. Borrowing funds from international capital markets can be viewed as a trading activity. A bank makes a long-term loan, but it simultaneously sells a product—the loan package. That loan package can be resold many times. Thus, borrowing funds is equivalent to importing a service. Beyond capital, though, the choices are more constrained. There is not, for example, as highly a developed market for technology that allows companies in developing countries to buy technology. Although firms in developing countries seek to "reverse engineer" products, it is becoming increasingly difficult to do so without violating intellectual property laws. Thus, for many countries, the choice lies between the traditional forms of wholly-owned foreign direct investment or the intermediate forms of international involvement outlined in this chapter.

COMPARING THE COSTS AND BENEFITS
OF INVESTMENT VERSUS INTERMEDIATE FORMS

The critical differences between foreign direct investment and intermediate or market forms of international business is that foreign direct investment transfers to the developing country capital, technology, management, and other potential benefits in the form of a package over which the foreign investor has, in the case of wholly owned foreign direct investment, complete control. As depicted in Table 9.2, the various intermediate forms of international business, on the other hand, transfer one or a few elements of the total package to a particular entity in a developing country. Thus, for example, licensing arrangements transfer only technology and brand names; and management contracts are primarily involved in transferring management skills.

The manner in which these resources are packaged, however, is of concern primarily because of the linkages between packaging structure and the effectiveness with which the resources are actually transferred to entities in de-

Table 9.2
The Benefits Sought from Foreign Linkages

Benefits Sought	Market or Intermediate Form	Investment Form
Capital	Loans, foreign portfolio investment	Foreign direct investment
Technology	Licensing, reverse engineering, foreign consultants, expatriate employees	Foreign direct investment
Market Access	Licensing of brand names, foreign consultants, expatriate employees, subcontracting	Foreign direct investment
Management Skills	Management contracts, expatriate employees	Foreign direct investment

veloping countries. On this note, developing countries have long felt that the resources that a foreign firm possesses are more effectively transferred to their countries through these intermediate forms of international business or through market forms than through foreign direct investment.

It is this perspective that has led to the calls for an "unbundling" of the foreign direct investment package. To the extent that foreign involvement is necessary to the development of the nation's industries, this argument suggests, this does not have to be channeled through the foreign direct investment package. Instead of seeking foreign direct investment, governments in developing countries should encourage their firms to borrow the necessary capital, license the appropriate technology, enter into contracts for the supply of any required management skills either through formal management contracts or through the hiring of particular expatriate employees, and gain access to markets through the efforts of foreign consultants or expatriate employees. This approach, the argument continues, will ensure that these resources are effectively absorbed by local entities that will endeavor to reduce their reliance on external resources over time. In fact, many governments tried to help their firms in this effort; and these governments were assisted, particularly in the technology acquisition component of this process, by the private development arms of the United Nations, for example, the United Nations Industrial Development Organization (UNIDO) and the UNCTC.

The assumption that absorption of the resources of foreign firms was more easily accomplished through these intermediate forms of international business was what motivated governments in developing countries to restrict the ability of foreign firms to establish wholly-owned facilities in their countries. In some cases, all forms of foreign direct investment were restricted. In others, restrictions occurred in particular sectors of the economy. In others, restrictions prevailed across sectors but stipulated that foreign investment was restricted to minority status in joint ventures with local entities.

These types of restrictions were employed quite extensively in Japan and Korea. Both countries placed restrictions on any form of foreign direct investment throughout a wide cross-section of the economy. Indonesia and India are examples of countries that required that all foreign investors had to enter into joint ventures with local firms. Brazil, on the other hand, limited its restrictions on foreign direct investment to particular sectors. This country's informatics policy, for example, restricted foreign direct investment in the computer and electronics industry.

The ultimate objective that countries have in seeking out foreign resources is to manage the acquisition and use of these resources in such a way that they lead to a self-sustaining cycle of resource generation and use that adds to the wealth of the country. It is usually felt that self-sustainability requires that indigenous entities, at some point, become involved in the generation of the resources. The efforts of these countries to use intermediate forms of international business to accomplish goals that it was felt might be more difficult to accomplish through the medium of foreign direct investment has met with mixed success.

A few countries, most notably Japan and Korea, have managed intermediate forms of international business very well. Both countries eschewed foreign direct investment and chose instead to restrict investment and trade. This created a situation in which firms seeking to gain access to the Japanese and Korean markets had little choice but to license technology to indigenous firms. Further, the domestic markets in these countries, but particularly in Japan, was large enough that it could not be ignored by foreign firms.

Even if the dominant firm in the industry, such as IBM in the computer industry, decided that it would not enter the market, there were always other firms seeking to gain an advantage against the industry's dominant firm that would be interested in entering licensing agreements. Further, Japan ensured that when technology was licensed, several firms were able to obtain the technology, thus creating competition among the firms designed to spur the development of these local firms and ensure that they could not become complacent given the protection their markets received from external competition. Japan's Ministry of Trade and Industry (MITI), however, did not allow these firms to bid for the licenses in an effort to ensure that the price of the license was not increased through a process of competitive bidding.

Other countries have not been as successful in their pursuit of this policy. This is because they have encountered several problems. One such problem is the lack of importance of the markets in some countries from the perspective of foreign firms. If the market is not particularly attractive and the foreign firm does not have access to the full range of options available for exploiting that market, the firm may simply decide not to enter the market in any form. In such situations, a country may have to give up its first-best choice of international business structure and allow firms to enter using the structure of their choice. Another problem is the difficulty of diffusion of the foreign firm's skills even when a government mandates, for example, that foreign firms have to enter via a joint venture.

The issue of market size is particularly relevant to small developing countries. These countries have found it much more difficult to mandate that foreign firms form joint ventures or that foreign firms license technology to local firms. For these small countries, the focus has had to be on foreign direct investment. This approach in some countries, Singapore representing the notable example, has focused on attracting wholly-owned foreign direct investment in export-oriented industries.

Even in those larger countries that were in a position to demand that foreign firms enter the country in joint ventures with local entities, the extent to which technology has diffused to local entities has not been significant. In some cases, the local firms have had little involvement in the joint-venture operations, often operating as silent financial partners only. Not surprising, in these instances, little diffusion of technology or managerial skill has taken place.

Even when markets are large and attractive enough that foreign firms are willing to engage in intermediate business forms, they often enter into a contractual relationship with a single entity: National champions used to be a popular description of these entities. From a government's perspective—and these single entities invariably have the blessing of the government—the idea of using such firms devolves primarily from the assumption that the most important variable affecting competitive success was the scale of a company's operations. Countries that have created national champions that have monopolies on local markets have discovered that competition is more important to the ultimate success of a company on world markets than is scale. This is particularly true in a world in which production is becoming less scale-sensitive.

Given the lack of success of countries in using intermediate forms of international business to achieve goals such as technology absorption, there has been a discernible movement away from intermediate forms of international business as a solution to the problem of diffusing technology and skills throughout a society. This trend was fueled by the debt crisis of the 1980s that reduced the ability of many developing countries to access the world capital market to gain the capital they needed and the movement toward export-oriented investment that not only reduced the bargaining power of developing countries vis-à-vis foreign firms but also made foreign direct investments more beneficial to the economies of developing countries, as discussed in Chapter 8.

The return to a focus on foreign direct investment, for pragmatic reasons if for nothing else, has not solved the problems of developing countries with respect to absorbing the resources that foreign firms bring to the country. Again, some countries have been successful in this absorption process. Returning once again to the example of Singapore, in that country indigenous industry has developed and benefited from the technology brought to the country by foreign investors. However, Singapore is the exception. In most developing countries, foreign direct investment for export operates in enclaves very similar to those created by the extractive foreign investment that dominated in an earlier period. There is very little diffusion of technology or of other resources. In general, it has proved very difficult to generate backward linkages with indigenous industry.

Some part of the solution of these problems rests in the management of local firms. Those that are involved in joint ventures with foreign firms must engage in proactive efforts to absorb the technology and other skills that their partners have to offer. A passive orientation to this task is unlikely to have the desired effect. To some extent, the problem can be solved only at a broader societal level. If education and technical training are inadequate throughout the country, this is going to have an extremely detrimental effect on the ability of any efforts to absorb technology from foreign firms, whether through investment or licensing.

Indeed, it is to this subject of technology transfer that the focus of this book shifts—from the concepts, institutions, and systems of international business to the manner in which firms in developing countries can manage their operations such that they become competitive on international markets. This examination is critical because, ultimately, the task of improving the competitiveness of the developing countries does not rest in Washington, D.C., or Geneva with the multilateral institutions; nor does it reside in New York, Munich, or Tokyo in the corporate offices of the world's multinational corporations. These entities can provide resources; but ultimately, the pace and extent of development in the world's developing countries will be determined in places like Mexico City, Sao Paulo, Istanbul, Kingston, Bombay, and Nairobi.

FURTHER READING

Gomes-Casseres, Benjamin. "Computers: Alliances and Industry Evolution." In *Beyond Free Trade: Firms, Governments and Global Competition,* edited by David B. Yoffie. Boston: Harvard Business School Press, 1993.

Oman, Charles P. "New Forms of Investment in Developing Countries." In *Investing in Development: New Roles for Private Capital,* edited by Theodore H. Moran. Washington, D.C.: Overseas Development Council, 1986.

Chapter 10

Managing Export Production

If the development dilemma for developing countries is not to be solved through regional integration efforts, through the reordering of North–South relations along the lines advocated by dependency theorists or the advocates of an NIEO, by the dedicated pursuit of the macroeconomic policy guidelines of the IMF or the WB, or through the attraction of an increasing share of the limited pool of available foreign investment, where, then, do the solutions to this dilemma lie? The really difficult work of improving the competitiveness of developing countries begins with the task of improving the production and operation capabilities of firms in developing countries, many of which will be indigenous firms. The objective of this process is that these firms should be capable of competing effectively, without protection, for their domestic markets and also for regional and world markets. Although subsidiaries of foreign firms can serve as important catalysts in this process, it is the extent to which indigenous firms are able to compete effectively that will dictate the pace of development in the developing countries of the world.

The focus of this chapter is on production and on exports for various reasons. The focus on production may appear odd, given the extent to which there is discussion today of the information revolution, the ascendancy of services, and so forth. Indeed, particularly for small developing countries, it is popular to suggest that these countries may as well forget about competing in manufactured goods and focus instead on services because they have no hope of competing in manufactured goods.

In developing this argument, its proponents typically focus on the problems of economies of scale that hamper the ability of small developing countries to compete in world markets. There are at least two problems associated with the prescriptions that are proffered by such analysts. The first is that small developing countries may be able to identify forms of competition that rely less on economies of scale, even as economies of scale generally are becoming less important in international competition than has been true in the past.

The second issue surrounds the basis of competition in services. There are many services in which economies of scale matter as much as they do in the production of goods. In the life insurance industry, for example, life insurance firms in developing countries selling policies at significantly higher costs than firms in the United States raise the size of the U.S. market as the principal reason why policies are much cheaper in that market—economies of scale in services.

Thus, rather than creating a false dichotomy between goods and services, the analyst in a developing country environment is better served by focusing on the manner in which firms of all types in developing countries need to position themselves in order to be competitive. This chapter begins this process by primarily examining production problems because, for most developing countries, this is where competition in external markets has been based to date. Services, in contrast, continue to be highly protected in most developing countries; and the success of service exports, with the notable exception of tourism, has been even less than the success these countries have experienced in the exports of goods.

The focus is on the export function for a variety of rather obvious reasons. Exporting is an important activity for all developing countries. Large developing countries find that if their firms are not engaged in exporting activity, it is usually a sign that their operations are not competitive. In such circumstances, these firms will have to be sheltered even within their own domestic markets from international competition. Most experiments in protection in developing countries, however, have resulted in a reduction in consumer welfare and a tendency for sheltered firms to become increasingly uncompetitive over time.

Exporting is even more important, though, for small developing countries. For these countries, it is the principal avenue for expanding national wealth. These countries will find that their domestic markets are too small to allow for the development of many types of industry. If the capital or consumption goods these countries cannot competitively produce domestically are to be imported, the country will only be able to afford such imports if it has a set of industries that are competitive on world markets.

In order to understand the production problems exporters from developing countries face, however, it is important to begin by examining important principles of production. Modern production processes trace their origins to the system of production developed in the United States in the early nineteenth century, in particular, the production of rifles in the Springfield Armory in Springfield, Massachusetts, in 1817. This system had two fundamental elements: the principle of interchangeability of parts and the system of production flow. The interchangeability of parts required that parts be produced by specialist machines according to precise specifications and in a separate manner from the products that would be assembled from these parts. This system replaced the hand production of parts by craftsmen.

The second important principle is that of production flow. Initially applied to the production of a single product, the principle of production flow allowed companies to produce goods in a system of continuous production. According to such a system, goods would not be produced utilizing batch production methods; instead, they would move from one stage of production to another with interchangeable parts added in a continuous manner throughout the production process. This process of continuous production flow required machines to be laid out properly according to the operations they were to perform. The idea was that each stage of the production process should be capable of processing material without being forced to produce to inventory.

Based on these principles of production, large, single-product plants were built by U.S. firms. It was these principles of production that allowed these firms to compete effectively with British firms, leading to the ascendancy of production in the United States, even though Britain had a headstart in the race for industrial development.

In more recent times, competing based on large plants gaining economies of scale in the production of single products according to the principles of interchangeability of parts and continuous production flow has been less successful. In large part, this has been as a result of a change in the approach to production that was spearheaded by Japanese firms. These firms, recognizing the opportunity to gain markets through the development of an ability to produce multiple products quickly and at low cost, have created plants that are much more flexible than the single-plant factories that worked well for U.S. firms in the heyday of U.S. industrial supremacy.

The production approach pioneered by the Japanese was an approach described as just-in-time (JIT) production, flexible production, or flexible specialization. Essentially, it applies the principles of production flow and interchangeable parts but to the production of multiple products rather than a single product. It does so by creating an organization in which all production workers are well trained in making decisions on the setting up and maintenance of machines. By relying on suppliers to provide supplies "just in time" to enter the production process, it avoids carrying raw material inventory. It then seeks to reduce the costs of producing multiple products by changing machine setup times quickly so that machines and workers can move from the production of one product to the production of another.

From the perspective of developing countries, so the argument goes, the new mode of production deemphasizes economies of scale and focuses instead on economies of scope, range, or time. That is, the new global competitors are not necessarily producing from large plants that allow significant economies of scale; rather, they are now producing from smaller, more flexible plants that produce multiple products with very short lead times. This type of production, the argument continues, is more conducive to the spatial and economic circumstances of most developing countries. It is against this background of the principles of modern production and trends in the application of these production principles that it is useful to examine the problems firms from developing countries experience as they seek to produce goods that will be competitive on export markets.

PRODUCTION SYSTEMS IN DEVELOPING COUNTRIES

Possibly the most fundamental problem faced by firms in developing countries that seek to produce for export markets is that many of these firms operate using craft-production systems or batch-production systems that employ neither the principles of interchangeability of parts nor those of production flow. In craft-production systems, the focus is on the specialist skills of workers. In most cases, these skills are unique to particular workers. These handcrafting skills can be and often are excellent, but they suffer from a critical deficiency: They do not typically allow for exact replication from product to product; that is, the parts produced in a craft environment are not interchangeable. These parts must be hand-fitted to a particular product. They cannot easily be produced in a specialized operation and then transferred to any available product.

Not only do these systems not employ the principle of interchangeability, but many also do not employ the principle of production flow. That is, rather than use production flow production systems in which a product travels from a start point to a finish point, with discrete stations along the way at which another element of value is added to the product, batch-production products would be produced in groups or departments; and intermediate products, as a group, would be shipped from department to department within the enterprise. Batch production does not allow for the specialization at production stations, the streamlining of product movement, and the elimination of in-process inventories that is possible in production flow systems.

Absence of a Focus on Product Engineering

Another critical problem faced by many producers in developing countries is an absence of a focus on product engineering. This problem is tightly linked with the problem of producing parts according to the principle of interchangeability. Interchangeable parts can only be produced in an environment where significant attention is placed on product engineering. Product engineering includes the specification of construction methods that simplify the manufacturing process. In the furniture industry, for example, construction methods that utilize dowels lead to an easier manufacturing process than those that use mortise and tenon joining techniques. Product engineering also involves the use of product specification sheets that specify the precise dimensions of the product, the machine operations necessary to produce the product, and the machine attachments that may be necessary. This process is complemented by the design of blueprints for each product and product component.

These two problems, in turn, lead to a number of related problems experienced by manufacturers in developing countries, but the problems are particularly significant for manufacturers that are seeking to export their products.

Consistency of Output

One of the fundamental production management problems associated particularly with the fact that component parts are often not produced according to the production principle of interchangeable parts is that of inconsistent product output. In many developing countries, local consumers are willing to tolerate output from a facility that is not consistent from product to product. Consistency relates to the quality of the product but also to its precise dimensions, form, and aesthetic attributes. For the export market, on the other hand, products within a particular export order must be consistent in form and be of consistently high quality. Thus, the furniture manufacturer must ensure that all drawers fit all desks of a similar type. Consistency is also critical from one order to the next.

Firms that do not produce according to the principle of interchangeable parts will find it particularly difficult to supply export orders. They may obtain orders based upon the quality of their samples; but they will find it difficult to expand production significantly beyond the stage of sample generation. It is this problem that leads to some developing countries being described as "nations of samples."

Timeliness of Production

Another consequence of the problem of an inability or unwillingness to produce using the principles of interchangeable parts and production flow is the lack of timeliness in the delivery of products. Again, this is a problem that is more acute for the exporter than for the firm oriented to the domestic markets of developing countries. The smaller volumes demanded by the local market make it easier to meet production timetables. Further, the conditions of scarcity that have been typical of many developing countries allow producers to get away with late delivery of products. The export market differs on both counts. The volumes can be quite large, and buyers are extremely intolerant of late delivery. Thus, export orders are likely to be relatively large and are likely to require delivery at a clearly specified time.

Delivery after a specified time may simply not be tolerated by the importer. Consider, for example, a garment producer in a developing country that is given an order to deliver particular products at a specified time. The retailer, eager to operate his retail establishment on JIT inventory principles, is not interested in inventorying these products. Instead, the retailer would like to receive them just in time to put them on display to coincide with a particular sale period. Delivery after the date of the sale period is not an option the retailer is willing to tolerate. If the producer tries to deliver after the agreed-upon date, he or she may find that all the products are returned.

The producer in a developing country that has been producing for the domestic market may find it difficult to move to a significantly higher level of production. There may, for example, be constraints on capacity that would not apply were the facility with its existing collection of equipment located elsewhere. Many companies move to shift operations to make maximum use of existing production capacity. Firms in developing countries, however, may find it more difficult to move to shift operations. Transportation problems for workers might not allow production during late shifts. Further, many of the production workers in export operations in developing countries are female. Shifts other than the regular day shift may pose problems for these workers. This is especially true for firms that operate in high crime locations.

The reason many firms find it difficult to expand production, however, relates not only to the problems outlined earlier, but also to the fact that many firms do not operate according to the production principles outlined. Consequently, expanding production is a much more difficult proposition than it would be if the production facility were functioning using these production principles.

Facility Layout

Instead, because of the problems of an inadequate focus on production flow, many production facilities in developing countries are poorly designed for efficient production flows. This occurs for various reasons. Facilities are often poorly laid out. The production facility was probably laid out, in phases, to accommodate craft- or batch-production methods. With poor plant layout and suboptimal arrangement of machines, work flow suffers and the company's costs of production are higher than they should be. A WB study illustrates the case of a foreign consultant guaranteeing that the output of a developing country firm involved in exports could be expanded by 100 percent with existing plant and equipment within one year through a process of reorganizing production methods, machinery layout, work flow, and other systems engineering aspects of production.

This problem is created largely because facilities that begin their life focused on batch-production methods tend to grow incrementally. Rarely during this pattern of growth is the firm likely to reexamine the optimal plant layout. Instead, new machines are placed in the most accessible location. It is not likely that attention would have been placed on designing an optimal facility to handle relatively large volumes. A move to export production does not automatically trigger a redesign of the firm's production facilities.

Materials-Handling Processes

Further, firms in developing countries have not gone far down the road of flexible production that relies upon the limited use of inventories. Instead, these firms often place inadequate emphasis on their materials-handling processes. Inventory supply systems are not well organized. Where firms in other countries have placed significant effort in developing JIT inventory systems or in focusing on a materials-requirement planning process that will closely align material needs and production activity, firms in developing countries have not tended to innovate in these areas. Consequently, they continue to hold relatively large levels of inventory.

Although one element of this problem relates to the organization of the work force and the attitudes toward production, one cannot ignore the critical infrastructural problems that may well limit the ability of firms in developing countries to move rapidly in this direction. Firms in developing countries that begin to move toward more streamlined and flexible operations that rely on JIT inventory processes often revert to their normal patterns of holding large quantities of inventory after their suppliers fail to provide supplies to them on time, and they are forced to shut down the operations of an entire plant. It is simply a fact that, in developing countries, the transportation and supply systems are not as advanced as they are in developed countries.

Buffer stocks represent the firm's insurance against supply disruptions that take place in developing countries to a greater extent than in developed countries. Even if the firm faces a high cost of capital, as do many firms in developing countries, they regard this as a price that must be paid to ensure that supplies are not disrupted. It is rather difficult to convince firms that have experienced these supply disruptions to move to flexible systems that take as their fundamental mode of operation a transportation and supply system that is different from the one that prevails in many developing countries.

Quality Control and Quality Management

Again, because of the nature of production processes in developing countries, most manufacturing entities in these countries also lag behind the best practice in developed countries in areas such as quality control and quality management. In the quality management approach that has been pioneered by Japanese firms in parallel with their movement to more flexible production systems, the focus is on producing a high-quality product throughout the entire production process rather than the more traditional quality control approach that focuses on sampling finished goods to determine which batches of goods might contain an unacceptable number of defective products. The quality management approach relies on an integrated team of trained production workers who are involved in decision making on the plant floor.

A quality sampling process, on the other hand, operates from the separation between production workers and quality control personnel that is typical of the separation of functions and production decisions that characterized the more standard production processes that dominated production around the world prior to the movement to new systems of production within the last two decades. The quality sampling approach accepts a certain level of defective products, whereas a quality management process has as its goal the complete elimination of defective products.

In general, the pronounced movement toward quality management that began in Japan and has taken hold in North America is only slowly filtering to the developing countries of the world. Indeed, many firms in developing countries had yet to master the traditional quality control procedures that dominated production management operations in North America, Europe, and Japan in the post–World War II period. One of the normal elements of assistance provided to exporters in developing countries by buyers from developed countries, for example, has been in the area of quality control. Like several of the problems discussed, the quality problem is particularly acute when the firm is dealing with very demanding export clients.

Waste and Wasted By-Products

The inadequacy of quality assurance systems and the nature of the production process in a developing country firm leads to a level of waste that tends to be unusually high when compared to the levels that prevail in firms in developed countries. Waste also extends to wasted by-products. Japanese firms, in particular, have focused on minimizing waste in their production processes and utilizing all the by-products that emerge from these processes. Many firms in developing countries have not placed significant attention in these areas.

One important element of waste in firms in developing countries is associated with the fact that these firms often do not utilize good housekeeping procedures. In the absence of good housekeeping procedures, such as clean work areas, appropriate storage sections, and so forth, much material is wasted with no indication of the area of waste. This problem is compounded by the lack of product engineering and material accounting systems. Were such systems in place, they would be able to specify the quantities of material that should be used in particular applications.

Deficiencies in Inputs

Last, firms in developing countries often experience deficiencies in the quality of the inputs they have to use in the production transformation process. The starting point for inputs, of course, is the trained production specialist. There is, in many developing countries—with the exception of countries such as India, Korea, Taiwan, and Singapore—a shortage of technically trained personnel. Further, even where countries can boast a large supply of engineers and technicians, these individuals are sometimes not exposed to plants using the newer forms of production systems that are used in other countries.

Firms in developing countries often also must contend with poor-quality inputs if they source locally or inputs at relatively high cost if they source from foreign companies. In the latter environment, it is difficult for the firm in the developing country environment to compete with firms in the country from which the inputs are being purchased, since firms in these countries can source equivalent products more cost-effectively. Firms in developing countries also face deficiencies in other forms of input. Erratic and high-cost energy supplies, for example, do not make it easy for firms in developing countries to compete with their rivals based elsewhere.

RESPONSES TO PRODUCTION-MANAGEMENT PROBLEMS

The origins of many of the problems associated with managing the production process of firms in developing countries suggest that the most important elements that would provide an environment for sound export-production management is the reordering of production according to the principles of interchangeability and production flow. This process is more likely to occur if firms are dedicated to the export function. Firms that are dedicated exporters can carefully examine their production processes and substantially reconfigure these processes to meet export production requirements. If firms are beginning with an export focus, this process is somewhat easier because such firms begin with a clean slate and can design their factory layouts and work flows for the most efficient operations.

The focus on the production process as the arena in which problems need to be solved reflects changes in the way in which value is added in the production process. The equipment used in most production establishments is fairly standardized. In this respect, equipment is now something of a commodity. Once a firm can raise the capital, this equipment can be purchased. This does not mean that acquiring the capital is a trivial exercise. The point is that once the equipment is obtained, even if it is the optimal equipment, this only solves part of the production problem.

Along with equipment purchases must come the technical ability and creativity that transfer the equipment into an effective production environment. It is the ability to manage the production equipment and the production process that has led many governments and firms in developing countries to rely on foreign investors to manage the entire package of activities. However, indigenous firms in developing countries have found that an emphasis on training of personnel in conjunction with careful equipment purchases can also be a recipe for successful export production. The importance of technical training at the factory level has also been demonstrated in studies that compare the efficiency of production processes in Japan and the United States.

In this regard, training is much more important than access to equipment. One study that demonstrates this conclusion, albeit in the context of the highly technical and automated manufacturing processes used in the United States and Japan, holds important lessons on the importance of training for developing countries. This study examined flexible manufacturing systems, or computer-controlled groupings of semiindependent workstations, operating in both countries. These systems are designed to allow the manufacture of multiple products by adjusting machine setup times rapidly and, in some cases, automatically by using computer numerically controlled (CNC) machines. Although the system configurations were essentially the same across both countries, as Table 10.1 indicates, the Japanese were able to use their systems to much greater advantage primarily because they used much more highly trained workers. Even with the same equipment that was available to their counterparts in the United States, the training to which the Japanese production workers had access allowed them to utilize fully the capabilities of these flexible manufacturing systems, producing nine times as many parts as those individuals working in the United States.

Developing countries will not quickly be able to move to flexible manufacturing systems that rely on highly automated machinery. Indeed, they will find it difficult even to move to the general principles of flexibility developed by the Japanese. At a minimum, flexible systems require interchangeability of parts, flexibility in machine setup, multiskilled workers operating within a business environment that allows them to make essential decisions on the plant floor, consultative supplier relations, and competition among firms within an industry.

It is not easy to put all these requirements in place; but firms in developing countries must begin to move in several of these directions if they are to compete effectively on their home markets and ultimately on world markets. For example, they must move to the principle of interchangeable parts if they are to be involved in more than the production of samples. The movement to this principle has important implications for the recruitment and training of production workers.

To state the obvious, it is unlikely that illiterate workers will have much success in understanding blueprints and in reading routing sheets. They may make excellent craftspeople; but if the production process is to be more than an entirely idiosyncratic one in which each item produced is a unique masterpiece, with little potential of creating many such masterpieces, then firms must move to a more systematic process of production.

Firms in developing countries also must move to more consultative relations with suppliers, creating vertically linked production networks. This is the only way for a firm in a developing country to reduce the risks associated with specialization. The changes in the nature of production systems reduces some of the barriers created by manufacturing scale in earlier years.

Table 10.1
Comparison of Flexible Manufacturing Systems in Use in the United States and Japan

System Features	United States	Japan
System development time	2.5 to 3 years	1.25 to 1.75 years
Number of machines per system	7	6
Types of parts produced per system	10	93
Annual volume per part	1,727	258
Number of parts produced per day	88	120
Number of parts introduced per year	1	22
Number of systems with untended operations	0	18
Proportion of workforce as engineers	8%	40%
Number trained in the use of CNC machines	25%	100%
Length of training to upgrade skills	x	3x

Source: Adapted from Ramchandran Jaikumar, "Postindustrial Manufacturing," *Harvard Business Review* (November-December 1986): 69–76.

Taking advantage of this new production environment, however, is quite difficult. Companies in developing countries are competing with companies in other parts of the world that have developed tight links along a vertical production chain that allows for flexibility, while reducing the administrative burdens, bureaucracy, and inertia typical of the industrial behemoths that are undergoing a metamorphosis around the world. However, firms in developing countries will find it very difficult to compete in these new markets without tight links to other firms that are similarly driven to high levels of performance and that can be relied upon to supply specialized materials as needed.

Little has been said about the need to acquire technology because, increasingly, the obstacle to competitive ability is not technology in the form of adequate machines. Clearly, for state-of-the-art processes, access to state-of-the-art technology will be necessary; but it is rare that the developing country will be competing in such markets. Most developing countries would be content to be competing effectively in world markets in the more mature industries of the world. This goal cannot be achieved without important changes in the orientation of these firms toward the production process.

Last, little has been said about the production choices faced by firms in developing countries. Firms from developing countries have a number of export strategies from which they can choose. They can opt for a strategy of producing relatively standardized products in which they are competing based on the availability of low-cost productive inputs, typically labor or raw materials. In such cases, efforts to increase productivity focus on obtaining production efficiencies that increase the volume of output per given set of inputs or decrease the quantity of inputs per a given volume of output. The traditional exports of agricultural and mineral products from developing countries fall into this category. Also in this category are many of the garments assembled and exported under the provisions of U.S. Tariff Code 807.

An alternate strategy is to export differentiated goods where the firm's competitive advantage in export markets derives less from its low-cost position and more from the distinctive nature of its product. Regardless of the strategy chosen, however, the principles and problems of production outlined in this chapter apply. Indeed, firms are increasingly being forced to accomplish both tasks simultaneously, that is, produce differentiated products that can be sold at low prices. In many respects, in fact, where such choices exist, they revolve as much around the firm's marketing strategy as its production strategy. Competitive production is required regardless of the firm's chosen marketing strategy.

FURTHER READING

Best, Michael, and Robert Forrant. "Production in Jamaica: Transforming Industrial Enterprise." In *Jamaica: Preparing for the Twenty First Century.* Kingston, Jamaica: Ian Randle Publishers, 1994.

Girvan, Norman, and Gillian Marcelle. "Overcoming Technological Dependency: The Case of Electric Arc (Jamaica) Ltd., A Small Firm in a Small Developing Country." *World Development* 18 (1; 1990): 91–107.

Jaikumar, Ramchandran. "Postindustrial Manufacturing." *Harvard Business Review* (November-December 1986): 69–76.

Keesing, Donald B., and Andrew Singer. *How Support Services Can Expand Manufactured Exports.* Washington, D.C.: World Bank, 1990.

Chapter 11

Managing Export Marketing

Export competitiveness requires that, in tandem with the challenge of producing goods that are on par with goods produced by competitors in other countries, developing countries identify appropriate export markets and buyers. Export marketing addresses issues such as identifying buyers and their product needs and ensuring that products are produced that meet the needs of these buyers and are delivered to the buyers in a timely manner in the quantities desired. Although easily identifiable, the tasks for firms in many developing countries are quite difficult in practice for the reasons that will be outlined. What is clear is that, for most firms in developing countries, there is an evolutionary dimension to their export activity.

The many empirical studies of the export activity of firms in developing countries are emphatic in their conclusion that firms, and those within the firm that make decisions about export activity, go through stages in the development of the firm's export activity. An early "stages" model of export activity of firms in both industrialized and developing countries was the Vernon–Wells product cycle model described in Chapters 2 and 8.

In another perspective on the stages of export activity, Reid indicates that firms and export decision makers move through a "hierarchy of effects" or an "adoption of innovation" model of export behavior, where these entities go through the process of export awareness (Stage 1), export intention (Stage 2), export trial (Stage 3), export evaluation (Stage 4), and export acceptance (Stage 5). At the final stage of this process, firms have demonstrated that they are "committed" exporters.

In another study, Wortzel and Wortzel also suggest the existence of a stages approach to the development of export markets, as indicated in Table 11.1. According to the Wortzel and Wortzel framework, exporters from developing countries go through five stages. The first (Stage 1) is importer pull, in which the firm has made no decision to pursue exports and is simply filling

Table 11.1
Stages in the Development of Export Markets

Marketing Activities	Stage 1: Importer Pull	Stage 2: Basic Production	Stage 3: Advanced Production	Stage 4: Channel Push	Stage 5: Consumer Pull
Internal design	1	X	X	X	X
External design	1	1	X	X	X
Package design		1	X	X	X
Quality control			1	X	X
Branding				1	X
Cost	X	X	X	X	X
Price to retailer				1	X
Price to consumer					1
Local promotion		X	X	X	
Foreign promotion (to importer)			X	X	X
Foreign promotion (to retailer)				1	X
Foreign promotion (to consumer)					X
Distribution to wholesale				X	X
Distribution to retail				1	X

Source: Heidi Vernon Wortzel and Lawrence H. Wortzel, "Export Strategies of NIC and LDC Based Firms,"
  Columbia Journal of World Business (Spring 1981): 53.

1: Partial responsibility
X: Full Responsibility

an order brought to it by a foreign buyer. In Stage 2, there is a switch from exporting being based upon importer pull to exporting based on an exporter push strategy. Here, the firm sells basic production and capacity, but it can also produce samples for customers and put in place a skeletal marketing team that seeks to contact buyers and engage in other marketing activities but primarily within its own country. In Stage 3, producers are selling advanced production and capacity marketing. Firms in this stage have begun to internalize several components of the mix of export-marketing activities. The firm undertakes these marketing activities both within the export countries and within its own country.

In Stage 4, product marketing and channel push, the firm has begun to use its own brand names instead of its customer's brand name. By so doing, it has begun the process of marketing a product based on nonprice features. In the preceding three stages, firms from developing countries sell exclusively based on price. Even in Stage 4, however, given the fact that the company's brand name is unlikely to be well known to consumers, price will continue to be the company's principal competitive weapon. This situation changes in Stage 5. In this stage, product marketing and consumer pull, the firm from a developing country becomes indistinguishable from its developed country counterpart. Firms in this stage take full control over all marketing activities.

In general, according to the conclusions of this study, exporters take increasingly greater responsibility for management of the export-marketing mix of export price, product, promotion, and distribution as they move from Stage 1 to Stage 5. Thus, firms operating in Stage 1 of the export-marketing development process would have full control over only basic production costs but no control over product design, packaging, quality control, branding, retail price, or any elements of the distribution process. Firms in Stage 5 of the export-marketing development process, on the other hand, would have full control over all elements of the export-marketing mix except for the establishment of the price to the consumer, over which they are likely to have only partial control.

Implicit in most of the approaches to identifying stages in the export development process is the issue of the exporting firm's commitment to the export function. Committed exporters will have gone through the five stages of Reid's export decision process and made a decision to accept exporting as an important focus of the firm's operation. Exporters in Stage 1 of the Wortzel and Wortzel typology have made only a negligible commitment to export operations. Exporters in Stages 3, 4, and 5 and, to a lesser extent, Stage 2 have made a significant commitment to export operations.

There is an important distinction, however, between the notion of commitment in both studies. Reid's work, like that of many other analysts that have focused on the export strategies of firms, examined export strategies in North American and European firms. In these studies, the issue of commitment focuses on whether the exporting firms desire to pursue an export orientation. In many cases, particularly in those studies of U.S. firms, these firms have an attractive local market; and export activity could easily be relegated to a secondary position. For such firms, the critical variables in moving the firm to an export orientation are changes in the perspectives of the managerial team that elevate the priority attached to exporting in the firms' corporate strategies.

For exporters from developing countries, the issues of commitment are somewhat more complicated. The orientation of managers continues to play a role. This is especially true for firms in developing countries that have historically pursued inwardly focused development strategies, often in concert with a restriction on domestic competition to promote economies of scale. Managers in such firms require a fundamental reorientation in order even to contemplate what is required for success on export markets. For these firms, however, the problem of succeeding on export markets is even more complicated because these firms are unlikely to have world-class products and an administrative heritage that involves engaging in sophisticated competitive marketing practices. Thus, beyond a change in the focus of management, firms in developing countries often need to solve specific production and marketing problems in order to be successful in their export activities.

The Wortzel and Wortzel typology, based upon empirical research in developing countries in Asia, illustrates the marketing approaches that firms from developing countries often pursue. In their initial forays into export markets (Stage 1), these firms are not engaged in export marketing, nor are they engaged in product design. Instead, they simply sell production capacity, opportunistically, to a buyer that may well have initiated the contact. The products sold are likely to be commodity-like, and the basis for competitiveness is invariably price. Exporting does not have to begin in this manner, but this form of exporting appears to help a firm in a developing country overcome the various production and marketing obstacles it is likely to encounter. If firms stay at this stage, however, this does not augur well for their future export prospects. They are completely hostage to the activities of the foreign buyers. If these buyers opt to move their operations, they are not organized to do anything other than await the next buyer that might have an interest in their ability to produce goods inexpensively because of their relatively low labor costs. From the perspective of the firm and the country within which it resides, Stage 1 firms represent a very fickle export capacity.

The fickle nature of Stage 1 exporting leads firms from developing countries to try to advance to other stages, but advancing to other stages is a not a trivial exercise for many firms. It requires moving to create new marketing functions and new levels of production and marketing expertise. In general, such advancement requires new investment. This is particularly true as firms move toward Stages 4 and 5 when they incur the marketing expenses associated with the establishment of brand names. As firms move toward these stages, they also incur the short-term financing costs associated with producing goods for inventory rather than customer orders and selling goods on open account rather than against letters of credit, issues to be discussed in more detail in Chapter 12. Thus, as with all matters of investment, the firm will have to examine the risk-return tradeoff associated with adopting new strategies.

In discussions on the typology of export-marketing strategies, Wortzel and Wortzel are emphatic that their typology is not normative; that is, it is not necessarily in the best interests of all firms in developing countries to progress sequentially from stage to stage until they arrive at Stage 5. Regardless of the stage of export development a firm in a developing country is in, it is likely to encounter a series of problems in its export-marketing efforts.

EXPORT-MARKETING PROBLEMS

Chapter 10 began a discussion of the problems exporters face as they seek to begin exporting and continue, over time, to pursue more sophisticated export strategies. The production problems are, in fact, interwoven with the problems of marketing. The linkage between these problems is most obvious in the area of product development and design. In essence, since both business functions seek to take responsibility for the product design and development component of the firm's activities, the difficulties firms in developing countries encounter in developing and designing products for export markets represent both an export-production and an export-marketing problem.

Having said that, export-marketing problems can be usually divided into three categories. One category comprises problems that affect the supply of exportable products, for example, product design and development and packaging and labeling. Another set of problems are those that affect the demand for exportable products, for example, the difficulty firms from developing countries face in gaining access to markets and market information and the problems of pricing, branding, and promotion. The final category includes issues of transportation and logistics.

Export-Supply Problems

Beyond the issues discussed in Chapter 10, firms from developing countries face additional problems as they seek to compete in export markets. Foremost among these problems is the need for improvements in the area of internal and external product design. For firms that have produced for the local market and are now contemplating entering export markets, improvements to the internal and external design of the product are often required in order to make this product competitive on export markets. With respect to internal design, the focus is usually placed on ensuring that the product performs its appropriate utilitarian function reliably. The external design issues, on the other hand, relate more to the aesthetic appeal of the product, including the impact of packaging and labeling on the product's appeal to consumers. Changes in these areas may represent a substantial investment for the firm from a developing country.

A firm in a developing country might be selling canned or bottled goods on the local market. In some developing countries, companies experience significant problems gaining the appropriate bottles and other forms of packaging they need from local suppliers. They accept bottles and other forms of packaging material that are less than ideal. Consumers in the country also accept goods bottled in inappropriate types of containers. Consumers in export markets are unlikely to be as tolerant of poor or inappropriate packaging.

In addition to the aesthetic attributes of packaging, if a product is poorly packaged, it can increase the costs of transporting the product, lead to a product that is delivered in poor condition, or make the product difficult to store before resale or use. In addition, export markets typically have labeling requirements that will differ from those that apply in the firm's domestic market. Examples of such requirements are those for language and for nutritional reporting information. Identifying these requirements and adhering to them is an obvious component of the firm's broader strategy of adapting the product it will export to the needs of the target export markets.

Not all firms in developing countries will face the issues of external and internal product design. Recall from the Wortzel and Wortzel typology that Stage 1 firms had little involvement in this aspect of the export-marketing mix; but the firm in a developing country that passively relies on foreign buyers to guide its products into foreign markets may experience a short-lived existence. Foreign buyers or other foreign firms should be regarded as catalysts from which the firm can benefit as it moves to internalize the necessary product design capabilities. However, it should so move if it desires long-term involvement in export activity.

Export-Demand Problems

If indigenous firms from developing countries are to move to the internalization of marketing activities or begin their export activities with these activities conducted in-house, they are confronted with the problem of how to gain access to export markets. The issue of market access has several dimensions. One such element is the issue of obtaining sufficient market intelligence to allow the firm to position and price the product properly. Another is the fundamental problem of gaining access to appropriate distribution channels. Still another element of market access is how to overcome trade barriers that are often raised in developed countries against imports of agricultural and manufactured products from developing countries.

Effective export-market intelligence requires appropriate and timely information and structured research into export markets. Firms in developing countries tend to be weak in both areas. For most exporters of consumer goods in developing countries, the market is not the ultimate consumer. Very few firms have the resource base that would allow them to promote their goods to the ultimate consumer and create within these consumers sufficient interest in these products that they would "pull" them off store shelves or out of warehouses. Indeed, Wortzel and Wortzel in reporting on their five stages indicated that Stage 5 was theoretical at the time of the study. None of the firms that they interviewed could be included in that stage. Today, possibly the only developing country firms that may have achieved Stage 5 status and may be involved in considerable attempts to promote consumer goods to final consumers are the Korean Chaebol, that is, Korean conglomerates, which typically couple manufacturing entities with trading companies such as Daewoo, Samsung, and Hyundai. These firms will need to engage in consumer marketing research in an effort to correctly position their products to meet the needs of consumers. These firms will also be involved in promotion to consumers to create brand awareness of their products.

For most exporters in developing countries, however, the effective consumer of their product is the distributor in the developed country rather than the final consumer. Market research must be focused on the needs of buyers, which are often intermediaries such as the large wholesalers and retailers. In addition, market intelligence must allow the firm in a developing country to assess the characteristics of competing producers that operate within that country or are based in other countries.

A firm's pricing decision should be made only after this type of market intelligence is obtained. Firms in developing countries often provide quotes to buyers based on an estimate (usually rather incomplete because of an absence of precise management accounting information) of the product's costs. In fact, however, product pricing decisions should also involve close examination of the pricing strategies of competing firms. This information is often not sought after by the firm in the developing country. To be sure, market information such as this is easily described but not as easily obtained. Firms in developing countries often do not have access to the types of market information databases that firms in developed countries take for granted. Further, even where databases exist, they may not contain the precise types of information required.

It is rare that the exporter will be able to gain adequate market intelligence without developing close contacts with institutions or individuals in the market to which the firm seeks to export. Such contacts do need to be nurtured in order to gain access to information that is critical to the firm's decision-making process. Routinely, firms in developing countries find that their ability to gain access to an international market revolves around personal contacts that are made between the firm's executives and buyers in that market. It is important to pursue and nurture such contacts, whether in an independent manner or with the assistance of foreign consultants or agents that are able to identify appropriate buyers and influence their buying decisions.

There is also an attitudinal problem that makes it more difficult for exporters from developing countries to acquire the necessary market intelligence they need to be successful in export markets. Many entrepreneurs in developing countries are used to operating in local markets under conditions of relative scarcity or conditions of monopoly. Under such conditions, little market research is necessary, since firms are able to sell virtually anything that they produce.

Firms in developed countries have been forced to shift to a marketing orientation in which products are geared to market needs. Because of the nature of the market environment, firms in developing countries have not moved as quickly toward a marketing orientation. For many companies in these countries, a selling or a production orientation has dominated. Only recently have there been shifts more toward a marketing orientation with the movement to liberalized trading environments and enhanced competitive structures in these countries. While these changes are taking hold, however, firms in developing countries that seek to export will continue to find that export customers are considerably more fickle and demanding than their local customers. Ascertaining precisely what these customers need is critical for a successful export strategy.

A final, but important, market-demand problem that many firms in developing countries face is the barriers that are imposed on their exports by the governments of developed countries. As indicated in Chapter 3, these trade barriers come in different forms: tariffs; volume restrictions, such as quotas; and NTBs, such as onerous customs or health and safety inspection requirements. These barriers pose a special problem of market access to firms from developing countries. In particular, they tend to exist in the sectors that play host to many exporting firms from developing countries. Stringent agricultural inspection programs, for example, are believed by many to be one mechanism that governments in developed countries use to protect their agricultural industries. Protection by developed country firms of their textile industries became so pronounced that an agreement—the multifiber agreement—was negotiated between the United States and many developing countries that produced textiles, whereby quotas are allocated to each developing country.

Although protection clearly constitutes a significant problem of market access, various companies from developing countries—particularly companies from East Asia—have found ways to ensure that their export prospects are not held hostage by protectionist tendencies. As reported in a seminal study of the issue by Yoffie, these companies used the fact that developed countries have developed protectionist policies in an unsystematic and ad-hoc manner. As a consequence, these measures contained many loopholes. Several East Asian nations took advantage of these loopholes, diversifying production marginally, for example, to take advantage of the fact that different protectionist measures would apply to very similar products. Indeed, these firms were able to turn the protectionist measures to their advantage as it spurred them to add value to their products in certain areas.

Transportation and Logistics

Even when exporters from developing countries have correctly identified appropriate pockets of demand and adjusted their supply arrangements so that they are appropriately positioned to meet the needs of the markets identified, they still must overcome the transportation and logistical barriers that make export activities more difficult in many developing countries. These logistical barriers include elements of the home government's bureaucracy that make it more difficult for exporters to pursue their business activities. Exporter registration and certification processes can be time consuming. Exporters utilize the nation's ports and customs facilities to a considerable extent. If these facilities are substandard or if the process of gaining access to port or customs services is particularly bureaucratic, then the exporter from that country is placed at a disadvantage vis-à-vis exporters from countries with more simplified and efficient processes.

The actual quality of the country's transportation infrastructure can also be a significant problem. In the 1980s, for example, Bangladesh's textile industry was booming; but the actual export of textiles was constricted by the country's transportation network. Feeder vessels called at Dhaka, the capital of Bangladesh, only once every two weeks. The demand for shipping being seasonal, during peak seasons the vessels had insufficient cargo space, and during off-seasons the ships left the country with partial loads. The feeder vessels, having left Bangladesh, would then call at Colombo (Sri Lanka) and there transfer freight to another vessel; and there would be at least one more transfer before the freight left for its eventual location in the United States. Of course, exporters faced highly erratic transit times, since their load could easily miss a connection given the complexity of the transfer process and the frequent lack of cargo space.

One might suggest that it might be possible for exporters to air freight their cargo. This is probably too expensive an option for all but the most time-sensitive cargo. Even here, there would have been no easy solutions to the problems of the Bangladeshi exporter. International flights to the United States from Bangladesh during the 1980s were sporadic for passengers and even more so for freight. Air Bangladesh flew to the United States twice per week, but the demand for its services was very high, creating a queue. Alternative carriers flew through their own international hubs where their domestic freight would take priority over Bangladeshi freight.

For those exporters of time-sensitive products that use air freight, there may be other transportation needs that are not always satisfied. Exporters of cut flowers, for example, require not only rapid shipment but also rapid shipment in refrigerated cargo holds. Not all commercial aircraft companies offer this type of facility. One of the key concerns of importers is that exporters be able to meet delivery deadlines; thus, solving these transportation problems becomes critically important to export success.

Responses to Export Problems

Exporters in industries in some countries, for example, have been able to form associations to arrange for infrastructural needs and lobby their host government for assistance in this area. This is clearly one of the ways in which exporters respond to the transportation and logistical problems they face in their efforts to sustain their exporting activity.

In addition, exporters often respond to the problem of accessing market intelligence by engaging in discrete activities such as attending trade shows or export fairs. These events can be useful to exporters, but they do not replace the need to have ongoing contacts with the export marketplace in order to ensure that opportunities are pursued. These discrete promotional events should simply represent one of several avenues through which an exporter begins the process of forming the personal and institutional contacts that are required to facilitate access to particular markets.

Another mechanism for both gaining access to markets and improving the quality of the product to be supplied is through the judicious use of catalysts. These catalysts could be foreign, coming in the form of foreign buyers, multinational corporations, and technical assistance from foreign firms or individuals. The firms operating in Stage 1 of the exporting-development process are clearly relying on foreign buyers. The point, however, is that firms from developing countries should view these buyers as catalysts; that is, they should provide the platform from which the firm can "take off" into self-sustaining export activity that is not reliant on the patronage of a single foreign buyer.

Export catalysts do not have to be foreign. They could also be public or private local institutions. One such candidate is the government through its export assistance program. Most developing countries have such a program in place. Several have been quite effective; others, as pointed out in Chapter 13, have been less effective. These programs, coupled with the financing activities discussed in Chapter 14, complement the production and marketing efforts in which companies engage in their efforts to generate products that are competitive on world markets.

FURTHER READING

Reid, Stan. "The Decision-Maker and Export Entry and Expansion." *Journal of International Business Studies* (Fall 1981): 100–111.

Rhee Yung Whee, and Therese Belot. *Export Catalysts in Low-Income Countries: A Review of Eleven Success Stories.* Washington, D.C.: World Bank, World Bank Discussion Paper, 1990.

Wortzel, Heidi Vernon, and Lawrence H. Wortzel. "Export Strategies of NIC and LDC Based Firms." *Columbia Journal of World Business* (Spring 1981).

Yoffie, David B. *Power and Protectionism: Strategies of the Newly Industrializing Countries.* New York: Columbia University Press, 1983.

Chapter 12

Financing Exports

For firms in developing countries, the mechanism by which export activity is financed deserves special attention because, similar to many export activities, it represents an area where many firms are entering into uncharted waters. Many of the problems identified in earlier chapters have financial implications to the exporting firm. This is true whether one focuses on the need for the exporter or prospective exporter to improve its technological operating base, the need for such a firm to produce in volumes larger than those to which it is accustomed, or the need for exporters from developing countries to engage in structured efforts to obtain essential market intelligence.

In addition, the exporter faces the potential problem of trade financing. This problem is much greater than the one faced by firms producing for the domestic market. The larger export volumes and the potentially longer lead times between the shipping of an order and the receipt of payment for such an order imposes upon the exporter a severe working capital constraint.

In general, the funding requirements of the exporter can be divided into the categories of capital funding, funding for export-marketing expenses, and funding for working capital expenses. In addition, like all businesses engaged in international business activities, the exporter must manage the company's exposure to exchange risk.

FUNDING FOR RETOOLING
AND EXPORT-MARKETING ACTIVITIES

Common to many exporters is the need to obtain funding in order to allow the company to retool its facilities to position itself to engage in competitive operations. As noted in Chapters 10 and 11, firms involved in exporting are under greater pressure to modernize their productive facilities than are their counterparts focused on production for particular domestic markets.

Similarly, funding export-marketing activities represents a potentially severe problem for many exporters from developing countries. As mentioned in Chapter 11, the potentially exorbitant cost associated with promoting products in export markets is one of the factors an exporter would have to consider in moving from a position of reliance on foreign buyers for marketing support to a position in which the export firm would undertake responsibility for marketing. The extent of the financing problem relates to how far along the continuum an exporter moves in the direction of taking over marketing responsibility for its product. The extreme situation, in the context of a consumer goods company, would involve the exporter establishing a brand and seeking to create sufficient brand awareness on the part of consumers through appropriate marketing activities that consumers would "pull" the exporter's product from retail outlets.

In seeking to engage in these retooling and external marketing activities, the exporter needs to identify appropriate sources of funding. Possibilities include equity from new or existing owners of the company. Some firms in developing countries tap into local stock markets as they seek to expand their base from domestic to export markets and engage in the production and marketing activities linked to such a transfer. A firm that has been closely held might decide that an export push represents the opportune time to open up investment opportunities to the public at large by listing the firm on the local stock exchange. Others might view the movement into export markets as an appropriate time to engage in a strategic alliance or a joint venture with a foreign company that can provide financing for retooling and export marketing in addition to technical assistance and enhanced access to overseas markets.

In addition to equity funding, firms may pursue their export-funding needs through commercial banks, development financial institutions, government export-financing programs, and multilateral financial institutions.

In relation to export financing, commercial banks perform their normal financing roles. Some commercial banks will have special schemes to provide financing for exporters. In many cases, the funding needs of exporters will be for foreign-currency loans. Commercial banks in developing countries, particularly those that are in the process of liberalizing their currency markets, are increasingly involved in providing such foreign-currency loans. The principal drawback of such loans from the perspective of the exporter, however, is that the interest rates on these loans are often several percentage points higher than rates on similar loans in developed countries. The exporter in a developing country may be unable to access the cheaper loans available in developed countries because the firm is not known to the lending community of the country in question.

Similarly, development financial institutions in developing countries may become involved in on-lending funds received from various sources to firms interested in obtaining financing for their export operations. Interest rates on these loans are sometimes marginally lower than interest rates that would prevail in commercial banks. Increasingly, however, developing countries under WB or IMF structural adjustment programs are unable to adopt a differential interest rate policy; where loans to particular types of business firms are materially different from other loans. This resistance on the part of the multilateral organizations to differential interest rates reflects a general philosophy that interest rates should reflect the true scarcity of capital and that governments should not intervene in factor and currency markets.

Governments do become involved in financing export operations directly. The export promotion agencies of many developing countries have programs of industry modernization and retooling in which the government promotion agency provides both technical and financial assistance in the retooling or industry-modernization exercise. A popular mechanism used to assist in the financing of the modernization process is for governments to allow companies that have retooled to gain tax credits for the capital expenses associated with retooling or to depreciate these expenses in an accelerated manner, gaining some tax relief in the process. Given that some firms in developing countries are concerned about investing in long-term ventures because of the environment of uncertainty created by inflation and government policy changes, such incentives might serve to assist in inducing investment. They do not, of course, substitute for an investment climate that is politically and economically stable.

These tax credit approaches have even been applied to marketing expenses. The government of Trinidad and Tobago, for example, has adopted a system in which investors can apply 150 percent of expenses incurred in promotion of products in new export markets as a credit against their tax liabilities. This is of particular assistance to some companies. Some exporting firms, for example, complain that they are forced by external auditors to expense all promotional expenses incurred in expanding into export markets. Such firms believe that this expense is actually an investment in much the same way that a firm invests in machinery and equipment, but this "investment" has no resale value. Allowing firms to apply such expenses as a credit against tax liabilities provides needed assistance in a promotional export drive.

The final source of financial assistance, particularly for retooling and modernization, is the multilateral financial organizations. As mentioned previously, these organizations lend money that is on-lent to business firms through development finance companies. There is also one multilateral organization discussed in Chapter 5 that becomes directly involved in financing the operations of firms in developing countries, including their export operations. The IFC will assist firms seeking to enter export markets by taking relatively small, short-term equity positions in these ventures.

After tapping into these sources of financing in an effort to retool production systems and engage in overseas marketing activities, exporters from developing countries still face an export financing problem. That problem is similar to one faced by many small companies operating domestically—that of financing working capital. For the firm from a developing country seeking to export, however, the financing of working capital becomes even more complicated, not least of all because the firm also must manage exchange risk as it seeks to solve its working capital problem.

METHODS OF TRADE FINANCING

The methods used to finance trade activity can be divided into categories based on the extent to which the exporter bears the credit risk. At one extreme, the investor bears all risk; at another, the investor is able to transfer all risk to financial intermediaries. In between these extremes, there are possibilities for the exporter to share risk with governments or private insurance companies or to transfer risk (at a fee) to financial institutions. Table 12.1 summarizes the range of options, some of which may be available to a particular exporter.

The exporter bears all the credit risk in consignment sales, sales on open accounts, sales relying on draft documents that call for payment after goods have been shipped, and in circumstances where working capital is financed by using export receivables as collateral to obtain secured bank overdrafts. The exporter can transfer these risks, at a cost, through the mechanisms of forfaiting or factoring. The exporter bears some of the risk in circumstances where governments provide export guarantees. Exporters pass on all credit risks to a financial institution through the use of confirming house facilities and letters of credit, buyer credits, or export leasing arrangements.

Table 12.1
Range of Options for Dealing with Credit Risk in Export Financing

Exporter Bears All Risk	Exporter Transfers Risk For a Fee	Exporter Shares Risk	Third Party Accepts Risk
Consignment transactions	Forfaiting	Government export insurance schemes	Confirming house facilities operating through letter of credit transactions
Sales on open account	Factoring		
Sales on sight or time drafts	Discounting of time drafts		Buyer credits
Secured bank overdrafts	Private insurance		Export-leasing programs

Financing Methods in Which the Exporter Bears All Risk

There are various methods of trade financing in which the exporter bears all the risk. In consignment transactions, the exporter or consignor ships the goods to the buyer or consignee. Title to these goods, however, is not transferred to the buyer. Title to the exported goods remains with the exporter until these goods are sold. Upon sale, the consignee forwards payment to the exporter after deducting amounts for expenses and sales commissions. In this form of arrangement, the exporter takes all risks. The buyer takes no risk, either commercial, financial, or foreign exchange.

Exporters also absorb significant risk when they sell goods on open account. The terms of such a sale typically involve an exporter sending goods to a buyer and then billing the buyer for the cost of the goods. Billing terms usually indicate that a buyer has a prescribed period, say thirty or sixty days, to pay for the merchandise that has been shipped. This procedure is identical to that used by most business entities in their normal transactions with customers. Similarly, it creates the same types of concerns, except that the international nature of the transaction exacerbates these concerns. Thus, for example, many companies that sell on open account locally find that their buyers pay their bills late. Essentially, there is an unspoken rule in many business circles that buyers can use credit from suppliers as a form of working capital financing. From the suppliers' perspective, delays in the payment of bills are even more severe in the context of export orders because of the additional time involved in the shipment of the goods.

For sales that rely upon draft documents, the exporter prepares a document demanding payment, essentially a bill, and sends this bill or draft along with the relevant shipping documents to the importer, usually via the importer's bank. The bank only gives the shipping documents to the importer after the importer has agreed that the draft represents a valid bill that he or she intends to pay. Of course, the buyer still does not have to honor this debt. In some cases, these drafts should be honored as soon as the importer sees the goods (sight drafts); in others, payment of the draft is scheduled to occur at an agreed-upon point in the future (time drafts). The exporter continues in both payment forms to be exposed to credit or default risk, although sight drafts should prove to be less risky than time drafts.

The final payment method that places all risk on the exporter is the secured bank overdraft. In these instances, in order to ameliorate the firm's working capital situation, the exporter obtains a short-term line of credit or overdraft facility from his bank and uses the receivable from the importer as collateral for the bank loan. Again, it is clear that if the importer reneges on its loan obligations, the exporter will still be responsible to the bank for monies borrowed under this arrangement.

Financing Methods in Which Exporters Transfer Risk at a Fee

Exporters can obtain financing in the form of bank loans and overdraft facilities, but there is also a variety of other financing instruments to which they have access that both provide financing and also transfer the credit risk to a financial institution. One such instrument is the discounting of time drafts. As discussed earlier, these drafts represent the importer's promise to pay the exporter for imported goods at a mutually agreed-upon time. These drafts represent negotiable financial instruments. As such, they can be sold at a discount from their face value to a financial institution or any willing borrower. The discount, of course, represents the reward directed to the purchaser of the time draft for accepting the risk of buyer default and the time value of money between the date of purchase and the date the time draft matures.

Another instrument used in a somewhat similar manner is that of forfaiting. This is a financing arrangement in which the cost of financing trade is passed eventually to a forfaiter. A typical arrangement has the buyer paying the exporter with a promise to pay (promissory note). This note is then guaranteed by a banker, typically in the importer's home country. The supplier then sells the guaranteed promissory note to a forfaiter at a discount. The discount is based upon the buyer's credit rating, the credit rating of the guaranteeing bank, and an allowance for the time value of money between the time the note is sold to the forfaiter and its maturity date. The forfaiter can sell the note on the secondary markets. When the note matures, the forfaiter presents it to the guaranteeing bank for payment.

Factoring presents yet another mechanism for obtaining export financing. Used in either domestic or international trading activities, it is a situation in which a third party provides immediate cash against a company's account receivables. The factoring institution charges interest on the amount extended in the form of a short-term loan secured by the company's receivables. The typical procedure is that an exporter approaches a factor requesting that the factor provide financing against the exports the company has made on open account. The factor establishes the credit rating of the importer and, if the rating is deemed satisfactory, purchases the exporter's outstanding receivables. The factor then takes responsibility for all future interaction with the buyer.

Financing Methods in Which Exporters Share Risk

In response to the magnitude of the risks involved for the exporter in normal trade financing methods, various institutions in many countries have become involved in designing programs that reduce the financing risks for the exporter. Government institutions in many countries provide export insurance and guarantee schemes. These guarantee programs are likely to provide exporters with payment for their exports in the event that an importer defaults on his or her payment obligation. However, these programs typically accept only part of the credit risk in order to ensure that the exporter has an incentive to act prudently in his or her choice of importers. It is in this respect that both approaches represent shared-risk financing methods.

Financing Methods in Which Third Parties Accept Risk

One method of transferring risk to third parties is through an export leasing agreement. In this agreement, the manufacturer sells products to a leasing firm. The leasing firm will then lease the goods to foreign users. The exporter receives payments for his or her exports immediately and transfers the working capital problem to the leasing firm.

Exporters can seek to transfer all risks to intermediary institutions in various ways. One method is by confirming house arrangements. In these circumstances, a bank in the buyer's home country confirms that it will operate as a principal by accepting liability for payment on orders placed by the buyer with the exporter. The bank is liable to pay the requisite amount to the exporter regardless of whether the buyer defaults on payment of the trade credit. This is typically true, for example, of letter-of-credit arrangements.

The letter of credit is possibly the most widely used instrument in trade financing that involves the passing of risk to a third party. There are several variations of letters of credit for exporters to consider.

A confirmed letter of credit, for example, is one in which a bank in the exporter's home country (called the advising bank and often the one in which the bank that issues the letter of credit has correspondent banking relations) confirms that it will pay the exporter on proof of the exporter's compliance with the details of the export arrangement. In such circumstances, it is the advising bank in the exporter's country that takes on the risk of default by the importer or inability to pay by the bank that issues the letter of credit.

Other variations in letters of credit exist. A revocable letter of credit is one in which the importer can cancel the letter of credit up until shipment of the goods. In contrast, under the terms of an irrevocable letter of credit, the importer cannot cancel the letter of credit once the exporter has been advised that it has been issued. Whereas most letters of credit require the exporter to present the letter of credit to the confirming or advising bank for payment, under a negotiable letter of credit, the exporter can present it to any bank for payment. The intermediary bank might accept the letter of credit for a fee and then present it to the confirming or advising bank on its own behalf. Most exporters dealing with unknown customers or banks would like a confirmed, irrevocable letter of credit. This form of letter of credit provides the most protection to the exporter.

In situations where goods are shipped to customers on a continuing basis, a revolving letter of credit might be issued. Such a letter of credit applies to the sale of multiple shipments over an extended period of time. In circumstances where nonfinancial intermediaries operate between the exporter and the importer, it may be appropriate to consider one of the various transferable letters of credit. In such a situation, the initial beneficiary of the letter of credit is able to transfer the shipment rights under the letter of credit to a third party. Thus, if a broker initially arranged the credit, that broker can transfer the credit to the actual manufacturer of the product through a transferable letter of credit. One type of transferable letter of credit is an assignment. An assignment letter of credit allows the exporter to assign a proportion of the credit's value to a manufacturer, even while stipulating that it continue to negotiate the credit directly.

In a back-to-back letter of credit, the export intermediary in whose name a letter of credit has been obtained uses this letter of credit as security to the confirming or advising bank as it opens its own letter of credit with the manufacturer. In such cases, the second letter of credit must match the wording of the first, except for the beneficiary, the price at which the goods are sold, and the date of shipment. As goods are passed from the manufacturer to the export broker to the importer, the export broker's letter of credit with the manufacturer is negotiated first, followed by the importer's letter of credit to the export broker. Back-to-back letters of credit are particularly useful if the manufacturer would like to conceal its identity from the importer. Thus, manufacturers in developing countries that are not well known to importers might export their products via a well-established intermediary by using back-to-back letters of credit.

EXPORT-FINANCING DOCUMENTS

In seeking to execute letters of credit, exporters need to be aware that they will only receive payment on their letters of credit after they have supplied all the documentation necessary for confirming that they have completed their responsibilities under the export contract. The principal document used in this respect is the bill of lading, of which there exist several types.

The bill of lading performs several functions. It is a contract between a transportation carrier and the exporter to take goods from the point of shipment to the point of delivery, the exporter's receipt for the goods that have been shipped, and the document that establishes control over the goods while they are in transit between shipment and delivery points. Various forms of bill of lading exist. A "received for shipment" bill of lading simply indicates that the goods have been received by the shipper. In contrast, an "on-board" bill of lading indicates that the goods have been loaded onto the vessel that will transport them to the prescribed destination. A "clean" bill of lading indicates that the goods have been received in what appears to be good condition; a "fouled" bill of lading suggests that the goods appear to be in unsatisfactory condition.

Other documents that might be required of an exporter when negotiating a letter of credit include a commercial invoice that identifies the goods being shipped, the cost of these goods, and the total amount owed by the importer. If the contract stipulates that the exporter is responsible for insuring the goods, then an insurance certificate must be submitted with other export documents. For foodstuffs or other products to be consumed or applied to humans or animals, the importer's government may require that the exporter furnish a health or sanitary certificate that attests to the quality and safety of the goods being exported.

The United States is particularly vigilant in this regard. The U.S. Food and Drug Administration (FDA) can stop the importation of any product that it views to be potentially harmful. In a number of developing countries, concern about rejected shipments, particularly of agricultural products, led exporting governments to negotiate with the U.S. FDA for permission to establish, with the U.S. FDA's cooperation, a preshipment system that would allow for the inspection and clearance of agricultural products in the exporting country.

MANAGEMENT OF EXCHANGE RISK IN EXPORT FINANCING

Developing-country exporters may also be exposed to exchange risk in their export financing activities. The nature of the risks they are likely to face and the instruments available to them for dealing with such risks are somewhat different from those that developed-country exporters would face. For the developed-country exporter, the exchange risk associated with export is that the exporter may accept payment (voluntarily or involuntarily as a consequence of competitive conditions, for example) in a currency other than the currency of his or her home country while the export shipment is priced in the currency of his or her home country. The risk under such circumstances is that the exchange rate between the exporter's country and the currency of the export contract changes between the date of negotiation of the contract and the date of the contract's consummation via payment. If the currency of the exporter's country appreciates vis-à-vis the currency of payment, the exporter experiences a foreign exchange loss. If the currency of the exporter's country depreciates, however, then the exporter experiences a foreign exchange gain.

Exporters from developed countries have a number of methods they can adopt in their efforts to manage this exchange-risk problem. One such management approach is to eliminate the foreign exchange risk or exposure by directly aligning the currency of operation and payment. Thus, if the exporter can arrange for payment in its own currency, then there is no foreign exchange risk. Beyond such arrangements, exporters can seek to hedge the foreign exchange risk.

Exporters from developed countries tend to hedge their foreign exchange risks by using forward exchange markets, option markets, or currency markets. An exporter would hedge in the forward markets by selling its expected foreign currency receipts in exchange for its own currency on the forward market. Upon buying such a contract an exporter would be obliged to deliver foreign exchange at a particular time (e.g., thirty or sixty days hence) and at a price predetermined at the time of negotiation of the forward contract. Such an exporter would no longer have foreign exchange exposure or risk, since, regardless of the exchange rate at the time of the payment, the exporter would receive its currency at the prenegotiated price.

Similarly, the exporter could hedge the exchange risk on the foreign exchange options market. The exporter could achieve this result by purchasing a put option, that is, an option to sell foreign exchange. Such an option is in contrast to a call option, that is, an option to buy foreign exchange. At the time at which the option is purchased, the price at which the option can be exercised (strike price) is determined, along with the length of the option and the amount of the currency the exporter has the option to purchase.

If the exporter's home currency appreciates vis-à-vis the currency of the export receipts, then the exporter would exercise the option of selling the receipts from the export contract rather than converting these receipts to its home currency at a rate that would result in a foreign exchange loss. If, on the other hand, the exporter's home currency depreciated against the currency in which the export receipts are denominated, then the exporter could choose not to exercise the option, choosing instead to benefit from the foreign exchange gain that would result from converting the foreign currency receipts into its home country on the spot market. An option, because of its flexibility, is more attractive than the use of the forward market; but the exporter must pay for this flexibility.

Another approach an exporter could use is to hedge foreign exchange risk via the currency markets. It could do so by borrowing a loan in the currency of its export receipts with a maturity date that coincides with the date it expects to receive those receipts. The amount borrowed could be converted to the home country currency at the current spot market rate and the proceeds of that conversion invested, either within the firm at its opportunity cost of capital rate or externally at prevailing rates of return. The export proceeds would be used to pay off the amount of the loan and accumulated interest. The cost of this hedging instrument would be the differential between the borrowing cost and the return that can be obtained on the sum that is borrowed.

These approaches to hedging foreign exchange risk are not used with similar frequency in developing countries for various reasons. First, many exporters in developing countries incur relatively little exchange risk. A typical Caribbean or Latin American exporter, whose principal export market is the United States, for example, would negotiate export contracts so that payment under the contract is made in U.S. dollars. These exporters, however, are unlikely to convert all of the proceeds from their exports to the currency of their home countries for various reasons. One critical reason is that many exporters use a high proportion of imported inputs in producing for export markets. Thus, since their imported inputs will probably be purchased using U.S. dollars, they keep a significant portion of their export proceeds for that purpose.

There are, of course, circumstances where exporters might wish to hedge the portion of the proceeds that they intend to convert to local currencies. This is unlikely to happen, however, in developing countries that have had a history of inflation and depreciation of the local currency relative to the world's "hard currencies." If the exporter expects movement only in the direction of depreciation of its home currency, as is true throughout most of Latin America, the Caribbean, Africa, and parts of Asia, there is little incentive to hedge foreign exchange risk. Exporters are only used to experiencing foreign exchange gains as a result of their foreign exchange exposures.

Even for those exporters that choose to hedge their risks, however, the opportunities for using hedging instruments tend to be fewer than those for the exporter from a developed country. In most developing countries, forward and option markets are not well established; and currency markets may also be far more limited than equivalent markets in the world's developed countries.

There are circumstances under which exporters in developing countries have faced rather large foreign exchange losses that could easily have been avoided. In 1991, for example, when the pound sterling faced a crisis within the European ERM and depreciated by a significant amount against the German mark and the U.S. dollar, among others, some exporters from Caribbean countries suffered extensive exchange rate losses. These losses occurred primarily because exporters that typically priced their products in U.S. dollars and sourced their production inputs from the United States negotiated contracts with importers in Britain and priced their exports in pounds based upon the existing exchange rate between the U.K. pound and the U.S. dollar. Between negotiation of the contract and payment of the contract, the pound/dollar exchange rate moved from approximately £1 = $2 to £1 = $1.50. Exporters, therefore, received on average 25-percent less than they expected (in U.S. dollars) from their export contracts. These exporters might have had difficulty hedging the risk of movement in the pound/dollar exchange rate in their home countries; but it clearly would not have been difficult to hedge this risk in several nearby financial centers. A simpler strategy would have been to eliminate the exchange risk by negotiating payment on export contracts in the currency of the country from which the exporter purchases most inputs—in the case in question, the U.S. dollar. Such a strategy, however, is not always possible.

In all matters of export financing, whether managing exchange risk or providing financing for the capital or the working capital aspects of the export venture, exporters from both developed and developing countries are often assisted by the governments of their home countries. Governments engage in these activities because they believe that assisting exporters in this manner will improve the country's exporting capability for the greater welfare of the country. It is the mechanisms that governments from developing countries use to assist the exporters that are discussed in Chapter 13.

FURTHER READING

Kim, Suk H., and Seung H. Kim. *Global Corporate Finance: Text and Cases.* Miami: Kolb, 1993.
Salorio, Eugene. *Note on Trade Finance.* Boston: Harvard Business School, 1987.

Chapter 13

Managing Government Export Assistance

In their efforts to improve the international competitiveness of their economies, governments from most developing countries have tried to put in place institutions dedicated to supporting the countries' exporters. One of the common complaints of both governments and firms in developing countries, however, is that the firms seem to be unaware of the assistance that governments are willing to provide or, if aware, unwilling to take advantage of these assistance programs because they are deemed to be ineffective. This chapter seeks to identify the types of export-assistance programs provided by governments in developing countries and the manner in which firms in developing countries might best take advantage of these programs of government export assistance.

EXPORT-ASSISTANCE PROGRAMS IN DEVELOPING COUNTRIES

Many developed and developing countries have created organizations to assist exporters. Indeed, at least 104 countries are believed to have such an organization. Of this number, eighty-two are developing countries and twenty-two are developed countries. In general, the organizations in developed countries predate those in developing countries. The earliest organizations in developed countries were created in Canada (1894), Finland (1919), and Italy (1926). Among developing countries, the earliest organizations were created in the Bahamas (1935), Mexico (1937), Thailand (1952), and Brazil (1953). (See Table 13.1, which lists export organizations in developing countries, the dates the organizations were formed, and the nature of the organizational structures.)

Table 13.1
Trade Organizations in Developing Countries

Country	Trade-Promotion Organization	Year Established	Type of Organization
Algeria	ONAFEX	1987	Autonomous
Argentina	DNPC	NA	Department of Ministry
Bahamas	BCofC	1935	Non-profit/Private
Bangladesh	EPB	NA	Autonomous
Barbados	BEPC	1979	Autonomous
Belize	BEIPU	1986	Non-profit/Private
Benin	CBCE	1988	Department of Ministry
Bolivia	IBCE/INPEX	1986	Autonomous
Botswana	TIDA	NA	Department of Ministry
Brazil	CACEX/ITAMARATY	1953	Department of Ministry
Burkina Faso	ONAC	1974	Autonomous
Burundi	APEE	1989	Autonomous
Cameroon	CNCE	1980	Autonomous
Chile	PROCHILE	1974	Department of Ministry
China	CCPIT	1952	Autonomous
Colombia	PROEXPO	1967	Autonomous
Costa Rica	CENPRO	1968	Autonomous
Cote d'Ivoire	CCIA	1984	Autonomous
Cuba	PROEX	1977	Department of Ministry
Cyprus	TD	1960	Department of Ministry
Dominica	DEXIA	1986	Autonomous
Dominican Republic	CEDOPEX	1971	Autonomous
Ecuador	DGPE	1974	Department of Ministry
Egypt	EEPC	1979	Autonomous
El Salvador	DGPDE	1981	Department of Ministry
Ethiopia	ECC	NA	Autonomous
Gabon	CGCE	1974	Autonomous
Ghana	GEPC	1969	Autonomous
Guatemala	DIRECOM	1968	Department of Ministry
Guinea	DAP	NA	Department of Ministry
Guinea-Bissau	SPE	1984	Department of Ministry
Haiti	PROMINEX	1986	Autonomous
Honduras	DGPEI	1988	Department of Ministry
Hong Kong	HKTDC	1966	Autonomous
India	TDA	1970	Autonomous
Indonesia	NAFED	1973	Department of Ministry
Israel	IEI	1958	Autonomous
Jamaica	JNEC/JAMPRO	1969	Autonomous
Kenya	KETA	NA	Department of Ministry
Korea	KOTRA	1962	Autonomous

Table 13.1 *(continued)*

Country	Trade-Promotion Organization	Year Established	Type of Organization
Lesotho	TPU	1978	Department of Ministry
Macao	EPD	NA	Department of Ministry
Malawi	MEPC	1971	Autonomous
Mali	CMCE	1977	Department of Ministry
Malta	METCO	1989	Autonomous
Mauritius	MEDIA	1985	Autonomous
Mexico	BANCOMEXT	1937	Autonomous
Morocco	CMPE	1980	Autonomous
Nepal	TPC	1971	Autonomous
Nicaragua	DIPEX	1983	Department of Ministry
Niger	CNCE	1984	Autonomous
Nigeria	NEPC	1976	Autonomous
Pakistan	EPB	1963	Autonomous
Panama	IPCE	1984	Semi-Autonomous
Paraguay	CEPEX	1967	Autonomous
Peru	ICE	1986	Autonomous
Philippines	BETP	1975	Department of Ministry
Rwanda	CCIR	1982	Department of Ministry
Saint Lucia	TS/EPU	NA	Department of Ministry
Senegal	CICES	1977	Autonomous
Sierra Leone	SLEPC	1981	Autonomous
Singapore	TDB	1983	Autonomous
Sri Lanka	EDB	1979	Autonomous
Sudan	EPD	1979	Autonomous
Suriname	IEB	1985	Department of Ministry
Tanzania	BET	1978	Autonomous
Thailand	DEP	1952	Department of Ministry
Trinidad	EDC	1984	Autonomous
Tunisia	CEPEX	1973	Autonomous
Turkey	IGEME	1960	Autonomous
Uganda	UEPC	1985	Autonomous
Union of Myanmar	TIS	1983	Department of Ministry
Uruguay	COEX	NA	Department of Ministry
Venezuela	ICE	1970	Autonomous
Vietnam	CDE	1982	Autonomous
Zaire	CCIZ	NA	Autonomous
Zambia	FTD	1980	Department of Ministry
Zimbabwe	MOTC	1981	Department of Ministry

Source: International Trade Center, *Selected Export Promotion Organizations* (Geneva: UNCTAD/GATT, 1986).

NA: Information not available.

Form of Export-Assistance Organizations

These organizations take different legal forms in the developing country world. A few trade organizations are created as private bodies. A more popular form is that in which the trade organization is part of the normal system of government, operating in the form of a particular department of government. The most popular form of structure, however, is that in which the trade organization is established as an autonomous entity within the government. This form of structure seems to be popular because, since export organizations provide a public good, they need to be funded by governments. On the other hand, in order to be responsive to the needs of their clients—existing and prospective exporters—trade organizations need a level of flexibility, autonomy, and marketing expertise that they might find difficult to achieve within the confines of the normal structure of the government civil service. In their marketing and customer service functions, these organizations differ from the more regulatory function that is typical of much of government activity. Accordingly, many countries have established export organizations that are funded by government but allowed to operate autonomously in keeping with the special mandate of the organization.

FUNCTIONS OF EXPORT-ASSISTANCE ORGANIZATIONS

Export-assistance organizations in developed countries were formed primarily to provide market information for firms in these countries that were not currently engaged in export activities. The presumption in forming these organizations was that the firms in question were producing a product of world-quality standards but that these firms were absorbed with the country's domestic market and felt no sense of urgency in expanding their horizons to encompass the markets of distant and unfamiliar countries. Given these assumptions, these organizations were set up as trade-promotion organizations with the function of marketing the potential of exports to export-shy firms and providing market intelligence about conditions in overseas markets to these firms.

Developing-country export organizations were created with the same goal of expanding exports from these countries. Indeed, to a large extent, early efforts by developing countries to create trade organizations followed closely (and with little thought) the efforts that developed countries had undertaken. Thus, these organizations were also created as trade-promotion organizations with the principal onus being to market exporting to nonexporting firms and to provide market intelligence that would assist firms to penetrate export markets. Over time, the export-assistance organizations of many developing countries have moved away from a focus that is placed solely on marketing issues to a broader focus that represents the reality of the circumstances of developing countries. The reality of these countries is that there do not exist legions of firms producing goods at world-quality levels and needing only persuasion and market information to enable them to gain access to world markets.

Consequently, export organizations in developing countries, though still often described as trade- or export-promotion organizations, are and should be involved in much more than the narrow marketing definition of promotional activity. They are also involved in programs designed to improve the productive capability of firms in developing countries. These programs are sometimes regarded as focusing on supply-side versus demand-related concerns. The term *promotion,* in these cases, relates to all efforts, export policy, production assistance, and export-marketing assistance, in which export-promotion organizations engage in their efforts to expand the volume of exports. Often in these countries, the focus is on expanding exports in nontraditional areas, that is, those in which the country does not have a long history of export activity and in which the products exported go beyond commodity-type agricultural and mineral products. Export organizations in these developing countries are typically funded either through a direct government subvention or through a portion of the tax revenue governments receive from international trade.

Export Policy

Export-promotion organizations in developing countries may have a role in determining policies toward exports. Government policies toward exports typically include a range of trade, investment, exchange, and other policies that affect the operations of exporters. Typical areas of focus are the level of a country's exchange rate, the access exporters have to foreign exchange, the level of import duties exporters have to pay on materials and other inputs and government incentives, such as tax relief, to exporters.

Governments interested in increasing nontraditional exports tend to pursue an exchange rate policy that ensures that the country's currency does not become overvalued relative to that of its principal trading partners. In countries that have fixed exchange rates, a typical mechanism for achieving this policy goal is for the country to devalue the currency periodically through a series of mini-devaluations if the country's inflation rate has been higher than that of its trading partners. Such a policy is based on the purchasing power parity model of exchange rate determination discussed in Chapter 4.

While some countries have used mini-devaluations or some other mechanism to ensure that exchange rates move to reflect the changing underlying economic circumstances of a country relative to its trading partners, other developing countries have sought to achieve the same purpose in a manner they view to be more direct; that is, they have allowed their exchange rates to be determined entirely by market forces. A movement to market-based exchange rates has been popular since the mid-1980s, although the initiative for such movements cannot be construed as coming entirely from the developing countries themselves. The Washington-based multilateral institutions, the WB and the IMF, have often insisted that developing countries seeking to adjust their economies through the assistance of their loan programs move to market-based exchange rates.

Another export policy related to foreign exchange is the policy of, in the context of exchange controls, allowing exporters to keep a portion of their foreign exchange receipts. Governments in many developing countries, and indeed governments in some developed countries, have used controls on the holding of foreign exchange by residents of the country as a policy instrument designed to protect the country's foreign exchange position. In most countries that have used such policies, however, it has created unintended consequences. Exporters faced with the prospect of either selling the foreign exchange they earn to national governments often at rates that do not reflect the true value of the foreign exchange or holding their foreign exchange overseas illegally have had little incentive to boost their foreign exchange earnings. The difficulty associated with obtaining foreign exchange in a system that combined, as often happened, exchange controls and exchange rates fixed at levels that overvalued the local currency, led to capital flight. Many of the country's residents would convert local currency to foreign currency illegally and export their capital to foreign financial centers.

Recognizing the problems associated with exchange controls, particularly from the perspective of exporters, several developing countries have gone beyond adjusting exchange control legislation to allow exporters to control the foreign exchange they earn. These countries have completely dismantled exchange controls and liberalized the country's foreign exchange markets. One outcome of this dismantling is that for the first time in these countries, residents of the country can legally maintain foreign exchange accounts in their home countries. Further, financial institutions that attract foreign exchange deposits are in a position to provide foreign exchange loans to exporters.

Other types of export policies seek to allow exporters from a particular country to compete with their counterparts in other countries by allowing them access to inputs at world market prices. To accomplish this, governments in developing countries wishing to increase exports have adopted trade measures in favor of exporters. A principal tool governments have used is the duty drawback program. In this program, exporters that use imported raw materials for which duties were paid are allowed a refund of those duties upon providing the government with evidence that the raw materials have been transformed into products that have been exported. More recently, some developing countries have recognized that duty drawback programs still place upon the exporter a burden of working capital financing and time loss related to negotiating relief under these programs. These countries, therefore, have moved to eliminate duties on raw material and equipment more broadly throughout the economy. The removal of these duties has, of necessity, been a part of a broader trade liberalization program. Were that not the case, of course, the removal of duties on raw materials for firms that produced finished goods for the local market that were themselves highly protected from import competition would simply transfer revenue to these producers, as shown clearly in the discussion of effective protection in Chapter 2.

Another broad area of export policy has sought to provide exporters from developing countries with preferential treatment relative to other firms within the country and possibly relative to the firms' competitors in other countries. This has operated through the mechanism of government financial-incentive programs. Governments provide tax relief to exporters and, in some instances, also provide export subsidies that come in a variety of forms. The more standard government incentive is tax relief. Most developing countries operate export-free zones that allow exporters tax relief, usually comprehensive relief, in perpetuity. Others provide multiyear tax holidays. Other countries operate tax allowance programs that allow exporters outside of the countries' free zones to gain tax relief that is proportional to their export activity.

Tax relief for exporters has become an accepted part of the world's trading system. Governments that seek to provide their exporters with financial subsidies, however, as many seek to do in both developed and developing countries, are likely to run in conflict with the world's trading system. If a government is found guilty of providing financial subsidies to its firms, the products exported by these firms face the prospect of being subject to countervailing duties applied by the government of the importing country. Such countervailing duties are one of the rare retaliatory actions countenanced by the world's trading organization, currently the GATT but soon to become the WTO.

Other export policies are tied closely to investment policies; that is, to the extent that countries are seeking to increase nontraditional exports in particular, export activity is likely to be linked with increases in investment of local and foreign firms. Thus, policies that create a more favorable investment environment are investment policies in the first instance but may well be export policies secondarily. Thus, policies that relate to ownership of investment operations, protection of investment from government expropriation, the proportion of the economy open to foreign investment, and the level and incidence of corporate taxation relative to levels in other countries are export-related policies in countries that anticipate that some significant component of increased exports are likely to be generated by new local or foreign investment.

Other issues that are important to exporters include the simplification of export clearance procedures, the liberalization of export- and import-licensing programs, and improvements in the infrastructure at the ports, both air and sea. Export-assistance organizations in developing countries should realize that the policies outlined have a potentially important influence on the scope of export activity. These organizations should regard the lobbying for an export-friendly policy climate as in important export-assistance function.

Export-Production Assistance

Export-assistance organizations in developing countries are increasingly involved in seeking to assist exporters in improving their productive capabilities. The principal areas of export-production assistance are training of production workers, assistance in quality management, and technical and financial assistance for modernizing productive facilities. Export-assistance organizations in several developing countries hold periodic training sessions for workers in particular industry sectors. These sessions are focused on providing practical information on how workers might improve their productive capabilities. These organizations also conduct training programs on how to improve the quality of the firm's product and how to adhere to quality standards. A popular program in recent times has been the ISO 9000 program, which focuses on adherence to international quality standards.

Some export-assistance organizations also provide technical assistance on facility layout, production techniques, and equipment procurement that is designed to improve the productive performance of the exporting firm. Technical assistance might be sourced by the export agency, from local or foreign sources. In some instances, the export-assistance agency is the conduit through which bilateral technical assistance is extended from the relevant donor agencies to the particular firm.

Critical to increased export performance for many companies in developing countries, however, is the modernization of existing machinery and equipment. For many firms, equipment might have been initially purchased many years ago during a period of emphasis on import substitution. Such equipment might simply be inadequate to the current requirements for effective export performance. Further, some equipment, possibly purchased second-hand, may currently be insufficiently flexible or inadequate in other ways to the requirements of current markets. For various reasons, a change in equipment may be essential to solid export performance. Export-assistance organizations might assist in this regard by managing incentive schemes that provide government assistance to exporters or prospective exporters that opt to modernize their capital equipment. Technical assistance is also provided in the areas of product design.

Notwithstanding a recent increase in the emphasis placed on export-production assistance, because of the heritage of export-assistance organizations in developing countries, the efforts at production assistance continue to be viewed in many countries as secondary to those of marketing assistance.

Export-Marketing Assistance

Export-marketing assistance by export organizations in developing countries takes the form of providing trade information services, analyzing foreign market opportunities, and preparing market and product profiles. The objective of the export-marketing assistance efforts is to find markets for products that are being produced by local firms, to gather market intelligence suggesting what market needs might exist, and to feed that information back to local firms that might be in a position to produce products that satisfy the market needs identified.

The marketing techniques used by these export-assistance organizations include periodic forays into international markets via trade fairs and conferences and more regular efforts at market intelligence gathering through trade representatives located on an ongoing basis in particular market centers. Export-assistance organizations also sponsor trade shows in the local marketplace to which foreign buyers are invited and arrange various seminars to provide exporters with information about changes in international market conditions. Many organizations run trade information centers that represent a repository of information about international markets, product and market trends, and standards and certification requirements in foreign markets.

In addition to the export-production and -marketing assistance functions, developing countries might engage in the registration of exporters, the certification of export products for various bilateral and multilateral market access programs, and the checking of the creditworthiness of foreign buyers. The functions of Jamaica's export-assistance agency, Jamaica Promotions (JAMPRO), identified in Table 13.2, illustrate the range of activities of an export-assistance organization in a developing country.

Company Responses to Government
Export-Assistance Programs

Corporate responses to government export-assistance programs in developed and developing countries have been quite varied. Some companies have clearly benefited from these assistance programs. On the other hand, there are many firms that are not even aware of these programs of assistance. Recognizing this problem, some government agencies have focused on marketing their assistance programs to exporters and prospective exporters. From the perspective of the companies these programs are designed to assist, it clearly is in their best interest to at least be aware of the nature of the assistance governments seek to provide.

Exporters in some developing countries indicate what is possibly a more fundamental problem. They contend that the export assistance provided by governments is not particularly helpful in solving their export needs. The technical assistance provided, for example, may not be useful because technical experts are too theoretical in their approach. Also, export-marketing services are not useful because the market intelligence provided is too general and not specifically related to the firm's own market intelligence needs.

It seems, in fact, that there is an incongruence of expectations and need recognition between government export-assistance programs and exporters.

Table 13.2
Jamaica Promotions' (JAMPRO's) Export Functions

Function	JAMPRO's Activities
Registration	JAMPRO registers all exporters.
Marketing	In order to help exporters locate and penetrate overseas markets, JAMPRO provides market intelligence and assistance with product promotion. The agency also monitors Jamaica's access to markets under preferential schemes, certifies exports and allocates quotas.
Certification	Certificates of origin that are among the requirements of bilateral and multilateral agreements (e.g., the CBI, GSP, CARICOM, CARIBCAN, the Jamaica/United States Textile Agreement and the International Cocoa Agreement) are issued by JAMPRO.
Product Compliance	JAMPRO assists the exporter to comply with international trade agreements and safeguard his exports by - conducting company and product verification. - conducting company audits to identify procedural weaknesses in export security systems. - advising on the installation of appropriate export and security procedures. - expediting release and inspection of legitimate export cargo held by overseas customs.
Credit Checks	JAMPRO arranges investigations on behalf of exporters to ascertain the credibility of overseas consignees.
Training	JAMPRO has an ongoing human resources development program to upgrade standards and skills in various sectors, through preset and customized courses. Areas covered by these courses include - engineering, footwear design, and pattern making; - furniture finishing, export procedures, and international trade practices; - export security compliance procedures, market development; and - managerial and supervisory techniques, safety, production flow, plant layout.
Industry Modernization	Assessment is undertaken and certification provided for manufacturers who participate in the Modernization of Industry Program. Such certification entitles the recipient to reduction of duties or duty exemption and access to technical assistance.
Technical Assistance	For business enterprises, JAMPRO sources assistance from multilateral and bilateral agencies and also provides counterpart staff to help with - in-plant consultancy, advice on production methods, and equipment selection, and - plant design and layout.
Product Design and Packaging	JAMPRO assists with product and packaging design.

With regard to expectations, exporters either appear to expect too little from these programs, thus making little effort to acquaint themselves with the programs, or they expect too much, in which case they lose patience with the programs if they cannot meet all their export needs. On the other hand, government export agencies are rarely as effective as they could be in identifying the critical needs of exporters and creating programs that will address these needs adequately. Often, these organizations are hindered in their attempts to be effective by inadequate funding or an obstructive government bureaucracy and negative government perceptions toward business activity in general. Clearly, there is substantial room for improvement of the government's ability to improve the effectiveness of export-assistance programs.

There is also much scope for exporters to use government assistance programs more effectively. They can do so by entering into active and ongoing discussions with government organizations on their needs in the area of export assistance. They can do so also by recognizing that these needs will not all be met through government programs but that associations of exporters and private initiative toward improving the firm's productive capability and acquiring the necessary marketing intelligence are going to be fundamental to the firm's success. Any assistance provided by government organizations can complement the firm's efforts but is not likely to replace the need for such efforts. Effective exporters will take this factor into consideration as they use existing government export-assistance programs and press for new and more useful programs.

One such program that is gaining in popularity is a program of matching grants to exporters by external funding agencies. These schemes operate from the presumption that technical and marketing advice is most effective if the firm that is to receive the advice identifies appropriate sources. Further, the effectiveness of the advice should be tested in the marketplace. Thus, if a firm is willing to pay a foreign consultant, for example, half of the costs associated with the advice and assistance that is provided, it probably means that the firm is finding this advice to be useful. The program is subsidized initially as a promotional tool to interest firms in using these services. The expectation is that if the services are useful, the firm will be amenable to paying the full costs.

These programs have been successfully introduced in several countries. Proponents of matching grant schemes contend that, often, the activities in which traditional assistance organizations engage are not effective because they are too general and overly concentrate on providing the same service to many players within an industry. Because these programs are often offered at negligible or no cost to the exporting firm, the inadequacy of the programs is not immediately apparent because of the absence of a market test.

Regardless of the particular approach adopted, there is clearly an important role for collaboration between the government and private firms in expanding exports from developing countries. Clearly, export activities generate externalities that cannot be captured by the private firm, so there is an important economic rationale for public-sector support.

Governments and firms that can improve their levels of profitability by moving into export markets have an incentive to work together to identify the most appropriate mechanisms for assistance. Possibly the most significant problem developing countries have discovered in this regard is that dialogue between the government and the private sector is inadequate. In particular, many governments in developing countries do not spend enough time and resources in truly understanding the basis for the competitiveness of the country because, in a manner similar to the multilateral institutions, they operate at too macro a level of analysis. This problem is exacerbated in many developing countries because of a history of, at best, ambivalent, at worst, hostile, relations between governments and private firms.

Export-assistance organizations in several countries have tried to move to a deeper level of sectoral analysis in seeking to understand the needs and constraints of particular firms, and some governments in developing countries are recognizing the critical need to develop closer, more collaborative relations with the private sector. A continued movement in this direction should augur well for improvements in the export-assistance services that are provided.

FURTHER READING

Keesing, Donald B., and Andrew Singer. "Why Official Export Promotion Fails." *Finance and Development* (March 1992): 7–15.
Seringhaus, F. H. Rolf, and Phillip J. Rosson. *Export Development and Promotion: The Role of Public Organizations.* Norwell, Mass.: Kluwer Academic, 1991.

Chapter 14

Managing International Investment

The ability to export systematically to an array of countries represents one indicator of the international competitiveness of a firm or industry in a developing country. The critical importance of exporting activity to international competitiveness is reflected in the focus, in the last few chapters, on the analysis of export activity in developing countries. There remains, however, another important indicator of international competitiveness. This is the ability of firms in developing countries to engage in foreign direct investment activities in other countries. This chapter examines the extent of such activity, the factors that explain its existence and success, and techniques that firms in developing countries can use in their efforts to expand their foreign direct investment activities.

FOREIGN DIRECT INVESTMENT
BY DEVELOPING-COUNTRY FIRMS

The reader familiar with the foreign direct investment activities of firms from developed countries is likely to wonder how pervasive is the phenomenon of firms in developing countries, the so-called third-world multinationals, investing directly in other countries. A 1993 study by the Program on Transnational Corporations in the UNCTAD estimated, in response to that question, that foreign investors from developing countries controlled US$110 billion in foreign direct investment in 1990. This represented 8 percent of the global stock of foreign direct investment. The report suggests that Hong Kong invests more abroad than developed countries such as Belgium, Denmark, and Norway and that Taiwan and Korea invested more in foreign countries than foreign firms invested in their countries. Other developing countries whose firms have been actively involved in foreign direct investment activities are Singapore, China, Argentina, Brazil, Colombia, India, Mexico, Pakistan, and Venezuela. Even Jamaica, a country not known for spawning international investors, has seen some increase in investment activities in recent years with the country's two principal indigenous hotel chains extending their operations to other countries in the Caribbean region and with companies from the country's financial sector establishing branches in North America and the United Kingdom.

Much of the foreign direct investment activity from firms in developing countries has occurred quite recently, but the phenomenon of firms from developing countries investing overseas has a rather long history. Indeed, there are examples of firms from Argentina engaging in foreign direct investment activities in the nineteenth century and the early twentieth century, although, during this period, Argentina was, relatively speaking, a developed country or on the verge of being so considered. Firms from Hong Kong have also had a long history of international activity. The origins of Indian foreign direct investment can be traced to 1960. By the early 1980s, Louis T. Wells, Jr., estimated that the stock of foreign direct investment by firms from developing countries was $5 billion to $10 billion in 1980 in the form of some 6,000 to 8,000 subsidiaries and predicted that the fact that so many investments had appeared in such a short time suggested that the overall numbers were likely to be impressive in a few years. This is a prescient statement, to be sure, given the increase to a stock of $110 billion in only a decade—a significant increase even when one considers that the increase is measured in nominal dollars.

Historically, much of the foreign direct investment by firms from developing countries has been of the South–South variety; that is, its destination has been other developing countries. In the Wells study, more than 65 percent of the subsidiaries identified were in countries with less value added in manufacturing in absolute terms than prevailed in the country that hosted the parent company. Similarly, most recipient countries were poorer than the capital-exporting countries as measured by per capita income levels. The only significant exception was India, whose per capita income level significantly understates the strength and size of that country's industrial sector.

This trend, however, has changed somewhat since the Wells study. As indicated in Table 14.1, the UNCTAD study estimates that in 1990, half of the investments from firms based in developing countries are now destined for developed countries.

As indicated in Table 14.1, of the $110-billion investment stock in 1990, $26.7 billion (24.3 percent) was located in the United States; $7 billion (6.3 percent) was located in the Netherlands; $6.5 billion (5.9 percent) was located in the United Kingdom; and $10.6 billion (9.6 percent) was approximately split among the developed countries of Australia, France, and Germany. These six developed countries comprised 46 percent of the total stock of foreign direct investment controlled by firms from developing countries. The largest

Table 14.1
Largest Recipients of Foreign Direct Investment from Developing Countries

Country	Stock of Developing-Country Foreign Direct Investment (U.S.$ Billions, 1990)
United States	26.7
Indonesia	11.7
China	10.0
The Netherlands	7.0
The United Kingdom	6.5
Australia	3.9
France	3.7
Germany	3.0

Source: United Nations, *Transnational Corporations from Developing Countries: Impact on Their Home Countries* (Geneva: United Nations, 1993).

developing country recipients of investment by firms from other developing countries were Indonesia, with a stock of $11.7 billion (10.6 percent of the overall stock), and China, with $10 billion (9 percent of the overall investment stock) of foreign direct investment. This shift in the destinations of foreign direct investments by third-world multinationals is likely to be linked to the factors that lead to the emergence of this form of economic activity.

FACTORS THAT EXPLAIN FOREIGN DIRECT INVESTMENT FROM DEVELOPING-COUNTRY FIRMS

The starting point for explaining the incidence of foreign direct investment by firms from developing countries is identical to that which explains the incidence of foreign direct investment generally. Third-world multinationals engage in foreign direct investment, like their counterparts in developed countries, because they have an ownership advantage(s) and because they choose to exploit that ownership advantage through transactions within the organizational hierarchy of the firm rather than through market transactions. The firm internalizes the cross-border market for its advantages by engaging in foreign direct investment rather than using market mechanisms such as licensing or trade to exploit its advantages. In engaging in foreign direct investment activities, these firms will choose countries that provide particular locational advantages. The reader finding it necessary to refresh himself or herself on the factors that explain foreign direct investment generally is referred to Chapter 8.

The principal differences between third-world multinationals and their counterparts from developed countries lie in differences in the nature of their respective competitive advantages. In essence, third-world multinationals are only likely to succeed in their foreign direct investment operations if they have competitive advantages relative to the advantages of the local firms in the countries to which they direct their investments and competitive advantages relative to multinationals from developed countries. Since multinationals from developed countries possess "first-mover" advantages with respect to international investment activities, to compete successfully, third-world multinationals may have to be capable of displacing these firms in some instances. In others, they may engage in niche strategies or strategies of differentiation that do not involve head-to-head competition.

Wells indicates the types of competitive advantages multinationals from developing countries are likely to possess. These include small-scale manufacturing capabilities, local procurement as a special competitive weapon, price as a competitive weapon, and the exploitation of ethnic markets. In addition to these differences, third-world multinationals also, like their counterparts in developed countries, might concentrate on seeking lower-cost production locations. A locational advantage that is quite prominent in the location decisions of some third-world multinationals has surrounded the issue of whether the prospective investment location has underutilized quota capacity in industries such as textiles, garments, and footwear.

Small-Scale Manufacturing Prowess

In many developing countries, the market for many manufactured goods is quite small. Consequently, the firms that have engaged in manufacturing activities in these countries have developed the capability of designing facilities and production processes to cater to the small size of the market. This is particularly true in cases where the firm has honed its productive capabilities initially in the domestic marketplace. Consequently, this capability represents a competitive advantage vis-à-vis suppliers from developed countries when these countries seek to enter the markets of other developing countries. Firms in these other developing countries usually cannot simply import en bloc the manufacturing processes used in developed countries. Such processes are likely to have been developed to support much larger production runs. They do not, therefore, travel well to developing countries with significantly smaller markets.

The typical entrepreneur in a developing country will have initially obtained technology from foreign sources. These entrepreneurs obtain a competitive advantage in technology based on small-scale manufacturing by adapting the technology they have acquired from abroad to the imperatives of small-scale manufacturing. The Wells study, for example, reports that of fifty-two Indian parent companies interviewed, forty-two indicated that they initially received their technology from a foreign company, but forty-seven also indicated that in excess of half of their technology was indigenous by the late 1970s. An Indian firm that processed edible oil indicated, for example, that it had purchased processing equipment from the United States in 1917 but that by 1976 it was using entirely Indian equipment that had been adjusted to be compatible with Indian conditions. It is this indigenized equipment that usually is transferred to other developing countries. Such equipment responds to the needs in these other developing countries in a manner that a supplier from a developed country would have a great deal of difficulty matching.

The extent of the competitive advantage is related to the manner in which these firms reduce the scale of the manufacturing process. In circumstances in which the primary unit of production is a single item of equipment such as a sewing machine or a loom, then there is little innovation involved in reducing the scale of a plant. One simply uses fewer units of production. Such types of reduction create little in the way of competitive advantage. In other situations, however, the degree of adaptation is greater as the developing country firm changes the nature of the production process entirely. Changes could occur from a capital-intensive process to a more labor-intensive process or from a relatively inflexible type of production equipment to a more flexible form of equipment. These latter forms of adaptation provide more in the form of a competitive advantage to the manufacturer.

Although this ability to adapt production processes to small-scale manufacturing capabilities represents a competitive advantage when third-world multinationals invest in developing countries to manufacture goods oriented to the markets of these countries, one should also recognize the disadvantages associated with this competence. The principal disadvantage is that, as pointed out in Chapter 11, processes oriented toward small-scale manufacturing are not likely to serve a firm well when it shifts to export production in the large volumes of relatively standardized products that is typical of the export activities of developing countries.

Local Procurement and Special Products

The special conditions of the marketplace of developing countries create other advantages in international direct investment for the firms that they spawn. Given the conditions of scarcity that apply in these countries and the foreign exchange shortages that have characterized the markets of these countries, the firms from these countries have innovated by developing production processes that conserve on scarce materials and make maximum use of indigenous materials. As these firms move to other developing countries with similar constraints, conditions of scarcity, and foreign exchange shortages, their ability to introduce production processes that respond to the developing country environment provide for them a competitive advantage vis-à-vis firms from developed countries. Third-world multinationals are likely to import less than their counterparts from developed countries.

Another form of advantage that accrues to firms from certain developing countries is the ability to engage in foreign direct investment projects that serve the needs of ethnic groups well understood by firms from the developing country. These "ethnic investments" are an extension of the "ethnic markets" that many developing country exporters seek to exploit. Indian firms cater to the needs of the Indian diaspora; Hong Kong, Singaporean, and Taiwanese firms to the overseas Chinese communities; and Jamaican firms to the pockets of Jamaicans scattered throughout the United Kingdom and North America.

Portfolio Diversification

A long-standing economic rationale for foreign direct investment is the desire of firms to diversify their markets. According to this argument, firms invest in other countries to eliminate the risks associated with concentrating their investments in one particular country. Given the fact that the investment climates of many developing countries are quite unstable, in both economic and political terms, the notion of investment to diversify risks cannot be ignored in the context of these countries. Foreign direct investment in order to diversify investment risks may be the most important factor in explaining the recent investments by Jamaican hoteliers in hotel establishments in other sections of the Caribbean.

Low-Cost Production Capabilities

A principal competitive advantage that third-world multinationals are able to exploit is their ability to produce goods at prices that are cheaper than those of their competitors from developed countries. The basis of this competitive cost advantage emanates from various sources. It results from the adaptive production processes described earlier. Often, since the production processes are more labor intensive than the processes used by their competitors that were not adapted to local environments, production costs are lowered by reduced labor costs. It also relates to the lower overhead costs with which these firms are able to operate. Overheads are lower because these third-world multinationals tend to be quite lean in their staffing structure and because their expatriate employees, usually a significant element of cost for foreign subsidiaries, are paid at much lower rates than the rates that apply to expatriates from developed countries.

Access to Markets and Skills

Firms from developing countries are often able to combine their low-cost production capabilities with access to export markets that they have developed in their export operations at home. This combination provides them with a formidable competitive advantage as they move investment to other countries. They may well seek to invest in countries with lower-cost production inputs than those that prevail in their own countries, but they are able to compete with other producers from that lower-cost country because of production capabilities and access to markets they have refined in their home operations. Similar to multinationals from developed countries, third-world multinationals from countries such as Korea, Taiwan, and Singapore have moved to lower-cost countries as the costs of production in their home countries has increased. Firms from these countries have all developed access to multiple markets.

In the 1970s and 1980s, a component of the investment of third-world multinationals has been investment that might be characterized as "quota hopping." Firms from Korea, China, and Hong Kong moved their investment operations to other developing countries in regions such as the Caribbean and Asia that had underutilized quotas in sectors such as textiles and garments. That is, under the multifiber agreement, countries such as the United States have allocated set amounts or quotas of specific goods that specific countries can export to the allocating country. When the national quotas in China, Korea, Hong Kong, and Taiwan became fully utilized, their firms moved operations to other countries whose quotas were not fully utilized. Much of the increase in garment and textile exporting in countries like Mauritius in the 1970s could be traced to the foreign investment operations of firms from Hong Kong. Similarly, a significant proportion of the textile industry in Jamaica traces its origins to the activities of Korean firms that moved to Jamaica in the 1980s, largely in a "quota-hopping" exercise.

While some third-world multinationals invest in a country to provide access to a market through underutilized quotas, others will invest directly in the markets in which they seek to gain access. This phenomenon of investing in order to gain market access best explains the increase in investment by third-world multinationals in the markets of developed countries. Recall that during the decade of the 1980s, the proportion of the investment of third-world multinationals that went to developed countries increased from about one-third of the total investment of these companies to closer to one-half of this investment.

Investment in these developed countries did not result primarily from a search for lower-cost production sites, nor does it relate to a competitive advantage in small-scale manufacturing or the ability to adopt production processes to the constraints of the typical developing country economic environment. Rather, these investments can be best explained as the efforts of these firms to gain access to the entire markets in these countries or the ethnic markets in these countries. These are the firms that have moved to another stage of value added in the Wortzel and Wortzel marketing framework discussed in Chapter 11. In some cases, access to skills are as important a motivator as access to markets. Firms may be interested in particular forms of technology or particular reservoirs of human, technical, or design skills, for example, that are found in particular developed countries.

MANAGING INTERNATIONAL INVESTMENT

Foreign direct investment by firms from developing countries, while once a rare activity, has lost its novelty because of the frequency with which it occurs. It remains, however, a very important economic phenomenon. It indicates a degree of competitiveness on the part of the investor not normally associated with firms in developing countries. It further provides broader benefits to the home country in the form of technology acquisition and the possibility of eventual diffusion, long-run foreign exchange earnings, and balance-of-payments support.

The study by the United Nations suggests that investing abroad has pushed firms from developing countries to restructure and rationalize their operations. In some cases, the study reports, domestic profitability has increased because of greater vertical or horizontal integration, portfolio diversification, the ability to spread fixed costs, and reductions in tax liabilities. Further, from the perspective of the home country, foreign investments have stimulated rather than displaced exports. This stimulation occurs through different mechanisms. One mechanism, however, is the linkages that are created between these investors and exporters in the developing countries. Recall that access to markets is a critical hurdle that needs to be overcome in the development of export markets. Foreign direct investment in the desired market by affiliates of the exporter certainly has the potential to assist in this process of gaining access to markets.

Further, some component of foreign direct investment by developing countries represents the establishment of a sales presence in the export market that directly facilitates exports. A furniture company from the Caribbean producing antique reproduction furniture for the U.S. market, for example, might invest in the United States by establishing a showroom for the display of its furniture. Although not a significant investment, this certainly represents a form of foreign direct investment.

Given these benefits associated with foreign direct investment from developing countries, such investment activities should be a goal of firms and be encouraged by the governments of developing countries.

The Perspective of the Firm

The exhortation that firms from developing countries ought to consider exporting as a process that can significantly increase the profitability of these firms can be repeated with equal intensity when the subject shifts to foreign direct investment. Firms from developing countries that engage in foreign direct investment are not only able to provide an indication of their competitiveness by so doing but also—and possibly more important—are able to improve competitiveness through the act of investment.

Improvements in competitiveness may take different forms. In some instances, they will come from the access to lower-cost inputs into the production process. In others, they will come from the benefits the firm gains from the access to foreign markets or to more demanding consumers in foreign locations. Further, improvements in competitiveness could come through the reduction of corporate risk associated with diversification of investment across various locations.

From the latter perspective, for example, Jamaican hoteliers Gordon Stewart and John Issa, by investing in hotel facilities outside of their home base, have reduced their companies' exposure to the political and economic vagaries of the Jamaican marketplace. Further, this diversification enables these companies to broaden their markets. When marketing their companies in the world's tourism markets, they can propose to serve the needs of the customer who is interested in a Caribbean vacation but is indecisive about the particular country in which to take that vacation. The tourism industry in the various countries of the Caribbean expect some diversion of tourism from the currently popular islands of the Caribbean, Barbados, Jamaica, Bahamas, Cayman, and the islands of the Eastern Caribbean to Cuba if and when Cuba normalizes relations with the United States. While such a diversion represents a concern to most of the hoteliers of the region, because John Issa's Superclubs chain has invested in Cuba this issue is of much less concern to that hotel chain.

In order to gain these benefits, however, firms must engage in the relatively difficult task of foreign direct investment. This typically requires a commitment of resources, including financial resources and management time, that can be quite significant. The extent of the commitment required suggests the need for a carefully planned and managed approach to foreign direct investment. Similar to the manner in which firms from developed countries have internationalized, it is perhaps appropriate to adopt a staged, sequential approach that begins the expansion process in neighboring countries in order to utilize the firms' scarce financial and managerial resources in the best way possible.

In addition, the process of gaining the benefits desired from the foreign direct investment process also requires structured management. In order to acquire needed technologies or better understand markets, firms will need to engage in active strategies designed to achieve these goals even after a process of foreign direct investment has begun. The benefits to be gained from foreign direct investment will not be obtained entirely by osmosis. Firms need to be aware of the principal goals of their foreign direct investment efforts and keep their attention focused on how these goals can be achieved once the basic structure of a foreign direct investment operation has been put in place.

The Perspective of the Home Government

In Chapter 8, in the context of the discussion of foreign direct investment, I focused on the perspective of host governments in developing countries, and the desirability of foreign direct investment from their perspective. In the context of third-world multinationals, we can engage in an interesting shift in perspective to that of developing country governments as home governments for foreign direct investment.

In fact, in the past, the governments of developing countries have not tended to view foreign direct investment activities of the firms in their countries very favorably. The prevailing perspective in many countries was that capital was very scarce; the country needed capital for its development; and so, therefore, it should not allow its firms to dissipate the country's scarce supply of capital by engaging in quixotic capital-spending adventures in foreign countries. The capital controls established by many governments in developing countries, and by Japan for several decades after World War II, were designed, among other things, to thwart the efforts of firms to export capital. Part of the concern, to be sure, was that domestic entrepreneurs might export capital to foreign banks rather than in the form of foreign direct investment. In countries such as Korea and India, however, foreign direct investment was also specifically frowned upon by home governments.

In general, there has been a change in the attitudes of governments in this regard. Most countries recognize today that the constraint on development is less a capital constraint than it is a constraint of ideas, of opportunity identification, of technology, and of market access. These areas are some of the very ones in which there can be direct benefits associated with outward (as well as inward) foreign direct investment. There are also other benefits that resonate deeply with home country governments in the more open trade and investment environment that describes the world of the 1990s. As mentioned earlier, for example, foreign direct investment can expand rather than displace exports. It is rare that a developing country is not interested in increasing its exports. These are benefits that foreign investors from developed countries have long been contributing to their home economies.

Given these prospective benefits, home country governments should be promoting foreign direct investment by the firms based in their countries rather than restricting this activity. In many respects, the requirements for such a process are similar to the processes in which governments need to engage in order to build internationally competitive firms, where competitiveness is evidenced by export activity rather than by international investment. They need to promote national education and infrastructure development, develop sound educational systems that have a strong focus on science and technology, create a country with stable economic and political policies, and allow organizations to be externally focused through their trade, currency, and technology policies.

FURTHER READING

United Nations. *Transnational Corporations from Developing Countries: Impact on Their Home Countries.* Geneva: United Nations, 1993.

Wells, Louis T., Jr. *Third World Multinationals: The Rise of Foreign Direct Investment from Developing Countries.* Cambridge: MIT Press, 1983.

Chapter 15

Prospects for Development
via International Business

The fundamental focus of this book has been the relationship between international business and development. This focus reflects the concern with development that permeates all aspects of the environment of the world's developing countries. The theme that permeates the book is that a principal, if not *the* principal, contributor to development is the international business activities of firms and individuals within the society. This is not by any means to suggest that development relates only to international business activities. Clearly, the social, political, and economic characteristics of a country provide an important foundation upon which international business activities can build; and managers in developing countries need also to assist in the building of this foundation. Indeed, one might argue that while social, political, and economic stability are necessary conditions for competitive success and development, the development of a range of internationally competitive industries is a sufficient condition for national competitiveness. Clearly, no country will find that all of its industries are competitive by international standards; but the more of such industries a country can boast, the more competitive the entire country is and the higher the level of development.

Yet managers in many developing countries have fundamental concerns, many of which have been identified throughout the book, about their ability to spawn internationally competitive industries. In examining the prospects for development via international business, it is useful to revisit some of these concerns, particularly in the context of an examination of factors that lead to the creation of internationally competitive industries and firms.

CREATING COMPETITIVE INDUSTRIES

The traditional perspective on the factors that spawned competitive industries within countries placed the primary focus on a country's endowments of resources in the form of the factors of production of labor, land, and capital. The Heckscher–Ohlin extension to the Ricardian theory of comparative advantage discussed in Chapter 2 focused on these resources as the critical components that identified the industries in which countries would have a comparative advantage; that is, these were the industries in which a country would be internationally competitive.

The discussion in Chapter 2, however, also pointed out that, increasingly, efforts to understand the industries in which a country would be competitive have meant adding to a natural resource explanation for the creation and expansion of competitive industries a broader group of variables. These variables have an important impact on the determination of which industries are likely to be competitive and over what period.

To a large extent, studies that found a role for factors other than a country's resource endowments in explaining the set of competitive industries in a country trace their intellectual origin to Vernon's product cycle study of 1966. That study, discussed in Chapters 2 and 8, found a role for home-country demand patterns in determining the industries in which a country would be competitive. It also introduced the notion of dynamism to studies of industry competitiveness; that is, a country does not inherit a set of competitive industries based on its resource endowments and then relax with the knowledge that it will always host these industries. Rather, competitive industries could be and often were created through timely innovations. These creations, however, can prove fickle; and these same industries are likely, at some point, to migrate to other countries.

Porter's study on the competitiveness of nations continued this tradition by indicating the factors likely to be important in determining the international competitiveness of a nation's industries and thus, by extension, the competitiveness of the nation. He identified a set of principal variables—factor conditions, demand conditions, firm strategy, structure and rivalry, and related and supporting industries—and a set of secondary variables—the role of government and the role of chance.

In developing the variables that appeared to have the most significant impact on whether a country was able to spawn competitive industries and identifying which particular industries might be generated in particular countries, Porter identified the critical role of resource endowments (factor conditions) as embodied in classical trade theories. He also focused on the importance of home-country demand patterns as outlined in the work of Vernon (demand conditions).

To these two sets of characteristics, Porter added another two primary determinants of national competitiveness. In the tradition of classical economists with their emphasis on the importance of competition in generating efficient economic activity, Porter emphasized the importance of rivalry among firms. He posited that a country was likely to be host to a competitive industry where competitive rivalry among the domestic participants in that industry was particularly intense. He suggested further that where an industry could draw upon the resources of other competitive industries that together formed a cluster, the industry and other related industries in that cluster of industries would be better able to compete internationally.

In addition to these four primary determinants of national competitiveness, Porter added two secondary determinants. He suggested that there was an important role for government but that this role was to influence the four primary determinants and that the role of government should not, of itself, be considered a determinant. Last, for completeness, Porter suggested that some countries were simply lucky in their development of competitive industries. Thus, he suggested a role for chance in determining national competitiveness.

CREATING COMPETITIVE INDUSTRIES
IN DEVELOPING COUNTRIES

These studies that place significant emphasis on the nature of the home market and industry structure in creating competitive industries might be viewed, from the perspective of the world's developing countries, as providing hope while creating despair. They provide hope in the sense that they emphasize the notion that a country born with few competitive industries, which is the case in most developing countries, has the possibility of adding to its portfolio of such industries over time. At the same time, they exude despair because the conditions they delineate as important to the creation of competitive industries do not, in large part, exist in many developing countries.

These conditions typically involve firms honing their skills while they produce products particularly oriented to the needs of a home market comprised of sophisticated consumers. Once they have been able to satisfy these consumers, they are well positioned to extend their operations to segments of consumers with similar needs in other countries. A related condition is that firms are able to hone their skills while producing products for large domestic markets. In producing for these large domestic markets, their expertise expands over time and with increases in the volume of goods produced. This gradually evolving expertise provides these first-mover firms with a competitive advantage over follower companies, including those from other countries.

For most developing countries, the notion of large markets comprised of sophisticated consumers demanding and willing to buy state-of-the-art or innovative products is a very alien condition. The markets of these countries tend to be small in terms of the number of consumers that can effectively demand products, that is, can add to an interest in a good the wherewithal to purchase that good. This is clearly true of small developing countries, but it is also true of some of the relatively large countries.

This is not to suggest that there are no exceptions to this general observation. The Brazilian company, Embraer, for example, was able to spearhead the development of a small-aircraft industry in Brazil in part because of the demand characteristics of the Brazilian environment. As a physically large country with a very rugged terrain that had led to an underdeveloped surface transportation network, Brazil placed significant emphasis on the use of small aircraft. Early in Embraer's history, guaranteed purchases from the Brazilian military provided a market that allowed the company to hone its expertise in its home environment. Embraer went on to develop models that were successfully sold in the United States, but Embraer's experience was an exception rather than the rule. The Embraer route is not the route most developing countries have traveled in creating competitive industries.

For the majority of developing countries, competitive industries have arisen almost exclusively from the natural endowments of those countries, whether in terms of climatic conditions in industries such as agriculture or tourism, or low-cost factors of production, primarily labor, in industries such as textiles, footwear, electronic assembly, and data conversion. Indeed, the developing countries have developed competitive industries in a manner very much in keeping with the implications of the Heckscher–Ohlin extension of comparative advantage trade theory and the industry migration effects of Vernon's product cycle theory. Even India's booming software industry fits a resource-based, rather than a home-market based, notion of industry competitiveness with that country's plentiful supply of trained but low-cost software programmers.

Indeed, the developing countries are not concerned so much about how they develop competitive industries as long as they are, in fact, able to develop these industries. The history of national competitiveness has demonstrated quite clearly that countries can improve their competitiveness over time (and also that countries can lose their competitiveness over time as the example of Argentina, among others, demonstrates quite clearly). The task then is for these countries to advance over time, adding additional competitive industries to their arsenals of competitive industries and upgrading the sources of competitive advantage upon which these industries rely.

In so doing, developing countries will be likely to go through stages. These stages take their starting point, however, with the development of competitive industries based upon the country's resource base, including the important resource of skilled labor. Porter's work addresses this issue of the stages countries are likely to go through in pursuit of the widest array of competitive industries based on increasingly more sustainable forms of competitive advantage.

As indicated in Table 15.1, Porter identifies four stages of national development through which countries may pass: factor driven, investment driven, innovation driven, and wealth driven.

Table 15.1
Stages of National Development

Stages	Characteristics
Factor driven	Based on natural resource endowments
Investment driven	Based on firms investing in state-of-the-art facilities
Innovation driven	Based on creation of new products
Wealth driven	Based on prior investments or prior innovation

Source: Adapted from Michael Porter, *The Competitive Advantage of Nations* (New York: Free Press, 1990), p. 546.

The factor-driven stage is one in which competitive firms and industries derive their competitive advantage from the country's endowments of resources. Firms operating in such countries export primarily standardized products. This stage of national development corresponds to the initial stages of export marketing described in Chapter 11. Countries in the investment-driven stage have established a set of firms that are willing and able to invest aggressively in the development of modern, efficient facilities with the best available process technology. Firms in the innovation-driven stage compete by creating new products and processes based on their resources of highly skilled and creative workers but also in response to the demands of highly sophisticated consumers. Competitive industries in this stage would draw their competitive advantage from all the sources of competitive advantage identified by Porter and other analysts. Last, in the wealth-driven stage, a country's competitive industries draw their competitiveness from prior investments and innovation. Firms in such countries rest upon their first-mover advantages but have lost the urge or ability to innovate in new areas. This stage has the potential of leading countries to ultimate decline unless the movement in this direction is arrested and countries are able to return to the innovation-driven stage of national development.

Most developing countries operate at varying points in the factor-driven stage. A few have moved from the factor-driven stage to the investment-driven stage. Those countries that have moved (e.g., Korea) gained the momentum for moving from their success in the factor-driven stage.

Korean companies, like the large conglomerate Daewoo, provide a firm-based example of how the entire Korean economy has moved from factor-driven to investment-driven sources of competitive advantage, with a corresponding expansion in the types of activities in which the company engages. Daewoo began its international life as an exporter of textiles and garments. In 1967, 100 percent of the company's exports comprised textile and garment exporters. By 1985, however, textile and garment exports constituted about 16 percent of total exports. By that time, Daewoo had become a well-known producer of ships, automobiles, rolling stock, and machinery—and even an installer of telephone lines. In the early 1990s, Daewoo's car imports were not at the level of its local competitor, Hyundai; but the company was exporting cars, primarily to developing countries around the world.

The immediate task for most developing countries, then, is to become internationally competitive, based on the country's resources, including skilled labor, in an array of industries. Once that goal has been achieved, these countries can seek to move to more advanced stages, where competitiveness is based on more durable advantages than low-cost factors of production. These countries, particularly the smaller ones, might also be able to move immediately to niche markets in which they can produce specialty products that have a competitive position built not on low costs but on the existence of unique, differentiated products.

IMPEDIMENTS TO THE CREATION OF COMPETITIVE INDUSTRIES

In moving in the direction of expanding their portfolio of competitive industries, and indeed in preserving the competitiveness of existing industries that have done well internationally, developing countries contend that they face many impediments and that these impediments retard their development prospects.

Access to International Markets

In order for firms in developing countries to take advantage of their competitive abilities, they need to have unimpeded access to the markets of other countries. In today's world, companies will receive no such guarantees. Protectionism, for example, as examined broadly in Chapter 3 and more narrowly in Chapter 11 in the context of problems faced by companies seeking to enter export markets, will continue to make more difficult the efforts of firms in developing countries to expand into developed country markets.

Here, it is important to note that developed countries have been largely unwilling to engage in the transition from one set of industries to another as the competitive imperatives within that industry change. Thus, an industry such as textiles in which firms in developing countries have a significant cost advantage relative to their counterparts in developed countries has seen the institutionalization of protection in order to shield producers in developed countries from their more cost-efficient counterparts elsewhere. Protectionism has been similarly rampant in agriculture sectors in the developed countries of North America, Europe, and Japan.

Developed countries have not been the only countries engaged in protectionist policies. Developing countries have also been extremely resistant to providing other developing countries with unimpeded access to their markets. The discussions have focused on the developed countries because of the significance of the developed country market.

For developing countries that are poised to become a part of one of the major trading blocs that are being spawned in different parts of the world, the problem of markets made inaccessible by government policy should largely disappear. Very few developing countries, however, are thus poised. Mexico is the first developing country to have obtained a secure position in a trading bloc. There may soon be similar opportunities for Chile and possibly Turkey prior to the end of the century. Other countries in Latin America and the Caribbean have indicated a desire for membership in NAFTA; and many Eastern European, Middle Eastern, and North African countries have been knocking on the door of the EU. It is hard to be as sanguine about the prospects for inclusion of these other countries, based on the dilemma of difference discussed in Chapter 4.

Beyond awaiting a more liberal trade climate in which trade barriers are eliminated, developing countries can only find relief in the fact that the protectionism of most developed countries did not stall the export thrust of the NICs in the 1970s and 1980s. As reported in Chapter 11, these countries found innovative solutions to the problems of protectionism.

There are, of course, significant implications to developing countries of the movement to a more liberal trade climate and to accession to major trading blocs. A more liberal trading climate and entry into major trading blocs that involve developed and developing countries is increasingly going to occur only on the basis of reciprocal trade concessions. Thus, developing countries will also be unable to protect their own industries, increasingly including their service industries.

Trends in Foreign Direct Investment

Even where countries do not impose barriers to imports from developing countries, there is still a concern that firms from developing countries will find it difficult to gain access to the markets of developed countries because they lack institutional linkages with those markets. One of the institutions that has been viewed as valuable in creating those linkages is the multinational firm. These firms, so the argument goes, can help the exports of developing countries gain access to distribution channels in developed countries. In light of this benefit, there are those in developing countries who express concern at the reduction in the flows of foreign direct investment destined for developing countries.

It is indeed true that, apart from a blip in the late 1980s and early 1990s associated with privatization, the trend shows declining flows of foreign direct investment to developing countries. This does not, however, represent as strong an impediment to the creation of competitive firms as it might appear at first glance. Clearly, more foreign direct investment designed to use developing countries as an export platform would assist these countries in their bid to develop international competitive industries, particularly if the skills of the foreign investor can be captured throughout the wider economy. The reality, however, is that the bulk of foreign direct investment in past years was not of that form. Rather, it was investment to serve domestic markets. In engaging in such investments, particularly where they were established behind high tariff walls, foreign investors were never major contributors to the international competitiveness of the countries that were their hosts. The loss of such investment does not, therefore, necessarily have a detrimental impact on national competitiveness.

What is true, on the other hand, is that developing countries in this new investment climate cannot look to foreign investors to provide the engine of growth for their economies. Virtually every developing country is wooing foreign investors. Thus, the demand for export-oriented foreign direct investment far exceeds the supply of this investment. Singapore, in particular, gained first-mover advantages by being the first developing country to attract export-oriented foreign investment. This country has reaped significant fruits from its boldness. A boldness that, among other things, involved guaranteeing a return for investors on their commercial operations. Other developing countries will find it difficult to replicate that strategy.

The Nonresponsiveness of the World Financial Community

Many in developing countries have bemoaned the lack of understanding of the world's financial community and its monetary systems. The lack of responsiveness of these institutions is viewed by many in the South to be an impediment to the development of the developing countries. The efforts at creating a new international economic order came directly out of the view that the current world financial order was stacked against the developing countries. The criticisms of the IMF, and increasingly of the WB with its structural adjustment policies, is another manifestation of the view that the world's major multilateral institutions are unconcerned about the plight of the developing countries.

The response of the multilateral institutions would be that they have actually assisted countries in embarking down the path of enhanced competitiveness with the structural reforms they have insisted upon as a condition of their loans and that, although these prescriptions may have had a bitter taste, their medicinal effects are now working, as evidenced by the extent to which many countries are now prescribing the same medicine for themselves outside of the context of loan programs. The experience of several Latin American countries, most notably Mexico, and even some countries in sub-Saharan Africa would be presented as evidence of the wisdom of eliminating budget deficits, reducing inflation, privatizing inefficient state industries, allowing local farmers to get market prices for their produce, and so forth.

Ultimately, however, the multilateral agencies and the bilateral aid organizations also must be accountable to the countries that provide the funding or that own their shares. In a competitive arena in which developing countries are pitted against developed countries, the developing countries can expect a degree of nonresponsiveness at times. This was aptly demonstrated in the significant reductions in the U.S. Agency for International Development (AID) financing of investment-promotion activities in Central American countries after a television program in the United States suggested that the agency was assisting developing countries in their efforts to lure U.S. investors to their countries. The U.S. population asked why U.S. taxpayers should contribute to what may eventually be job losses within the United States. Developing countries might respond by saying that such an activity could well lead to enhanced productivity within the United States as U.S. workers make a transition toward jobs requiring greater skills. They would be likely, however, to encounter a nonresponsive organization.

The Limitations of South–South Economic Integration

As the efforts to create an NIEO floundered, developing countries placed much hope on the possibilities of development via South–South economic integration. The individual markets of developing countries might be too small for efforts at self-sufficiency or the scale required for production for export markets, but the combined markets of several countries might allow for efficient production.

The limitations of these efforts became readily apparent, however, since neighboring developing country economies basing their competitive activities on resource endowments have found that they have similar economies, whose products substitute for each other—this in contrast to the more appropriate base for economic integration efforts, that is, economies that produce a broad range of dissimilar products and are complementary to each other. Thus, the integration efforts of developing countries are unlikely to allow for self-sufficiency with any more effectiveness than the efforts of an individual economy to seek such self-sufficiency. This is especially true of the groupings of particularly small countries such as that of the Caribbean countries of CARICOM.

The Limitations of National Government Policy

Managers of private firms in many developing countries would regard the most significant impediment to the country's attempts at national competitiveness to be inept government policy. There is, to begin with, a major controversy on the appropriate role for government in developing competitive industries within a country. Porter argues for a supportive but unobtrusive role for government that involves creating the requisite infrastructure and enforcing competition while avoiding the temptation to engage in intrusive efforts at subsidizing particular industries. The work of strategic trade theorists, albeit in a limited number of special cases, sees the possibility of governments influencing which industries the country gains a competitive position in through subsidy and incentive policies that help firms gain a first-mover advantage relative to their rivals elsewhere.

For developing countries, there are two general areas of potential government involvement. The first involves creating a climate that is conducive to productive economic activity. This is largely ignored in studies of developed countries or of the more successful developing countries because this role is taken for granted. In concluding, for example, that the role of government was secondary, Porter based this conclusion on the situation that prevailed in the countries that he studied; but he studied the following ten countries: Denmark, Germany, Italy, Japan, Korea, Singapore, Sweden, Switzerland, the United Kingdom, and the United States.

For countries that have not reached the level of development of these ten countries, the role of government is likely to be much more fundamental. It seems reasonable, for example, to expect that a government will not allow inflation rates of 2,000 percent per annum. These expectations are not always met. Inflation rates at that level were seen in several Latin American countries during the 1980s. In such a situation, the role of government in solving the inflation problem is the most important factor in putting the country on a path that may lead to development. Many governments in developing countries enact policies that lend no economic, social, or political stability to the country. Stability of this type is a necessary prerequisite to the vibrant economic activity that is associated with the development of internationally competitive industries.

Once such stability is achieved, there still remain other roles for government. In pursuing these roles, governments should focus on activities that are socially beneficial but in which profits are not easily captured by a private firm. There are many critical areas of a society, from infrastructure to primary education, which are critical to a society's well-being but in which there would be underinvestment in the absence of collective investments managed by a central government. Several of the export management–assistance programs discussed in Chapter 13 provide more specific examples of the types of assistance that a government might usefully provide in an effort to develop competitive industries.

The more controversial role for government surrounds its discriminating in favor of one industry over another in an effort to pick the industry that is most likely to be internationally competitive and provide support for that industry. Here, the evidence is mixed. Many see the Asian success stories as vindications of the appropriateness of an activist government policy. Others argue that there was less intervention in these cases than is generally believed and that many of the examples of intervention failed.

THE PROSPECTS FOR DEVELOPMENT

The prospects for development of the world's developing countries lie as much in the ability of public- and private-sector managers in these countries as they do anywhere else. This is not to say that the external environment is unimportant, but it is to say that the managerial challenge is to make the best use of one's resources given a particular set of environmental conditions. Developing countries could bemoan the unattractiveness of the external environment unceasingly; but these moans will not change the environment, as the experiment with the NIEO demonstrated. In fact, they might not even be heard. A recurring theme of this book is that the development of developing countries is in the hands of the individuals that manage institutions in those countries.

Developing countries do, of course, have a fundamental choice. A developing country might suggest that it is too difficult to compete on international markets or that it does not believe that it is possible to develop a sufficiently wide array of internationally competitive firms to support the expectations of its population. The option such a country has is to retreat from the international marketplace and seek self-sufficiency or autarky. Such a country would endeavor to satisfy the expectations of its population in that manner. To a large extent, this is a less risky strategy for a country to pursue. The country will remove itself from the vagaries of the international marketplace and from the "clutches" of the international monetary system. The larger the country, the more desirable such a strategy might become. In many respects, it is a strategy that India pursued for many years.

There are, however, obvious problems associated with this "low-risk" strategy. As pointed out in Chapter 1, it is more viable for larger developing countries than for smaller developing countries. Such a strategy is also more viable for large countries that are already developed, but it is not a viable strategy for smaller developing countries. Even India, the second largest developing country in terms of population, has moved away from this approach beginning in 1991 with the liberalization program of the Rao regime. India's change in approach was as a result of the "low returns" associated with its "low-risk" strategy. India was simply developing far too slowly to accommodate the legitimate expectations of its citizenry.

The options for most developing countries, therefore, are few. Their success in creating competitive industries will rest on two interrelated managerial phenomena. The public-sector managers will have to manage the economy and society well, creating an economic and social environment that is stable and conducive and engaging in the provision of socially useful services that would be underprovided were the state not so engaged. The provision of these services and political, social, and economic stability should make the national environment conducive to the pursuit of international business opportunities.

Thereafter, the international competitiveness of the country will rest on the shoulders of entrepreneurs within these countries who are prepared to find opportunities and to pursue these opportunities relentlessly. These are not individuals who become complacent once they can provide an adequate standard of living for themselves. Rather, these entrepreneurs are desirous of doing as well as their counterparts in other countries of the world and are creative in their pursuit of opportunities. This is a creativity that will increasingly have to be imbued to citizens of developing countries through educational systems, training programs, and a general societal orientation. Some developing countries have gone far down the road to development through the pursuit of international business activities. Others can continue that trend but not by replication; rather, by innovation and creative application. Indeed, in today's competitive world, there may be no other route to development.

FURTHER READING

Porter, Michael. *The Competitive Advantage of Nations.* New York: Free Press, 1990.

Selected Bibliography

Beckford, George L. *Persistent Poverty: Underdevelopment in Plantation Economies of the Third World.* Oxford: Oxford University Press, 1972.

Beckford, George, and Norman Girvan, eds. *Development in Suspense.* Kingston, Jamaica: Friedrich Ebert Stiftung, 1989.

Best, Michael, and Robert Forrant. "Production in Jamaica: Transforming Industrial Enterprise." In *Jamaica: Preparing for the Twenty First Century.* Kingston, Jamaica: Ian Randle Publishers, 1994.

Bhagwati, Jagdish. *The World Trading System at Risk.* Princeton: Princeton University Press, 1991.

Dunning, John H. "Toward an Eclectic Theory of International Production: Some Empirical Tests." *Journal of International Business Studies* (Spring/Summer 1980): 9–25.

General Agreement on Tariffs and Trade (GATT). *Text of the General Agreement.* Geneva: GATT, 1969.

Girling, Robert Henriques. *Multinational Institutions and the Third World: Management, Debt and Trade Conflicts in the International Economic Order.* New York: Praeger, 1985.

Girvan, Norman, and Gillian Marcelle. "Overcoming Technological Dependency: The Case of Electric Arc (Jamaica) Ltd., A Small Firm in a Small Developing Country." *World Development* 18 (1; 1990): 91–107.

Gomes-Casseres, Benjamin. "Computers: Alliances and Industry Evolution." In *Beyond Free Trade: Firms, Governments and Global Competition,* edited by David B. Yoffie. Boston: Harvard Business School Press, 1993.

"The IMF and the World Bank." *The Economist* (12 October 1991): 1–30.

International Finance Corporation. *IFC Annual Report, 1993.* Washington, D.C.: International Finance Corporation, 1993.

Jaikumar, Ramchandran. "Postindustrial Manufacturing." *Harvard Business Review* (November-December 1986): 69–76.

Keesing, Donald B., and Andrew Singer. *How Support Services Can Expand Manufactured Exports.* Washington, D.C.: World Bank, 1990.

Keesing, Donald B., and Andrew Singer. "Why Official Export Promotion Fails." *Finance and Development* (March 1992): 7–15.

Kim, Suk H., and Seung H. Kim. *Global Corporate Finance: Text and Cases.* Miami: Kolb, 1993.

Krugman, Paul. *Rethinking International Trade.* Cambridge: MIT Press, 1990.

Lessard, Donald R. *International Financial Management: Theory and Application.* New York: John Wiley & Sons, 1985.

Lewis, W. Arthur. *The Evolution of the International Economic Order.* Princeton: Princeton University Press, 1977.

Manley, Michael. "Killed by a Smile." *Jamaican Sunday Gleaner,* 17 May 1992, p. 15.

Manley, Michael. *The Poverty of Nations.* New York: Andre Deutsh, 1990.

Oman, Charles P. "New Forms of Investment in Developing Countries." In *Investing in Development: New Roles for Private Capital,* edited by Theodore H. Moran. Washington, D.C.: Overseas Development Council, 1986.

Porter, Michael. *The Competitive Advantage of Nations.* New York: Free Press, 1990.

Prebisch, Raul. *The Economic Development of Latin America and Its Principal Problems.* New York: United Nations, 1950.

Reid, Stan. "The Decision-Maker and Export Entry and Expansion." *Journal of International Business Studies* (Fall 1981): 100–111.

Rhee Yung Whee, and Therese Belot. *Export Catalysts in Low-Income Countries: A Review of Eleven Success Stories.* Washington, D.C.: World Bank, World Bank Discussion Paper, 1990.

Rodrick, Dani. "Conceptual Issues in the Design of a Trade Policy for Industrialization." *World Development* 20 (3; 1992): 309–320.

Sachs, Jeffrey D., ed. *Developing Country Debt and the World Economy.* Chicago: University of Chicago Press, 1989.

Salorio, Eugene. *Note on Trade Finance.* Boston: Harvard Business School, 1987.

Seringhaus, F. H. Rolf, and Phillip J. Rosson. *Export Development and Promotion: The Role of Public Organizations.* Norwell, Mass.: Kluwer Academic, 1991.

Singer, Hans W. "The Distribution of the Gains from Trade between Investing and Borrowing Countries." *American Economic Review* 40 (May 1950): 473–485.

Stonehill, Arthur I., and David K. Eiteman. *Multinational Business Finance.* 6th ed. Reading, Mass.: Addison-Wesley, 1993.

"A Survey of Third World Finance." *The Economist* (25 September 1993): 1–40.

Todaro, Michael P. *Economic Development in the Third World.* New York: Longman, 1989.

United Nations. *Transnational Corporations from Developing Countries: Impact on Their Home Countries.* Geneva: United Nations, 1993.

United Nations Development Program. *Human Development Report, 1994.* New York: Oxford University Press, 1994.

Vernon, Raymond. "International Investment and International Trade in the Product Cycle." *Quarterly Journal of Economics* (May 1966): 190–207.

Vernon, Raymond. "The Product Cycle Hypothesis in a New International Environment." *Oxford Bulletin of Economics and Statistics* 5 (1980): 255–268.

Vernon, Raymond, and Louis T. Wells. *The Manager in the International Economy.* 6th ed. Englewood Cliffs, N.J.: Prentice-Hall, 1991.

Wells, Louis T., Jr. *The Product Life Cycle and International Trade.* Boston: Harvard University, Graduate School of Business Administration, Division of Research, 1972.

Wells, Louis T., Jr. *Third World Multinationals: The Rise of Foreign Direct Investment from Developing Countries.* Cambridge: MIT Press, 1983.

Wells, Louis T., Jr., and Alvin G. Wint. "Marketing Strategies to Attract Foreign Investment." In *Multinationals in the Global Political Economy,* edited by Lorraine Eden et al. London: Macmillan, 1993.

Williamson, Oliver. *Markets and Hierarchies: Analysis and Antitrust Implications.* New York: Free Press, 1975.

Wint, Alvin G. "Liberalizing Foreign Direct Investment Regimes: The Vestigial Screen." *World Development* 20 (10; 1992): 1515–1529.

Wint, Alvin G., and Louis T. Wells. *Indonesia: Choice of an Industrialization Strategy.* Boston: Harvard Business School, 1987.

Wint, Alvin G., and David B. Yoffie. "United States Trade Law." In *International Trade and Competition: Cases and Notes in Strategy and Management,* edited by David B. Yoffie. New York: McGraw Hill, 1990.

World Bank. "Adjustment Lending: An Evaluation of Ten Years of Experience." Washington, D.C.: World Bank, Policy and Research Series No. 1, 1988.

World Bank. *World Bank Annual Report, 1991.* Washington, D.C.: World Bank, 1991.

World Bank. *World Bank Annual Report, 1992.* Washington, D.C.: World Bank, 1992.

World Bank. *World Development Report, 1987.* New York: Oxford University Press, 1987.

World Bank. *World Development Report, 1991.* New York: Oxford University Press, 1991.

World Bank. *World Development Report, 1993.* New York: Oxford University Press, 1993.

Worrel, Delisle, et al., eds. *Financing Development in the Commonwealth Caribbean.* London: Macmillan Education, 1991.

Wortzel, Heidi Vernon, and Lawrence H. Wortzel. "Export Strategies of NIC and LDC Based Firms." *Columbia Journal of World Business* (Spring 1981).

Yoffie, David B., ed. *Beyond Free Trade: Firms, Governments and Global Competition.* Boston: Harvard Business School Press, 1993.

Yoffie, David B. *Power and Protectionism: Strategies of the Newly Industrializing Countries.* New York: Columbia University Press, 1983.

Index

ABOUT THE AUTHOR

ALVIN G. WINT is a Professor of Management Studies at the University of the West Indies, Jamaica. Prior to his appointment to a chair at the University of the West Indies, he was an Associate Professor of International Business at Northeastern University. Professor Wint holds a doctorate in international business from Harvard University. He has published extensively and been a consultant to the World Bank, the United Nations, and several national governments in the area of international business–government relations.

ISBN 0-89930-929-1

90000>

EAN

9 780899 309293

HARDCOVER BAR CODE